THE FALKLAND

Also by G. M. Dillon

COMPARATIVE DEFENCE POLICY MAKING
DEPENDENCE AND DETERRENCE

The Falklands, Politics and War

G. M. Dillon

Lecturer in Politics
University of Lancaster

MACMILLAN
PRESS

First published 1989

Published by
THE MACMILLAN PRESS LTD
Houndmills, Basingstoke, Hampshire RG21 2XS
and London
Companies and representatives
throughout the world

Typeset by Vine & Gorfin Ltd,
Exmouth, Devon

Printed in Hong Kong

British Library Cataloguing in Publication Data
Dillon, G. M.
The Falklands, politics and war.
1. Falkland Islands—History   2. great
Britain—Colonies
I. Title
997'.11   F3031
ISBN 0–333–44865–0
ISBN 0–333–44866–9 Pbk

Contents

List of Tables

List of Figures

Preface

This is not a book of revelations. It is bound, therefore, to disappoint those who have been weaned on the many exposures concerning Britain's part in the Falklands conflict, especially if they desire only further leaks and sensations. Instead, the following study is a detailed analysis of British policy making in respect of the Falkland Islands. Its principal objective is to examine the large volume of Parliamentary and other evidence that is now available concerning the outbreak of the Falklands war, much of it conflicting, and in particular to evaluate the role of the Prime Minister, other Ministers and Whitehall officials in the conduct of British policy. It concentrates on the political causes of the conflict, rather than the conduct of the military campaign, and the study effectively ends with the British counter-attacks of 1 May together with the sinking of the Argentine cruiser, the *General Belgrano*, the following day.

Historically, Britain's possession of the Islands, and claim to sovereignty over them, was always a function of its foreign and defence policy goals as well as the changing national and international circumstances in which these had to be pursued. Hence the conduct of Falklands policy, and the fate of the Falkland Islands, cannot be understood without reference to the politics of defence decision making in the United Kingdom. That, in turn, cannot be understood without considering the operation of power at the centre of British Government and the influence of the political culture within which this takes place.

During the United Kingdom's imperial ascendancy, for example, British policy was premised on: the practical value of the Islands as an imperial asset; the legal claim to prior discovery and earlier settlement, which was later supplemented by the principle of prescription; the non-negotiability of sovereignty, and hence the refusal to allow international arbitration to resolve the dispute with Argentina; and the desire to maintain a low profile on the issue in an effort to protect Anglo-Argentine relations. In the final analysis, of course, continued possession of the Islands relied upon the intimidatory effect of Britain's imperial power.

The question of sovereignty was by no means immutable and the matter of the Islanders' right to self-determination did not figure until the late 1960s. Formerly based upon discovery and settlement, for example, Britain's claim to the Falklands shifted, in the 1930s, to the principle of prescription, as the inadequacies of the earlier arguments became all too evident. The interests of the Islanders themselves only entered into discussion in 1968. In part this was a response to the Parliamentary opposition aroused by a Government proposal to cede sovereignty to Argentina without consulting the Falklanders. But 'self-determination' was also a convenient diplomatic riposte to the anti-colonial sentiments of the postwar world, particularly with respect to the UN's involvement in the matter. There, Britain found it useful to espouse a principle it had been forced into conceding elsewhere, particularly as the UN forum had allowed Buenos Aires to strengthen Argentina's case by construing the dispute as a question of 'decolonisation'. Thus, even at the level of international debate, the Falklands issue exposed conflicts of political value which were also to distinguish it in both Port Stanley and London.

The United Nations was in favour of 'decolonisation' and the Falkland Islands, of course, were a Crown Colony. But, equally, the UN was in favour of 'self-determination', and there seemed little doubt about the Falkland Islanders' determination to remain under British rule. Not surprisingly, therefore, the two parties were left to find their own reconciliation of the political principles involved.

While in the abstract a reconciliation might have appeared impossible, in practice it was entirely feasible, if difficult, because by the late 1960s the Islands had lost their strategic significance for Britain. Increasingly throughout the 1970s the colony became both socially and economically untenable for the Islanders. There was thus a two-fold incentive for Britain to negotiate with Argentina. Regeneration of the Islands' economy, as well as strategic withdrawal from the South Atlantic in accordance with the contraction of Britain's defence commitments, both argued in favour of a settlement of the sovereignty dispute. In response to this challenge, and unusually in cases of decision making, the importance of political leadership in the conduct of policy was clearly exposed. For what was required, in addition to bureaucratic expertise in the form of sound intelligence advice, policy analysis and diplomatic inventiveness, were some basic political skills, including the courage to bear the inevitable political and economic costs of a settlement.

All policy making requires a measure of political direction. But the Falklands issue was especially dependent upon political control because it was a deeply political matter, rather than a mere legal or strategic question. First, it comprised a number of conflicts of political interest and perceptions for those involved in British policy-making. These included a basic conflict of interest between successive British Governments, who wished to reduce Britain's overseas commitments, and many Falkland Islanders, who wished to see British power retained in the South Atlantic. Actors in both London and Port Stanley also experienced that basic political dilemma of recognising what was sensible but fearing its political consequences. Finally, again in both Port Stanley and London, there was a basic conflict of view between those who were willing to accept the political consequences of the decline of British power and those who were not.

In addition, however, the development of British policy, and ultimately of the dispute itself, was to be determined not only by the course of Anglo-Argentine relations, but also by the operation of three closely related domestic political processes. First, there was the politics of Britain's imperial retreat, the complex cultural and political process by which the United Kingdom has tried to come to terms, physically and symbolically, with the decline of British power and the demise of the British Empire. Next, there was the politics of British Government, through which, under Prime Ministerial supervision, political authority is normally employed to secure acceptance of Cabinet policy in the House of Commons and in the country. Added to these processes was the politics of the Falkland Islands themselves, a small collection of tiny colonial settlements on the brink of social and economic extinction.

This study, therefore, explores the nature of the Falklands as a political issue and the interplay between the political processes which determined its fate. A minor imperial possession, and a small anomaly in the context of postwar British defence policy, the future of the Falkland Islands nevertheless received high level political attention as well as routine bureaucratic consideration in Britain. Because all policy issues are more or less mobile, this one, like others, moved up and down the hierarchy of decision making, and across Government Departments, in response to various factors. Routinely, officials worked out the details of policy at the bureaucratic level, but options were regularly put to Government Ministers. Proposed courses of action were similarly reviewed by these political superintendents of the policy process and sanctioned by the Cabinet before being implemented. Detailed advice about the military situation was also regularly available from the Government's Joint Intelligence Committee (JIC), which furnished the Cabinet with intelligence briefings.

The course of the issue, however, would provide a particularly explicit example of how officials manage policy in a way that is materially influenced by a climate of opinion set by Ministers. It also showed that without the investment of adequate political resources, in the form of political authority and control, manageable international disputes can degenerate rapidly into military confrontations. In illuminating the relationship between domestic and international politics, the Falklands dispute thus revealed as much about the post-imperial politics of the United Kingdom, and the character of British policy-making, as it did about the nature of international crisis and conflict. It is this particular combination of insights, and the wealth of documentary evidence which illustrates them, that lends the Falklands affair such academic as well as political significance in understanding the way foreign and defence policy-making is conducted.

The evidence of the Falklands conflict, however, has relevance beyond the confines of British decision making, because it emphasises the political character of international disputes, the importance of political skills, especially the role of political judgement, in policy-making, and the dangerously independent power of the logic of conflict. In the end, however, the Falklands story is an account of a failure of political leadership in the conduct of Cabinet Government. It is a story also of how that failure led to a military confrontation, whose independent dynamics were as responsible for the outbreak of war as the political limitations of those responsible for British policy, or the machinations of Argentina's Junta.

Acknowledgements

I would like to thank my colleagues at Lancaster who read and commented upon my manuscript. Hugh Tinker's advice was especially wise, concentrating my mind on the central theme. Ian Bellany, Harro Höpfl and Richard Little also gave valuable help; and particular thanks are due to Richard for certain suggestions about the organisation of the text. Macmillan's anonymous reader also proved to be a hard, but fair, task master. I am grateful to them all.

More than usually, however, this book and its arguments are the author's responsibility. It took time for me to assess the evidence and come to a view. In the process I consciously avoided all those who, for whatever reasons, had already decided where they stood in relation to the Falklands War. My greatest debts, therefore, are personal ones. Indeed, in this respect, I was blessed with the support of some remarkable women. Without them I would not have survived.

Susan Riches typed more drafts than she or I care to remember; nonetheless we stayed good friends. That alone is a remarkable testament to her patience and sense of humour. She is incapable of letting anyone down, and I drew upon her loyalty and commitment to a scandalous extent. I cannot thank her enough.

My daughters, Jayne and Sarah, suffered all my long absences in my study with an understanding beyond their years, and welcomed me back from them with undiminished love and enthusiasm. Their encouragement to finish the book was indispensable.

Most of all, however, I wish to acknowledge my debt to my wife. This book is dedicated to her, a token of my love and appreciation.

G. M. Dillon
Lancaster 1987

List of Abbreviations

AEW	Airborne Early-Warning
ASW	Anti-Submarine Warfare
DOPC	Defence and Overseas Policy Committee
FCO	Foreign and Commonwealth Office
FIEC	Falkland Islands Emergency Committee
FIC	Falkland Islands Committee
FICo	Falkland Islands Company
FOSIC	Fleet Ocean Surveillance Information Centre
JIC	Joint Intelligence Committee
MEZ	Maritime Exclusion Zone
MOD	Ministry of Defence
MOU	Memorandum of Understanding
OSUS	Ocean Surveillance United States.
ROE	Rules of Engagement
SSN	Nuclear Submarine, Hunter Killer
TEZ	Total Exclusion Zone
UKFIL	United Kingdom Falkland Islands Committee

1 A Post-Imperial Problem

Between 1965 and 1979 officials in the British Foreign Office devised a variety of formulas to accomplish British withdrawal from the South Atlantic. There was acceptance at Ministerial and Cabinet level that withdrawal was necessary, but a way had to be found to discharge the United Kingdom's political obligations to the Islanders.[1] With the exception of the first direct attempt to transfer sovereignty to Argentina, in the late 1960s, the general strategy was to concede as little as possible, consistent with avoiding a crisis in Anglo-Argentine relations. In this way it was vainly hoped that the Islanders might somehow be persuaded to accept that the sovereign status of the Islands would eventually have to change, and that Argentina would have to be included in the new arrangements.[2]

These formulas included direct transfer of sovereignty on the basis of minimum consultation with the Islanders; functional integration in the form of certain Communications Agreements; condominium (considered only very briefly); Shackleton's Survey, a comprehensive socio-economic survey of the Islands; and finally trade-off— distinguishing between the South Atlantic Dependencies (such as South Georgia and South Thule) and the Falkland Islands themselves, with the intention of trading-off the Dependencies to win more time for a resolution of the Falklands dispute.

Many other suggestions were also canvassed from time to time but only one other had much significance. This was lease-back and it was informally considered on many occasions. Between 1977 and 1979 the British Cabinet concluded that eventually it would have to resort to such a scheme but it was only when the fifth strategy (trade-off) failed that lease-back became the principal option.

DIRECT TRANSFER OF SOVEREIGNTY

In 1966 the Defence and Overseas Policy Committee of the Cabinet (DOPC) authorised the start of diplomatic negotiations with Argentina, after considering a paper from the Foreign and Colonial Secretaries (George Brown and Fred Lee), which outlined the United Kingdom's position and the dilemma it faced: the Islands were barely defended and Argentina could easily occupy them by force.[3]

At the first diplomatic meeting authorised by this Cabinet decision, in November 1966, the United Kingdom proposed a 'sovereignty freeze' for a minimum of 30 years, after which time, allowing for the improvement of relations between the Islands and Argentina, the Islanders would be free to choose British or Argentine rule. This proposition was promptly rejected by Buenos Aires and in response the British Government stated formally, for the first time, that it would be prepared to cede sovereignty if certain conditions were met and the Islanders' wishes respected.[4] With this important breakthrough for Argentina, and historic shift in the character of British policy, further talks were held to draft a 'Memorandum of Understanding' (MOU). This was intended to serve as a basis upon which further negotiations could proceed, and agreement was reached at official level in August 1968.[5]

London insisted, against Argentine objections, that the publication of the memorandum be accompanied by a unilateral British declaration, emphasising that any transfer of sovereignty would be subject to the wishes of the Islanders. According to Argentine sources, a timetable was also agreed whereby Argentine sovereignty would be acknowledged after four and within ten years.[6] However, details of a draft version of the MOU were leaked by members of the Falkland Islands Council, who also sent an open letter to MPs and the press in London, stating that negotiations were proceeding 'which may result at any moment in the handing over of the Falkland Islands to Argentina'.[7]

The then Minister of State at the Foreign and Commonwealth Office, Lord Chalfont, had visited the Islands in November 1968 to explain Government policy, but on his return both Houses of Parliament, alerted by the councillors' leaks, received the Government's statements with considerable hostility and the proposals were condemned in the press.[8] Under domestic pressure the British Cabinet then sought to make Argentine conditions for the acceptance of the MOU a publicly acceptable reason for discontinuing the talks, although it recognised that failure to reach an agreement with Argentina 'carried the risks of increased harassment of the Islanders and the possibility of an attack.'[9] It decided to continue negotiations while maintaining that the Islanders' wishes were paramount, and Michael Stewart, the Foreign Secretary, announced this to the House of Commons immediately after the Cabinet decision.[10]

From the beginning, therefore, the political character of the issue was apparent. The use of force had either to be deterred by force or pre-empted by negotiation. To make diplomatic progress the Government would have to confront the Islanders, the Falklands lobby and Parliament with the realities of the decline of British power. Alternatively, if the Islands were to be provided with effective protection and their long-term economic future secured at British expense, the Government would have to resist the economic and political logic of imperial retreat.

Only Ministers had the authority to make the choices necessary, willing the means as well as the ends of policy. Strengthening the defences of the Islands meant taking costly financial decisions which also ran counter to the priorities of foreign and defence policy. Insisting on progress towards a transfer of sovereignty meant confronting the political influence of those who opposed it, including not only many Islanders but also some sections of Parliamentary and press opinion. Using negotiations as a tactic to gain time, in order simultaneously to forestall Argentine aggression and provide an opportunity for opinion in the Islands and Britain to change, also required sound political intelligence, and the employment of political resources to educate Island and domestic opinion. The military threat had to be monitored closely, public opinion had to be informed and the overall situation carefully monitored. Otherwise, as the Joint Intelligence Committee (JIC) had warned even at this early stage, the dispute would rapidly deteriorate and become a military one.[11]

From the beginning a basic contradiction had emerged at the centre of British policy which was to increase the political complications of the dispute and confound all subsequent attempts to solve it. How were British interests to be reconciled with those of the Islanders when, in a hastily improvised attempt to defuse Parliamentary hostility, the Government had committed itself to a formula that accorded paramountcy to the Islanders' interests? If there was a way out of that political impasse, it also could only be found by Ministers.

FUNCTIONAL INTEGRATION

Following the rejection of the Memorandum of Understanding, talks were resumed in 1969 under what was termed the 'sovereignty umbrella'. In effect each side agreed to shelve the sovereignty issue for the time being, and the talks went ahead 'without prejudice to either side's position'.[12] Economic reliance on the mainland was now encouraged, both to arrest the serious decline in the Islands' economy and to foster the development of some future political relationship between the Falklands and Argentina.

As with all functional strategies, however, political change was expected to come about through some automatic process of assimilation, unaided by political argument designed to change peoples' perspectives and symbol systems. Nevertheless, certain Communications Agreements were signed in 1971 and a variety of other measures were negotiated subsequently to encourage closer links between the Islands and the South American mainland. The results seem to have been mixed. Some Islanders apparently welcomed the new social and economic developments; others merely became suspicious of the increased reliance on Argentina and its attempts to exploit its position for political purposes.[13]

Thus the agreements soon ran into the three other characteristic problems. First, Britain expended too little money and political effort in the attempt to make them work. Second, closer ties eventually increased rather than diminished the Islanders' loyalist hostility to the Argentine. Finally, Argentine nationalism forced the pace of progress and sovereignty quickly became a political issue once more.[14]

CONDOMINIUM

As Argentine politics became more nationalistic and sovereignty became a central question again, Anglo-Argentine relations deteriorated and the functionalist experiment collapsed. Fearing economic or military action against the Islands, and in need of some response to United Nations pressure, Britain's Cabinet Defence Committee decided in January 1974 to consult the Governor of the Falklands about the possibility of a condominium (a form of joint sovereignty and administration). Before this could take place the administration was defeated at the polls and a new Government was returned to office, with Harold Wilson as Prime Minister and James Callaghan as Foreign Secretary.

Wilson and Callaghan endorsed the view that the costs of effective defence could not be justified, given the search for defence economies and Britain's adjustment to regional power status. By the mid-1970s, the contraction of Britain's global commitments had been confirmed and the Royal Navy withdrawn from Simonstown, the base from which defence of the Falklands had previously been deployable. The new Cabinet therefore authorised the continuation of attempts to find an acceptable compromise.[15]

Condominium, however, immediately proved unpopular in the Falklands. The Islands' Council indicated 'that it would raise no objection to talks on condominium going ahead, provided that there was no Islander participation initially'. The subject was then raised with the Argentine Government, but 'in the face of the Islanders' continuing refusal to participate it was decided that there would be no purpose in proceeding without them'. As a consequence, the topic was dropped and Argentina was duly informed in August 1974.[16]

The condominium idea lasted barely eight months. It revealed little that was not already well known but illustrated that, short of abandoning the Islands altogether, the Foreign Office was willing to explore a variety of formulas to extract Britain from its commitment.

SHACKLETON'S SOCIO-ECONOMIC SURVEY

After condominium the Foreign Office held internal discussions in order to reconstitute policy and discover a course of action which would mollify Argentina, by moving negotiations forward, without ceding much if anything on the central issue of legal title to the Islands.[17] There was, however, an additional and related difficulty. The Communications Agreements had not only failed to seduce the Islanders into accepting Argentine sovereignty, but also to stimulate the Islands' economy. At issue, therefore, was the future economic development of the colony, together with its social survival as well as its political status. As a result it was decided to commission an extensive study of the Falklands, to buy time and satisfy the Islanders' demands for attention from London. Conceivably, it was thought that the conclusions might also contain something that could be exploited to extract Falklands policy from its impasse.

Set up in October 1975, and entrusted to a team led by Lord Shackleton, the commission reported in June 1976.[18] Providing a detailed portrait of the social and economic division of the Islands and the extent of their decline, Shackleton's report amounted to a comprehensive indictment of their colonial structures. Monopolistic exploitation of its mono-crop economy by the Falkland Islands Company had been accompanied by a patrician but niggardly form of colonial administration. The result was a dependent and 'feudalistic' community, riven with internal jealousies, which was beset by economic disinvestment and depopulation. Shackleton's principal recommendations, including the improvement of the Islands' airport, were rejected by the Government on grounds of cost. However, the report's basic conclusion, that the sovereignty dispute overshadowed all proposals for the Islands' future, confirmed the political wisdom of existing policy advice.[19]

In effect Shackleton's survey had only represented a pause in the political development of the dispute. Indeed, his visit to the Falklands and the interruption of negotiations with Argentina had actually precipitated a military confrontation of the sort which the Joint Intelligence Committee had predicted. As a consequence, the Cabinet authorised the resumption of diplomatic talks.

TRADE-OFF

In response to the increase in tension, Callaghan, who had recently become Prime Minister, initiated a fundamental reappraisal of all aspects of policy, including military as well as diplomatic questions.[20] The implications of the military developments will be considered shortly and the British response to them analysed. For the moment, however, we need only deal with the diplomatic aspects because these introduced the final attempt to resolve the dispute before Mrs Thatcher's Government took over in 1979.

In March 1976 the DOPC agreed to Mr Callaghan's proposals for a new diplomatic initiative, and Argentina was informed that the British were prepared to resume negotiations 'including discussion of sovereignty'.[21] Confidential exploratory talks were conducted at official level in July and August 1976. By then Argentina was under military rule following the *coup d'etat* of 23 March and Buenos Aires continued to maintain pressure, both militarily and diplomatically.

On 2 February 1977 the new British Foreign and Commonwealth Secretary, Anthony Crosland, made a comprehensive statement to Parliament, announcing the results of the Cabinet's policy review. Britain would reserve its position but sovereignty was not to be formally excluded from the negotiations. Any changes had to be acceptable to the Islanders. His statement was received without controversy.[22] At a subsequent DOPC meeting, therefore, FCO Minister of State Ted Rowlands was authorised to visit the Falklands and consult the Islanders before re-opening political discussions with Buenos Aires.

Before meeting Argentine representatives, Rowlands visited the Falklands, in February 1977. He held an extensive series of meetings there and was, by all accounts, a popular figure. A lease-back solution was raised informally, although it was not official policy. From these discussions Rowlands concluded that the Islanders' agreement to that idea could not be secured. The Islands' Council nevertheless did agree to co-operate in working out terms of reference for formal negotiations 'covering political relations including sovereignty and economic co-operation, provided that the talks were covered by the "sovereignty umbrella" and that the Falkland Islanders were fully consulted'.[23] It was, of course, a familiar if thoroughly ambiguous undertaking: to talk about sovereignty as well as not to talk about it. But at least it kept open the prospect of some progress. For their part the Islanders would rather have had the political dimension excluded altogether. As it turned out, they showed that they were more adept at exploiting the ambiguity of the formula than either Ministers or officials in London.

Detailed terms of reference for the new talks were announced in the House of Commons on 26 April by Crosland's successor at the Foreign Office, David Owen.[24] A promise was made to consult the Islanders during the course of the negotiations, the position of each side with respect to sovereignty was formally reserved and it was thought that working parties might be set up to consider specific issues. At a meeting of the DOPC in July 1977 Owen submitted a paper outlining the revised strategy for the talks. This duly received full Cabinet approval because it was accepted that

> serious and substantive negotiations were necessary to keep the Argentines in play, since the Islands were militarily indefensible except by a major, costly and unacceptable diversion of current resources.[25]

The DOPC accepted that it would eventually be forced to return to some variation of lease-back, linked to a programme of joint economic co-operation, although it was not yet ready to negotiate on that basis. All intelligence assessments confirmed, however, that some material concessions would have to be made if military tension was to be reduced. The problem, therefore, was now to be broken down into more manageable proportions with the intention of trying

> to retain sovereignty as long as possible, if necessary making concessions in respect of the Dependencies and the maritime resources in the area, while recognising that ultimately only some form of leaseback arrangement was likely to satisfy Argentina.[26]

Five rounds of talks between officials were held over the next year and a half: in Rome (summer 1977); New York (December 1977); Lima (February 1978); Geneva (December 1978); and finally in New York again (March 1979). At the first round of talks the British proposed that sovereignty over the Dependencies and the Falklands should be considered separately. In New York in 1977 the UK accepted the setting-up of two working parties, one to consider sovereignty and the other to deal with economic co-operation. For this concession Rowlands was pleased to report that he was able to avoid raising the idea of lease-back. The Islanders were duly informed of the progress of the talks when Rowlands met some of the councillors in Rio de Janeiro on 18 December 1977.[27]

The following year, in Lima, the British proposed an arrangement for Anglo-Argentine scientific co-operation in the Dependencies. This device was partly designed to legitimise an Argentine landing on South Thule which had taken place in November 1976. The working parties set up in New York had run into difficulties, however, because Buenos Aires maintained that the maritime resources at issue already belonged to Argentina by virtue of its claim to sovereignty over the Islands. Between the Lima and Geneva meetings this issue was sorted out and discussion both of maritime zones and continental shelf rights was admitted to the agenda. As a consequence, at Geneva Rowlands was able to accept an agreement in principle for the scientific co-operation proposals which had earlier been formulated in Lima.

When this draft agreement was put to the Falkland Islands councillors they recognised it for what it was—the thin end of a long wedge—and they rejected it. At the resumption of diplomatic negotiations in New York in March 1979, therefore, the British delegation had to announce that 'owing to the Falkland Islanders' suspicions of the motives of the Argentine Government, it was not possible to sign the agreement'. The trade-off strategy then also collapsed.[28]

In addition to confirming the character of the issue, this episode indicated the degree to which policy had become subject to the will of the Falkland Islands councillors. Incorporated into the policy-making process through consultations and discussions, they refused, however, to accept the logic of negotiations. In the absence of a consistent political determination on the British side to take account of British as well as Island interests, they found themselves in a position to veto any progress in attempts to solve the dispute peacefully, without having to offer any alternative.

MILITARISATION OF THE DISPUTE

According to the Franks Report

> over the period from 1965 to 1975 assessments [of the military threat
> to the British territories in the South Atlantic] were made by the
> Joint Intelligence Committee, usually about once a year but more
> frequently at times of increased tension.[29]

The early reports in this period concluded that official military action
by Argentine forces against the Falklands or the Dependencies was
unlikely until diplomatic means of settling the dispute had been
exhausted. There was, however, a continuing risk of unofficial action.
With the progress of diplomatic talks in the 1970s, and in particular the
signing of the Communications Agreements, the danger of official
military action by Buenos Aires was discounted altogether, and even
the likelihood of unofficial extremist adventures was considered to be
very slight. A review in 1974, conducted in response to the hardening
of Argentine attitudes after the return of Peron, concluded that
adventurist operations were still the main threat but that the Argentine
Government was now less likely to discourage them. Official military
action, also, was not ruled out. But it was still thought to depend upon
the character of negotiations and especially upon whether Britain was
willing to negotiate about sovereignty.

The experience of the 1960s and early 1970s generally confirmed the
wisdom of this advice. When negotiations broke down entirely, or
when direct discussion of sovereignty disappeared into some indefinite
future, Argentina sought ways of drawing attention to the issue. This
usually took the form of increased diplomatic pressure via representations to London and protests at the United Nations. It also included
exploiting the nationalist passions of Argentine extremists who
engaged in private adventures, while disclaiming any official
connection with, or reponsibility for, the various incidents which took
place.[30]

With the decline of progress after these functional agreements, and
the advent of a more nationalistic regime in Argentina, however, there
was a significant change in the military situation. While the British
turned their attention to the social and economic problems of the
Islands, Argentina intensified the dispute by resorting officially and
repeatedly to military challenges to the British position in the South
Atlantic. British decision makers responded in kind to this dangerous

development by taking their own military measures and reviewing their military position.

Tension first mounted towards the end of 1974. It was signalled, in particular, by an Argentine press campaign run by the newspaper *Cronica*, which advocated an invasion of the Falklands. This, and other incidents, prompted the British Government to instruct its new Ambassador to warn the Argentine Government in April 1975 that 'an attack on the islands would meet with a military response'.[31]

However, it was the despatch of the Shackleton mission which was to precipitate a diplomatic crisis between the two countries. In January 1976 Shackleton's team, *en route* to the Falklands, was denied permission to fly to the Islands through Argentina. The British Ambassador in Buenos Aires was also informed that the two countries 'were rapidly moving towards a head-on collision.' Callaghan, as Foreign Secretary, replied on 12 January by sending what was described as a 'conciliatory' note in which he referred to the issue as a 'sterile dispute'. The Argentine Foreign Ministry objected to the tone of the British message and, detecting no 'positive elements' in it regarding the re-opening of sovereignty negotiations, broke off diplomatic relations. Weeks of hostile press comment followed in Buenos Aires, much of it officially inspired. Staff who remained in the British Embassy, after the withdrawal of Ambassadors, monitored these reports but they concluded that the tenor of press comment was predictable and that the Argentine Government seemed willing to control the displays of anti-British sentiment. There had been no threats or demonstrations against the Embassy itself, for example, and no repetition of *Cronica's* invasion campaign of December 1974.[32]

Instead, the first serious military escalation of the dispute came at sea in February 1976, although advance warning of it had been given (in December 1975) by the Chief of the Argentine Naval Staff. He had advised the British Naval Attaché in Buenos Aires that RRS *Shackleton*, an unarmed British research vessel, would be arrested if she entered Argentine waters, which in Argentina's view included the waters around the Falkland Islands. The British ship was duly intercepted during the first week of February 1976, by the Argentine destroyer *Almirante Storni*, 78 miles south of Port Stanley. The destroyer fired shots at the *Shackleton* in an unsuccessful attempt to arrest her, but she refused to stop and eventually reached the safety of the Falklands' capital.[33]

London's intelligence sources later confirmed that the plan to intercept the vessel had been in existence for about six weeks prior to the incident, and that the action had been inspired by the armed forces rather than the Argentine Government. The JIC concluded, nevertheless, that Argentina's military commanders were opposed to military invasion and that a policy of 'continued pin-pricks' rather than a precipitate attack was likely. Rowlands was newly appointed Minister of State at the Foreign Office at the time and Callaghan had only just taken over as Prime Minister. The attack was a baptism of fire which left a salutary impression on both of them. Rowlands was instructed to keep a special watch on what remained of Britain's overseas commitments, in the firm belief that big problems arose out of small issues, and it was the *Shackleton* incident which finally led to Callaghan's comprehensive review of British policy.[34]

At the beginning of 1976, recognising the need for military precautions as well as a fresh political impetus (the trade-off negotiations), Callaghan also requested 'a full and up to date military assessment on possible military options and limitations'.[35] In addition, two other decisions were taken to bolster Britain's military position in the area. First, HMS *Endurance*, armed with two 20 mm Oerlikon guns and carrying two helicopters equipped with air-to-sea missiles, was retained on station. She had been brought into service in 1967 to replace HMS *Protector* as ice-patrol vessel and guardship in the region. As a consequence of the 1974 Defence Review a decision had been taken to withdraw the ship from service, but the RRS *Shackleton* incident saved her for a further year. It was also decided to strengthen Britain's naval presence in the South Atlantic. The Prime Minister proposed that a frigate and a Royal Fleet Auxiliary support ship should be sent to join HMS *Endurance*.[36]

This measure was designed, in particular, to strengthen Rowlands' hand in his meeting in New York with the Argentine Foreign Minister. Rowlands' task was to lower tension between the two countries and to obtain assurances that Argentina would not interfere with the final leg of RRS *Shackleton's* programme. Presumably he was also to indicate that a new British proposal to re-open negotiations would soon be announced. Finally, given that Britain's naval forces in the South Atlantic were being reinforced and that a comprehensive review of Britain's military options was being conducted, Rowlands was also under strict instructions to make it plain that Britain 'would defend the Islands if the Argentines attempted to use force'. In the event, he obtained the desired assurances and both parties agreed to a resumption of the dialogue on the dispute in due course.[37]

Callaghan's request for a major re-assessment of the military position in the South Atlantic demanded consideration of a range of possible deployments in a number of different circumstances, including a determined Argentine assault upon the Falklands. A report was drawn up and approved by the Chiefs of Staff on 19 February. It was then circulated as an annex to a paper which was prepared for the DOPC. The report drew attention to the fact that airborne reinforcement of the Falklands was ruled out by the limitations of Port Stanley's airstrip, the adverse weather conditions to be expected in the Islands, the distance from the nearest usable air base on Ascension Island, and the fact that South American airfields were unlikely to be available to British aircraft in a conflict with Argentina.

The Franks Report summarised this report's findings, and its synopsis makes an interesting preface to what was to happen in 1982:

> To dislodge Argentine occupation of part of the Falkland Islands or the Dependencies would require an amphibious force with embarked troops. It would not be practicable to provide, transport and support the force necessary in the Islands to ensure that a determined Argentine attempt to eject the British garrison was unsuccessful. To recover the Islands by military means, though far from impossible, would be a major operation at very long range. The least force for this purpose would be of Brigade Group strength, the transport of which would entail the use of all the Navy's amphibious resources, a sizeable Task Force, including HMS *Ark Royal* and substantial logistic support.[38]

In sum, an effective defence of the Islands against a determined assault was impracticable, in the context of current defence priorities, while retrieving them would require the deployment of all the United Kingdom's amphibious capabilities and more besides.

With the announcement in March 1976 that political negotiations were to be resumed, officials concluded that 'the threat of military action [had] receded'.[39] Events were to show, however, that they were mistaken. Relations between Britain and Argentina did not return to 'normal' even while the trade-off discussions were being conducted. Indeed throughout 1976 and 1977 Argentina kept Britain under sustained military as well as diplomatic pressure. In February 1976 there was the *Shackleton* incident. In November, as we shall see, Argentina occupied one of the British Islands in the South Sandwich group. Finally, in September/October 1977 there was an incident involving Soviet and Bulgarian fishing vessels (see below). These were the main military incidents but, in addition, there was an accumulation of intelligence information documenting the change in Argentina's military posture. Thus the character of the Falklands dispute changed significantly and for the worse in the mid-1970s. Although British intelligence recorded these developments, it did not fully appreciate their significance, despite the advice contained in its own reports that official involvement in military adventures would signal a dangerous shift in Argentine policy.

Some time in November 1976, under the orders of the Naval Commander-in-Chief, a small Argentine military presence was established on the British Dependency of South Thule. A helicopter from HMS *Endurance* discovered the Argentines on 20 December, and on 5 January 1977, an explanation was requested from the Argentine *chargé d'affaires* in London as well as from Buenos Aires. Argentina's reply, that the operation was designed to establish a station for scientific investigations 'within the jurisdiction of Argentine sovereignty' and that the duration of the presence would depend upon the feasibility of the work, provoked a formal British protest on 19 January. Accepting Buenos Aires' claim that the presence was merely a scientific exercise, London pointed out that the UK had a right to expect prior notification of what was technically a violation of British sovereignty. It 'looked forward' to being told when the scientific programme was to be ended. All this took place in confidence, and the British Government did not acknowledge the Argentine presence on the Island publicly until May 1977. However, the British were aware at the time that the Argentine Navy was involved in the affair and that it was part of a developing Argentine military threat.[40]

It was known, for example, that the original intention had been to announce the existence of the base in mid- or late March, by which time it would have been too late, given the region's weather, for British ships to enter that part of the South Atlantic. In addition, British intelligence knew that Buenos Aires had expected a stronger British reaction (after the base had been discovered in December 1976). It was also known that should the British attempt to evict the Argentines, Argentine forces intended to capture the British Antarctic Survey party on South Georgia as a reprisal. Moreover, it was recognised that South Thule was not an isolated incident. British intelligence had also reported that there was an Argentine naval contingency plan for the joint air and naval invasion of the Falkland Islands, which was to be combined with a diplomatic initiative at the United Nations. All of this

information was available to British decision makers by the end of
January 1977, and the Joint Intelligence Committee summarised it for
the DOPC and its Ministers on 31 January.[41]

This JIC report confirmed that the occupation of South Thule was
officially sponsored, and not a private adventure, and that Argentina's
intentions were:

> (i) to make a physical demonstration of Argentine sovereignty over
> the Dependencies;
> (ii) to probe the British Government's reaction to such a
> demonstration; and
> (iii) to obtain a bargaining counter in the forthcoming discussions.[42]

It concluded that the Argentine Government was unlikely to withdraw
the station without achieving some concession, and that

> depending on the British Government's actions in the situation,
> [Argentina] could be encouraged to attempt further military action
> against British interests in the area.[43]

Although the British Government knew that it was being put to the
test, its response was subdued for several reasons. The island was
remote and no civilian population was involved; certain military
responses to other Argentine challenges had been made and others
were to be considered; Argentina was closer to the area and much
better placed to take advantage of any escalation of the incident; and,
finally, the British did not want to jeopardise the trade-off talks which
were planned for later in 1977.

In the light of the South Thule incident, however, and of a further
intelligence assessment which advised that if the trade-off talks broke
down, or ended in deadlock, Argentina might decide to take military
action against British shipping or the Falkland Islands themselves, the
Cabinet considered 'whether any precautionary measures should be
taken'. Ministry of Defence officials pointed out that a Royal Navy
task group of six warships, three support ships and one submarine
would be *en route* from Gibraltar to the Caribbean at the time of the
talks. It was agreed that should Argentina threaten the use of force in
the course of the negotiations, Rowlands would respond by making
reference to the availability of this task group. In the event he was able
to manage without having to rely upon it in his discussion.[44]

Buenos Aires, however, continued to maintain a high military profile when, in September/October 1977, Argentine naval units arrested seven Soviet and two Bulgarian fishing vessels which were sailing in Falklands waters. During this operation an Argentine ship fired on one of the Bulgarians, wounding a member of its crew. British intelligence reported that Admiral Massera, then Naval Commander-in-Chief, had given orders to sink the vessel if necessary and had stated that there would be a similar riposte to intrusions by any other flag carrier in the area. The Argentine naval attaché in London, Admiral Anaya (who was later to succeed Massera as Naval C-in-C, and become a member of the war-time Junta), drew Admiral Massera's statement to the attention of the Foreign Office.[45]

Meanwhile the British *chargé d'affaires* in Buenos Aires was subjected to a barrage of *aides memoire* and *bouts de papier*, demanding evidence of progress and British good intent, through the establishment of working parties, before the next round of trade-off talks began in New York in December. Within the Foreign Office it was also concluded that Argentina's failure to make progress on two other major foreign policy issues—the dispute with Chile over the Beagle Channel, and with Brazil over the River Plate Basin—had increased the Junta's desire for some success with respect to the Falkland Islands.

A close intelligence watch was kept on these developments and an intelligence assessment prepared by the JIC for the Cabinet on 11 October 1977. It revealed that the Argentine presence on South Thule was to be reinforced with the landing of another naval party at the end of the month. Nonetheless, the report argued that 'military action' against the Falklands was unlikely, pending the progress of the negotiations, although it anticipated that Admiral Massera might act unilaterally against any Royal Fleet Auxiliary vessel going to South Thule.

A fuller assessment of the situation, on 1 November, provided a summary of what had now become conventional intelligence wisdom relating to the military threat and the political development of the dispute. The militancy of the Argentine Navy was emphasised, as was the increasing frustration and resentment of the Argentine Foreign Ministry at Britain's delaying tactics. Although Argentina was now under military rule, the JIC assessment also concluded that the Junta would prefer to resolve the dispute through peaceful negotiation rather than by military means. But, again, this held good only so long 'as it calculated that the British Government were prepared to negotiate seriously on the issue of sovereignty'.[46]

Little had changed in these intelligence appreciations; they simply reinforced the old message. If negotiations broke down or led nowhere then 'there would be a high risk' that Argentina would use force. The intelligence assessment did specify precisely what sort of harassment or military action might be anticipated. On the evidence of the recent past, action against British shipping was likely to be the most serious risk. A second prospect was further action against the Dependencies, specifically a move against the British Antarctic Survey Base on South Georgia. A third possibility was a private adventurist operation against the Falklands, such as that of 'Operation Condor' in the 1960s, which the Junta might exploit or feel obliged to support. Finally, although the JIC thought it less likely, a full-scale invasion of the Falkland Islands themselves 'could not be discounted'.[47]

Such a sober intelligence assessment, and the continuing deterioration of the dispute as the Argentine Navy cut fuel supplies to Port Stanley and declared that its ships would no longer fly the British flag in Falkland waters, prompted the Foreign Office to ask the Minister of Defence for a paper on the defence implications of the Argentine threat. The previous Chiefs-of-Staff paper, produced at Callaghan's request in February 1976, was then revised and circulated by the MOD on 4 November. The new paper 'followed closely the lines of the paper prepared the previous year . . . and, in relation to the main threats, reached broadly similar conclusions'.

At a further DOPC meeting on 21 November it was agreed that 'a military presence in the area of the Falkland Islands should be established by the time the negotiations began in December.' Opposition from the Ministry of Defence was overruled by the Prime Minister, and a force of one SSN nuclear submarine and two frigates was ordered to be deployed to the South Atlantic, the submarine close into the Falklands, the frigates to stand off 'about a thousand miles away'. Rules of engagement were also drawn up, including plans for an exclusion zone around the Islands. The commander of the force was Admiral Leach, later First Sea Lord at the time of the Falklands war.[48]

Whether Argentina learnt about these naval deployments, and whether this helped to put an end to the military incidents, is debatable. The Franks Report simply records that 'we have found no evidence that the Argentine Government ever came to know of its [the Task group's] existence'.[49] There are indications from other sources, however, that the Junta was allowed to discover that the force had been sent, even though its despatch was never officially disclosed.[50] In the event the trade-off talks passed off without further incident.

Consideration was later given to deploying the force again, at the Lima negotiations, in February 1978, but the situation by then had stabilised and it was not required.

CONCLUSION

There are a number of much more important factors to consider than whether Argentina learnt about the British naval deployment at the end of 1977. The first concerns the changed nature of the dispute and what British intelligence made of it. The second concerns the way the British policy process operated at Cabinet and Prime Ministerial level. The third concerns the intrinsic political weakness of British policy.

Intelligence failures

It has been argued that British intelligence regarded the 1977 naval deployments as an excessive response to a low level threat and that they were, therefore, less inclined to recommend the use of force in the 1980s.[51] This is a plausible suggestion but it is difficult to substantiate. What is quite evident, however, is that political and intelligence advisers made some more simple but basic errors of judgement.

First, military incidents were treated as the best indicators of a threat requiring a British military response. Yet, according to a close reading of all intelligence reports, this conclusion was quite wrong. For over ten years intelligence reports had in fact stressed that the critical variable for anticipating the level of military threat was *not* the incidence of military actions *but the progress of negotiations*. The crucial variables, in short, were political ones; and those variables included the politics of the Falkland Islands and the United Kingdom, in addition to that of Argentina. Military incidents, of course, were important signs of increasing tension. But they were only proximate indicators of deeper political difficulties, and the intelligence community was to become disastrously insensitive to the political immobility which was to afflict policy under the Thatcher administration.

Second, and ignoring their own advice, which was nonetheless ritually repeated in all their reports, intelligence analysts also underestimated the importance of the shift from privately inspired Argentine adventures to official ones. As Franks concluded:

the military threat to the Islands varied in the light of the course of
the negotiations; it also changed character from "adventurist"
operations in the Islands to wider and more aggressive forms of
military action by the Argentine Navy.[52]

That shift was recorded in intelligence briefs but it did not lead to any
appreciable change in the evaluation of the threat to the Falklands.

Although no JIC assessment ever discounted an invasion of the
Islands, they all underestimated the possibility in the light of the
1975–77 developments. In short, Argentina began to experiment with
exercises in brinkmanship during the 1970s and the logic of that
process entailed the seizure of the Falklands, as the JIC's own report
on the South Thule incident actually revealed. There was, therefore, a
novel danger to be taken into account from now on. The slow and
deliberate pace of political developments contrasted with the rapidity
with which military incidents gathered momentum. Brinkmanship
contains within it the speed and uncertainty which distinguishes
military crisis and conflict. Argentina's Junta was beginning to gamble
on such factors and, increasingly, could no longer be relied upon to
control or resist them as other Argentine regimes in the past had done.

Finally, it was concluded in Britain that the Falklands problem had a
rhythm in which peaceful negotiations alternated with periods of
tension. But that view was also quite wrong. The political context and
thus the character of the dispute changed in the 1970s and it was to
change further in the 1980s. In general terms the balance of forces
between Britain and Argentina shifted in accordance with the
reduction of British power. While Argentine politics also became
more brutal and nationalistic, its Falklands policy became more
volatile. All this was reflected in the heightened tension of the period.

Thus the dispute became more militarised as the 1970s wore on, and
the political options were progressively reduced as one episode
succeeded another Increasingly, the Falklands question presented
ever greater challenges to the political judgement of British
policy-makers if they were to continue to avoid conflict in the South
Atlantic. For they had to exercise greater degrees of political direction
and control in order to retain some initiative over the course of the
dispute, both politically and militarily. That meant dealing firmly not
only with the Junta but also with the Islanders and with Parliament.
Otherwise events would be dictated entirely by Argentina and what
passed for politics under its military dictatorship.

Political leadership

Under Prime Ministerial leadership, political impetus was restored to the search to find a diplomatic solution to the Falklands dispute. In addition, Callaghan had taken the political initiative in organising Britain's military response to the increase in tension. The military situation was thoroughly reconsidered by the Chiefs of Staff, the JIC and the Cabinet Defence Committee. Britain's military presence in the South Atlantic was retained and reinforced at appropriate moments. Military backing for diplomacy was also provided as circumstances demanded. This occured not once but on three separate occasions: after the *Shackleton* incident of January/February 1976; in June/July 1977 in order to support Rowlands; and in December 1977, again to support Rowlands in his negotiations with Argentina. During this period, therefore, military considerations were an integral part of the Prime Minister's and the DOPC's handling of the dispute. And they figured from the beginning, with the first serious signs of tension, not after a long build-up of incidents.

The military response, however, was not sufficient to remove all doubt about Britain's willingness to defend its possessions. Failure to respond to South Thule, especially, undermined the force of Callaghan's decisions and left a question mark over Britain's determination to resist military challenges in the future. The Argentines were to remain on the island until evicted in the course of the British recapture of the Falklands and South Georgia in 1982. Equally, although Callaghan regained a measure of political control and stabilised the dispute, that political control was not used to any lasting effect. The trade-off strategy was also defeated in due course by the combination of political irresolution in London and hostility to change from Port Stanley.

Whether these measures were adequate or not is, therefore, arguable. Be that as it may, senior policy-makers were alert to the dangers of the dispute and took some prudent military as well as political measures to control it.

Intrinsic weakness of British policy

Its Falklands policy had provided the British Government with a framework for dealing with Argentina but not, as it turned out, for dealing with the Islanders or its own Parliament. The final effort to resolve the dispute on the basis of an indirect (trade-off) strategy contained the one weakness which had frustrated all previous efforts. It could buy time in which to mobilise support in the Islands for political change, and marginalise those members of the House of Commons who retained illusions about the decline of British power and the changing nature of British interests. But it contained no means for employing that time to achieve these objectives. Only the investment of political and economic resources could do that: offering the Islanders an attractive economic and political package, and managing the House of Commons in the usual way, through the exercise of party discipline. But neither was employed, because ultimately each amounted to the same thing, the maintenance of a consistent political impetus behind the conduct of policy-making.

By 1979 there was only one other prominent solution which was likely to avert military conflict with Argentina, and that solution was lease-back. It, too, required political support from Britain and the Falkland Islands if it was to have any chance of success. However, such a proposal required a new and very large injection of political capital if it was to succeed, because it addressed the political issue directly. Alternatively, the cost of the defence of the Islands would have to be borne and the likelihood of some military confrontation with Argentina accepted.

At this important juncture in the development of the Falklands dispute there was a change of Government in Britain. The Foreign Office now had the additional burden of educating a new and inexperienced team of political supervisors in the options which they faced. Thus a particularly high premium was placed upon political skills and political initiative at a time when a Government dedicated to a new style of politics gained power in the United Kingdom.[53]

2 Ministerial and Cabinet Politics

Falklands policy falls into two distinct periods under the Thatcher administration. The first ran from May 1979, when the Government took office, to January 1981, when it decided to abandon sovereignty negotiations. The second ran from January 1981 to 2 April 1982, when Argentina seized the Islands.

The first period showed how reluctant the new DOPC was to re-open negotiations with Argentina, and how it grudgingly accepted a proposal that the Foreign Office should explore lease-back as the basis for further discussions. When support for the scheme was withdrawn, following its hostile reception in the House of Commons, Foreign Office Ministers suffered a political defeat from which they never recovered. Thereafter, events were to illustrate the frustrating, and ultimately fatal, impact that political immobility was to have on British policy.

FALKLANDS POLICY 1979–81

When the new Conservative Government came to office, the nature of the Falklands dispute was well documented and, in accordance with standard practice, the new Foreign Office Minister responsible *inter alia* for Falklands affairs, Nicholas Ridley, was briefed and presented with a familiar range of options.

He could recommend that Her Majesty's Government break off negotiations and be prepared to defend the Islands against Argentine harassment or worse. Alternatively, the Islands could be given up and the Islanders resettled elsewhere. This, it was suggested, would be 'politically and morally indefensible'. Third, he could go through the motions of negotiation merely to prevaricate and delay. Finally, he could continue to negotiate in good faith in search of an arrangement which 'might ultimately prove acceptable to the Islands and Parliament'. Discussions between Ridley and his Foreign Secretary, Lord Carrington, followed and together they concluded that the Minister of State should visit the Islands and Argentina to confirm for himself what official advice had outlined.[1]

21

Ridley went to Buenos Aires first. There he met Comodoro Cavandoli, Argentina's Deputy Foreign Minister, and emphasised Britain's interest in economic co-operation. Cavandoli repeated that sovereignty had to be part of the negotiations. In July the British party travelled onto the Falklands. The Islanders were duly reassured that no deal would be made without their approval, although the advantages of co-operation with Argentina were brought to their attention. The Islanders' Council proposed instead that a lengthy 'freeze' be imposed on sovereignty negotiations, and showed no enthusiasm for lease-back, which was again discussed informally. Ridley then returned to Buenos Aires, where he arranged for the reinstatement of Ambassadors, so restoring normal diplomatic representation, disrupted since January 1976.[2]

Two false starts

On Ridley's return to London, the Foreign Office reviewed the position and a new policy proposal was prepared for submission to Cabinet. This outlined the two negative options facing the Government. These were what, even then, seems to have been referred to as 'Fortress Falklands', or delay and prevarication. It recommended instead 'substantive negotiations on sovereignty', ceding title to the Islands in principle but leasing them back for a period. The terms and conditions of a lease-back agreement would be difficult to negotiate in detail and would take some time to achieve but the proposal met Argentina's claim, and left only the timing and safeguards to be worked out. It was preferred because it would 'make an unpredictable and possibly violent Argentine reaction less likely'.[3]

The Foreign Secretary decided not to take the proposal to the DOPC immediately but to minute its members (on 20 September 1979), indicating the merits of the scheme and seeking their agreement to talks which would lead in that direction. The idea was that Carrington would then be able to inform Argentina's Foreign Minister (at a meeting scheduled to take place in New York at the end of the month) that talks would be resumed. Moreover, he would be able to do this without having to make an issue of the Falklands, hardly a priority anyway, so early in the life of the new Government. The tactic failed, however, because the Prime Minister blocked it by concluding instead 'that a decision of principle on the Government's approach to the problem could not be rushed but should be discussed at an early meeting of the Defence Committee'.[4]

Carrington had then to explain to his Argentine counterpart that he was not yet in a position to propose a solution to the sovereignty dispute 'while other pressing foreign policy problems remained outstanding'.[5] He was told in return that the Falklands were nevertheless at the top of Argentina's agenda. It was then agreed that a programme of weekly contacts between Ambassadors, twice yearly meetings of Junior Ministers and an annual meeting of the two Foreign Ministers should be instituted. A formal structure for continued negotiations was thus established even if they had very little of substance to consider, and Argentina seemed willing to allow the new British Government time to come to a view on the question.

On 12 October the Foreign Secretary circulated another memorandum to the DOPC, in anticipation of a meeting the following week, at which it was expected that the Falklands would be discussed. His paper repeated the arguments contained in his Minute of 20 September, but the dangers associated with failing to make any progress in negotiations were explained in greater detail. The paper was also supported by an annex which contained a political and military analysis of the Argentine threat. In particular it was noted that both Fortress Falklands and a decision to continue diplomatic talks without making concessions on sovereignty 'carried a serious threat of invasion'. Carrington ended by again recommending that talks be resumed at Ministerial level 'to explore, without commitment and without seeking to rush matters, political and economic solutions'.[6]

Once more the Foreign Office was frustrated by the Prime Minister, who now insisted that the dispute would have to wait until the Rhodesian question had been settled, and so the discussion was postponed.[7] In November, therefore, Ridley had to decline an invitation from Argentina for a further informal exchange of views because the British had no politically authorised views to exchange.

A new JIC assessment, dated November 1979, had also been prepared for the incoming Conservative Cabinet. This new review concluded that the level of threat had diminished for two reasons since the last report had been issued two years previously. The British Government had engaged in serious negotiations, and the Argentine Government had become more preoccupied with other foreign policy issues; especially its dispute with Chile over the Beagle Channel. Nevertheless, the latest assessment emphasised that Argentina remained determined to extend its sovereignty over the Falklands. It also repeated the warning of all other reports that 'the overriding consideration for the Argentine Government remained their perception of the British Government's willingness to negotiate about, and eventually to transfer, sovereignty'.[8]

These false starts not only demonstrated that the Falklands was a relatively unimportant issue; they also illustrated the basic lack of sympathy for negotiations in the DOPC. Moreover, they determined the role which Carrington was to play throughout the conduct of policy. Acting as an intermediary between his Department and his Cabinet colleagues, he continually had to judge what proposals he could put before them and when. In practice that meant dealing with the Prime Minister, whose influence appeared to be decisive.

The launch of lease-back

The new Defence Committee had been warned twice in its first seven months in office about the dangers surrounding the Falklands dispute. Yet the Government had still not authorised any action, and the issue did not finally come before the DOPC until 29 January 1980. Prior to this first meeting the Foreign Secretary circulated a further Minute, advising that 'exploratory talks with the Argentine Government should be started soon since to continue to stall could be risky'.[9] However, the DOPC merely authorised the Foreign Secretary to seek written confirmation from the Falkland Islands Council that it agreed to fresh negotiations. He was then to propose new terms of reference for any future discussions, since the Committee had concluded that 'it was undesirable that talks should be resumed on the basis of the terms of reference announced by the previous Government in April 1977'.[10] These negotiations had broken down, in any event, before the Government had come to power, and Carrington had already proposed new terms of reference in the form of lease-back. Clearly the Prime Minister (and presumably other members of the DOPC) had no liking for this suggestion, and was countering Carrington's representations with her own delaying tactics.

The Islands' councillors agreed to talks, however, and on 15 April 1980 the Foreign Office announced that discussions would be resumed later that month in New York. No new terms of reference had yet been approved by Cabinet and consequently the New York meeting, which was also attended by an Islands' councillor, was described as 'exploratory'. It ended with an anodyne statement to the effect that talks should continue for the time being and that further discussion of co-operation in the development and conservation of the resources in the South Atlantic should also take place.[11]

Only after two additional meetings did the DOPC agree to further action. Carrington delivered a report on the results of the New York talks to the first meeting, in July 1980, and finally obtained an agreement 'to reach a solution of the dispute on the basis of a lease-back arrangement'. At the second meeting, on 7 November, Ridley was authorised to visit the Falklands to discover what degree of support there was for such a scheme amongst the Islanders.[12]

According to some reports, Mrs Thatcher's reaction to Carrington's first suggestion that sovereignty should be negotiated had been 'thermonuclear'. She is also thought to have pressured Ridley to withdraw lease-back altogether before submitting it to Cabinet discussion.[13] As there was no coherent alternative and no suggestion that military protection be increased, however, the Prime Minister seems ultimately to have been unable to resist the logic of the Foreign Office's argument. It was evident, nonetheless, that Cabinet support for lease-back fell far short of unqualified approval.

The fate of lease-back

On 2 December 1980 Ridley made a Parliamentary statement about his visit to the Islands and to Buenos Aires. He told the House of Commons that lease-back was one way of seeking a negotiated settlement, and repeated the usual assurances that any agreement would have to be acceptable to the Islanders.[14] All accounts agree that his reception was a savage one, and that the Government suffered the political embarrassment which some of its members had wished to avoid. Almost all the MPs who spoke, however, betrayed a basic ignorance of the history of the Islands and of the predicament of the Islanders. Many were unaware of the Foreign Office's close liaison with Island councillors and of the consultations it had had with the Falklands lobby.

Peter Shore, Labour 'Shadow' Foreign Secretary, for example, talked about 'a territory which was originally uninhabited', and Russell Johnston for the Liberals declared 'that there is no support at all in the Falkland Islands' for any of the 'shameful schemes' which sought a peaceful settlement. Others displayed an equal ignorance of the dynamics of the dispute. Labour elder statesman Douglas Jay wanted to know 'why cannot the Foreign Office leave the matter alone?' Julian Amery, his Conservative opposite number, displayed less interest in the Islanders and more in the opportunity to indulge his own view of international relations. Advising the Minister that 'it is almost always a great mistake to get rid of real estate for nothing', he suggested that Ridley 'look back at the cost to us in terms of oil prices of the surrender of Aden and the Persian Gulf'. The Falklands commitment, he argued, would be cheaper for Britain to keep in the long run. Shore insisted that the paramountcy of the Islanders' wishes be maintained. As an epitome of Parliamentary ignorance and wishful thinking on foreign affairs, the discussion could hardly have been bettered.[15]

Ministers considered their position the next day at a Defence Committee meeting and later, on 4 December, at a full Cabinet session. According to Franks,

> the Cabinet noted that this was a highly emotive issue for Parliamentary and public opinion in Britain, where the Islanders' hostility to Mr Ridley's approach seemed to have been exaggerated: it would be tragic if the Islands' chances of escaping from economic blight were to be diminished by the attitude of their champions at Westminster.[16]

What tentative Cabinet support there had been for lease-back crumbled, and the collapse of the initiative was confirmed on 29 January 1981, when the Defence Committee endorsed the Foreign Secretary's lame conclusion that, although 'a freeze of the dispute was unlikely to be acceptable to the Argentines . . . the aim should be to keep negotiations going; and while applying no pressure to let the Islanders come to see the need to explore a realistic settlement based upon lease-back'.[17]

Emboldened by the Parliamentary opposition in the United Kingdom, and by success in local elections, the Islanders' new Council also passed a resolution, on 6 January 1981, opposing sovereignty negotiations. Ridley, however, had arrived back from Port Stanley, convinced that about half of the Falkland Islanders were prepared to consider the idea, and few dispute that many Islanders did see it as a viable solution even if they were not enthusiastic about it. In London the Falklands lobby recommended rejection of the proposal only by a bare majority, and Argentina was apparently 'well disposed' towards it in principle.[18]

The Cabinet, however, did not have the courage of the Foreign Office's convictions, and it was not prepared to encourage those in the Islands who acknowledged the merits of the scheme. Although it was intimidated by the hostile Parliamentary response, the real difficulty was that the Defence Committee's commitment to lease-back was minimal. The proposal seems to have been brought to Cabinet against the Prime Minister's political instincts and given a limited political remit only because the alternatives were less acceptable. Parliament's response merely added high political cost to minimum political support as reasons for abandoning the idea. The Cabinet did not have the political will to secure a settlement.

The causes and consequences of political defeat

There can be little doubt, given its composition and *modus operandi*, that the Prime Minister was primarily responsible for lease-back's rejection by the DOPC, and for its complete failure to give any consideration to the consequences of the non-decisions of December 1980 and January 1981. Thereafter, politically immobilised by the defeat of their Ministers, Foreign Office officials were unable to engage even in effective damage-limitation and contingency planning.

After the Parliamentary savaging of Mr Ridley, Falklands policy drifted without effective political direction or proper Cabinet supervision until Argentina seized the Islands. A series of desultory negotiations occupied the next 16 months. Britain had nothing to offer Argentina by way of progress on sovereignty, and Argentina slowly came to the view that it was getting nowhere through diplomatic channels. Relations between the two countries then drifted towards conflict as the JIC had predicted they would; save only that Argentina did not engage in all the preliminaries identified in JIC intelligence reports.

In stark contrast with 1975–77, no direction was given from Downing Street. Indeed, when that period is compared with 1981–82 two very significant differences stand out. The first was the complete absence of effective Prime Ministerial leadership. The second was the way in which the Prime Minister's anticipated hostility to Foreign Office advice frustrated all subsequent attempts to avoid catastrophe, ensuring confusion and contradiction when the long-predicted crisis with Argentina finally arrived at the beginning of 1982. There is no evidence to suggest that the Prime Minister's wishes were frustrated by the Foreign Office's commitment to negotiations. On the contrary, the lack of any alternative political lead frustrated the Foreign Office and compromised its subsequent attempt to review contingency plans for the Islanders.

There was a further contrast which also revealed something about the influences at work on Cabinet politics during this period, and the impact they had on the Falklands. Rhodesia was one of the Government's major preoccupations at this time. On that issue, however, the Prime Minister was persuaded, reportedly against her political preferences, to oppose the internal settlement agreed between Ian Smith and Abel Muzorewa, because it would lead to a break with the US over the renewal of sanctions and jeopardise British interests throughout black Africa. Instead, her authority was enlisted in support of the broader political settlement, embracing the Patriotic Front, which was recommended by the Foreign Office. A settlement was then reached 'through a combination of Mrs. Thatcher's political will and readiness to deal with any internal party problems, together with Lord Carrington's skill in handling the subsequent Lancaster House talks'. This might have been a recipe for success in the South Atlantic. On Rhodesia 'the Thatcher administration took the risk, rejected by its predecessors, of sending troops to monitor the ceasefire in the interim period before elections and full independence in spring 1980.'[19] On the Falklands no lead of any description was given.

Some have argued that this was the peak of Carrington's domestic political career. In staking his political capital on a Rhodesian settlement which was thoroughly disliked by many in the Conservative Party, he enhanced his international reputation. Paradoxically he also diminished his position within the Party as well as his influence over his Prime Minister and his Cabinet colleagues.[20]

The political ambience in which the Foreign Office had to work on the Falklands dispute from January 1981, therefore, undermined the conduct of policy at official level. Although that ambience was a specific product of the defeat over lease-back, it was also influenced by the general political sentiments which determined Cabinet politics under Thatcher, and the shifting politics of reputation within the Government as Ministers dealt with their agenda of major political issues. In short, aware of his depleted political resources, the Foreign Secretary made feeble attempts to restore political impetus to the management of the Falklands dispute and was unable to resist the implosion of policy which followed.

FALKLANDS POLICY AFTER LEASE-BACK

The bankruptcy of Government policy was displayed in all areas and its impact was cumulative as the dispute approached and then passed crisis point. The only decisive choice made about the Falklands during the interval between the lease-back initiative and the attack on the Islands was President Leopoldo Galtieri's decision to invade.[21]

A Departmental review of Falklands policy revealed the political impotence of Ridley and his officials as they tried to mobilise fresh political resources for the management of the dispute. Limited contingency planning, stimulated mostly by official concern and constrained by the absence of political direction, illustrated the continuing lack of political urgency about the implications of abandoning sovereignty negotiations. Withdrawal of HMS *Endurance* demonstrated that there was political will available to secure financial savings in endorsing the MOD's decision to withdraw the ship, despite the known consequences, which included the hostility of the House of Commons and Argentina's conclusion that this was an important indication of Britain's reluctance to maintain its position in the region for much longer.

As tension between Britain and Argentina rose at the beginning of 1982, lack of political attention allowed the mounting crisis to gain momentum, and significantly increased the danger of conflict. Political insensitivity to the deterioration of the dispute was increased still further by the scarcity of JIC reports and the inadequacy of those which were available. Intrinsic weaknesses in the Committee's intelligence reviews seem to have been compounded, in turn, by the political immobility which characterised the handling of the dispute at this stage. No new threat assessment was requested, for example, even when it became evident in March 1982 that Thatcher, Carrington and the Secretary of State for Defence, John Nott, had lost faith in the outdated JIC analysis which was available to them. On the eve of the invasion the increased volume of worried but conflicting reports about the turn of events concentrated attention on the Argentine landing on South Georgia. South Georgia, therefore, finally provided a model display of confusion and indecision in reactions to the crisis as Ministers in London failed to coordinate their responses to warnings of an imminent danger of military confrontation.

The Foreign Office review of policy

Faced with collapse of its policy the Foreign Office stalled Argentina at two further diplomatic meetings, in New York in February and in Paris on 15 June 1981. Meanwhile it took steps to reconsider the entire Falklands situation. A senior official, John Ure, who was the relevant

Assistant Under-Secretary of State, was despatched on a visit to the
Falklands and to Buenos Aires. His task in Argentina was to reassure
the Junta that Britain sought a peaceful solution and to persuade
Argentina 'not to force the pace'. In Port Stanley he reviewed the
dispute with the Islanders, in preparation for the forthcoming
reappraisal of policy required since the collapse of the lease-back
initiative.

The review took place in the Foreign and Commonwealth Office on
30 June 1981, at a meeting chaired by Ridley. Aware of the scale of its
political rebuff, the Foreign Office had decided to mount a powerful
response and the meeting included Sir Michael Palliser, the Permanent
Under-Secretary of State, the Deputy Under-Secretary of State (John
Ure) and Robin Fearn, the Head of the South American Department.
The British Ambassador to Buenos Aires, Anthony Williams, and the
Governor of the Falkland Islands, Rex Hunt, were also recalled. The
agenda was provided by a comprehensive summary from Ure which
was also supported by a long diplomatic telegram from the
Ambassador. This had been sent on 10 June, following his strong
recommendation in May that at least one further round of talks,
including a discussion of sovereignty, should be undertaken.[22]

Ure's paper, a classic piece of policy analysis, made three basic
points. First, he had concluded from his visit to Buenos Aires that the
Argentine Foreign Office was 'reasonably relaxed about progress—or
lack of progress—on the Falklands negotiations and well disposed
towards the lease-back idea'. He warned, however, that the military
leadership was much more unpredictable and might demand 'a more
"forward" policy at any time'. Second, he 'had formed the impression
that opinion amongst the Falkland Islanders had not hardened
irrevocably against lease-back'. In order to secure agreement for such
a proposal he recommended that a genuine effort would have to be
made to educate 'Islander and United Kingdom opinion about the
danger of inaction and the safeguards on which the Government would
insist in any lease-back arrangements'. Such a campaign would have to
include: assurance to the Islanders on access to the United Kingdom; a
resettlement scheme for those dissatisfied with any arrangements
reached; further land distribution schemes; and the initiation of more
productive economic schemes for the Islands. Third, if this approach
was unacceptable, he recommended that fuller contingency measures
for the defence and development of the Islands would have to be
considered.

Williams, the Ambassador, supported the idea of negotiation but was more blunt in urging that the initiative should be regained from the Islanders. In his view 'Islander opinion of the realities of the situation had been allowed to slide back'. He was also much less sanguine about Argentina's patience and warned that the risk of Buenos Aires using Britain as a scapegoat for its domestic troubles would be 'much more threatening' by the end of 1981. It was now 'less possible to depend on continued Argentine patience and understanding'. The British Government had to be more visible in support of a negotiated settlement.[23]

The discussion must have been a lively one since the Governor proceded flatly to contradict Ure and claimed that the Islanders wished to have 'nothing whatsoever to do with the Argentines'. He did not believe that 'any terms which could be arranged for a lease-back settlement could ever provide them [the Islanders] with the guarantees they wanted'. Such a stark and uncompromising report did not accord, however, with many other accounts of divided opinons amongst the Islanders; and it took no account of the cost of the alternatives or the risks which they entailed.[24]

Without reconciling these differences of opinion the meeting agreed that 'the immediate aim should be to play for time'. In addition,

> the new Falkland Islands legislative council, when elected, should be persuaded to allow talks to continue; . . . a paper for the Defence Committee should be prepared recommending a major public education campaign; and . . . up-to-date contingency papers, both civil and military, should be prepared as annexes to it.[25]

There was no recommendation that lease-back should be revived, but the debate must have reinforced Ridley's views since he decided to re-enlist his Foreign Secretary's support for the scheme. Minuting Carrington on 20 July 1981 he argued that there was no alternative to lease-back. While he recognised the strength of Island opposition he calculated that it might only be possible to stall Argentina for one more round of talks. Indeed he warned that

> if Argentina concluded, *possibly by early 1982*, that the government were unable or unwilling to negotiate seriously, retaliatory action must be expected: in the first instance through the withdrawal of communications, fuel and other facilities which it provided; in the longer run through some form of military action.[26] [Emphasis added]

He further suggested that in September the Defence Committee should be asked to consider a public education campaign to educate Island and domestic opinion about the facts of the dispute, the consequences of a failure to negotiate, and the corresponding advantages of a negotiated sovereignty solution on the lines of lease-back. His proposals were then drawn up in the form of a draft submission to the DOPC.

It was not until 7 September, however, that the two Ministers met to discuss this document. They were then also joined by officials and the Lord Privy Seal, Sir Ian Gilmour, who was there to provide a 'wider political view'. Carrington rejected Ridley's paper arguing that he would be unable to persuade his Cabinet colleagues to accept it. To attempt to do so would be 'counter-productive'. There was 'no immediate danger of hostile Argentine reactions'; hence there was no prospect of the Foreign Secretary securing the DOPC's support.

When the British Ambassador in Buenos Aires was notified of the 7 September decision, he despairingly protested that the Government had 'no strategy at all beyond a general Micawberism'. Warning that Argentina was unlikely to concede negotiations for much longer, he advised that 'If it was no longer possible to negotiate meaningfully about sovereignty, it would be better to tell Argentina frankly and face the consequences'.[27]

Appreciating his low stock of political capital in relation to the dispute, Carrington elected to keep the DOPC informed of events through a series of Minutes, only abandoning the tactic a week before the invasion. The first of what were to be five Minutes in all was sent on 14 September 1981.[28] Carrington used it merely to point out that 'there was little prospect of doing more than keeping some sort of negotiations with Argentina going'. The others followed on 2 December 1981, 15 February 1982, 24 March 1982 and 30 March 1982.[29]

Consequently, 'after January 1981' Government policy was never 'formally discussed outside the Foreign and Commonwealth Office'. The DOPC failed to discuss the Falklands at all in the 14 months between the end of January 1981 and the beginning of April 1982. During 1977 alone it had considered the issue on three separate occasions (in February, July and November).[30]

If the Foreign Secretary carried immediate responsibility for this, he was clearly responding also to his appreciation of the temper of the DOPC, the timing and agenda of whose meetings were 'ultimately a matter for the Prime Minister, advised by the Secretary of the Cabinet and the Cabinet Secretariat'.[31] Callaghan had not required much lobbying from his Foreign Office team to use the DOPC as an agent for refurbishing Falklands policy. Mrs Thatcher's interventions, however, were perfunctory and indecisive.

As in the 1970s, so in 1981–82, somebody had to give a lead to the DOPC and to the JIC to ensure that they took appropriate account of the implications of the January 1981 decision. Carrington did not believe that he could do so, and the Prime Minister apparently did not try. Yet, as Franks acknowledged,

> it could have been advantageous, and fully in line with Whitehall practice, for Ministers to have reviewed collectively at that time, September 7th or in the months immediately ahead, the current negotiating position; the implications of the conflict between the attitudes of the Islanders and the aims of the Junta; and the long-term policy options in relation to the dispute.[32]

The review of contingency planning

Foreign Office officials not only conducted a major review of policy in an unsuccessful attempt to regain the political initiative; they also began to review contingency plans for the protection and supply of the Islands. This was done as part of the staff work required in the preparation of Ridley's draft DOPC paper. Conducted through the usual inter-departmental channels the review was motivated more by sensible bureaucratic considerations than political priority. It proceeded at a deliberate administrative pace, therefore, unhurried by any political urgency.

In May 1981 officials consulted the Overseas Development Administration about a variety of matters including civil contingency measures for the Falklands: such as the possibility of extending Port Stanley's runway to accommodate long-haul jets, the provision of alternative sea communications, and the cost of providing better medical facilities. The Civil Aviation Authority provided estimates of the cost of extending the runway to different lengths, and the Department of Trade reported on the feasibility of various forms of sea service. This material was assembled into a comprehensive note which provided an annex to Ridley's proposed DOPC paper. It specified the costs of the measures and outlined some of the problems they would encounter. For example, South American countries would be unlikely to allow the provision of alternative air routes or services. Assuming that Argentina would refuse to allow its airfields to be designated as alternatives to Port Stanley for long-haul jets from South Africa, the annex concluded that only an alternative sea service was viable, at the charter cost of £8000 per day.[33]

Military contingencies were also reconsidered. At the request of the Foreign Office, the MOD prepared a 'short politico-military assessment of the United Kingdom's ability to respond militarily to a range of possible Argentine actions, the implications of responding in a particular way and the chances of success, with some indication of the possible cost'. The review was similar to that prepared for Callaghan's Government in 1977. It summarised Argentine military strength, noting that Argentina deployed some of the most efficient armed forces in South America, and examined the response needed to cope with the list of military options which the July 1981 JIC report had identified.[34]

The paper, however, was not so much concerned with how Britain should demonstrate its resolution but with what level of military combat it might have to engage in. To deter a full-scale invasion, for example, the paper argued for a large balanced force 'comprising an Invincible class carrier with four destroyers or frigates, plus possibly a nuclear-powered submarine, supply ships in attendance and additional manpower up to brigade strength, to re-inforce the garrison'. And the paper also concluded that a counter-invasion 'would require naval and land forces with organic air support on a very substantial scale, and that the logistic problems of such an operation would be formidable'. Preparation of the report naturally drew attention to the exposed position of the platoon of Royal Marines who formed the Falklands Garrison. This aroused some anxiety within the MOD, but not sufficient to encourage it to recommend that reinforcement was required.[35]

Although the report was drawn up on the understanding that it would provide an additional annex to Ridley's paper, the work was only approved by the Chiefs of Staff on 14 September—the week after Lord Carrington had declined to go back to the Defence Committee.[36] Consideration of its contents, therefore, never proceeded beyond the planning level and in February 1982 the UK Commanders-in-Chief's Committee accepted the advice of the Assistant Chief of the Defence Staff (Operations) that 'pending consideration of the Chiefs of Staff Paper (14 September 1981) by the Defence Committee, there was no enthusiasm in the Ministry of Defence for detailed contingency planning'.[37]

Preoccupied with stringent budget cut-backs, the MOD was in no mood to expend the time and energy required on a minor defence commitment, unless a much higher priority for that commitment was imposed upon it by the Defence Committee. But, as the DOPC was not to meet to discuss the Falklands no such pressure was to arise. It was therefore evident, as early as September 1981, that officials in both the MOD and the Foreign Office were looking in vain for Ministers to 'review the outcome of the contingency planning they had done in view of a potentially more aggressive position by Argentina'.[38]

The withdrawal of HMS *Endurance*

Of all the British actions which were thought to have influenced the Argentine decision to invade the Falklands, the announcement that HMS *Endurance* was to be withdrawn was considered decisive. In fact, it was only one in a series of important decisions and omissions remarkable for their political insensitivity. Although the ice-patrol ship had limited military value it was a source of important intelligence information about Argentine activities, and it was the only regular Royal Naval presence in the South Atlantic. As a token of Britain's commitment to the defence of the Falkland Islands, therefore, its deployment had a symbolic value far in excess of its military capabilities. This, as we have seen, had been acknowledged in 1976 when the first attempt to withdraw the vessel (as part of the economy measures introduced by the 1974 Defence Review) was reversed. HMS *Endurance* was kept in service, after representations from the Foreign Office, until it was ultimately decided to end her deployment following the 1981 Defence Review.

General financial and strategic considerations, of course, determined the MOD's priorities. It was under pressure both to save money and to employ the resources it had to best effect in support of Britain's continental defence commitments. The deployment of the ice-patrol ship was an unjustifiable expense in these terms. In the past, however, the Foreign Office had successfully persuaded the Ministry of Defence to keep *Endurance* on station because withdrawal would have had a significant impact on the conduct of Falklands policy. But in 1981–82, the coincidence of economic and strategic demands, together with the political demotion of the South Atlantic, brought about by the collapse of Falklands policy, allowed the MOD to defeat the Foreign Office in the new round of ministerial politics concerning the future of the ship.

Operating in politically straitened circumstances, the Foreign Secretary proved unable to reverse this decision.

Carrington protested to Nott on 5 June 1981. He pressed for the retention of *Endurance* on the grounds that a withdrawal would be interpreted by the Islanders and Argentina as a reduction in the United Kingdom's commitment to the Falklands. In addition, he argued that although the ship was nearing the end of her working life she ought to be replaced by a similar vessel. This ministerial exchange was followed by a meeting between Foreign Office and Defence officials, after which Carrington's representatives concluded that there was 'no prospect of the decision being reversed'.[39]

On 26 June the Falkland Islands Council objected strongly to the announcement, urging that 'all possible endeavours be made to secure a reversal of this decision'.[40] The Falklands lobby in London also took issue with it. Meanwhile, in July, the British Embassy in Buenos Aires submitted an official report on Argentine press reactions to the news. There was no doubt that the withdrawal was regarded as a decision to abandon 'the protection of the Falkland Islands'. This was confirmed by an intelligence report in September 1981, which noted that Argentina had concluded that the decision must have been a deliberate political gesture, rather than an economy measure, because the implications for the Islands and Britain's status in the South Atlantic were so fundamental.[41]

The issue provoked almost as much hostility as lease-back had exactly a year earlier. On 16 December, for example, 150 MPs signed a motion in the House of Commons objecting to the decision, and there was a debate in the House of Lords which was also critical of the Government. In an attempt to exploit this opportunity to gain political leverage, Carrington challenged the decision a second time. He made it clear (in a letter to Nott) that the withdrawal was being interpreted in Argentina as a deliberate move in a British disengagement from the South Atlantic and abandonment of the Falkland Islands. Nott, however, rejected Carrington's request for a meeting to discuss the issue and insisted that the decision could not be reversed.[42]

Ultimately Mrs Thatcher had to arbitrate and in doing so she had to exercise her political judgement, by running risks and signalling priorities, as well as making calculations of cost and benefit within the wider context of Goverment policy and under the pressure of its business. In the event, the Prime Minister elevated financial stringency above the minimum expenditure necessary for the successful management of a long-standing and potentially dangerous international dispute. She made this clear in response to worried Parliamentary questioning from Callaghan on 9 February.[43] Furthermore, she took this step despite the sort of opposition which had led to political capitulation in December 1980, and presumably in full awareness (with her Ministers) of the construction which the Argentine Government would place upon it.

The Foreign Secretary's last resort was to appeal to the DOPC. He reserved his right to do this in a letter to Nott on 17 February. (However, the balance of political argument was now heavily weighted against the Foreign Office in the conduct of Falklands policy, and so Carrington held to his judgement that the evidence currently available was not sufficient to persuade the Defence Secretary or the Prime Minister to change their minds.) He indicated to Nott that he would await the outcome of another round of talks with Argentina, arranged for the end of February 1982 in New York, before deciding to lodge his appeal. By then, he calculated, Argentina's response to the lack of progress might give him the additional leverage which he required.[44]

Unable to reconcile the diplomatic fears and demands of his Department with the political fears of his Cabinet colleagues, the Foreign Secretary had decided to bide his time and allow Argentina to make his case for him. Just as this made him a prey to Argentine actions, so it placed an extremely high premium upon the ability of intelligence services 'to quantify the degree of instability in a given situation and chart its development'. In particular, it demanded that they be able 'to indicate as precisely as possible when that development will precipitate a trauma'.[45] Such an ideal of intelligence reporting, however, is seldom realised in practice. Events are never so predictable and intelligence signals are rarely so clear. They are also likely to be confused by the 'noise' created by the other side's attempts to deceive, and by what Robert Jervis calls 'the masking effect' which makes it difficult to distinguish bluff from genuine preparations for attack.[46] Ministerial and Cabinet politics, therefore, demanded a degree of precision from intelligence analysts which was unlikely to be achieved even in the best of circumstances.

Diplomatic crisis, December 1981–March 1982

Buenos Aires could hardly have been expected to conform to all the options which the JIC's ladder of escalation had specified. Nonetheless, at the turn of the year and throughout the next few months the Junta did raise the level of tension in several of the ways which had long been anticipated: notably by inciting a hostile domestic press campaign which predicted an Argentine invasion of the Falklands; by interfering with communications to the Islands; by initiating, or at least exploiting, a private enterprise operation which raised the question of British control over the Dependency of South Georgia; and by taking a much tougher line in diplomatic negotiations. Moreover, intelligence made it clear that the Argentine Navy, long the most militant of the Argentine armed services, was deliberately forcing the pace of Argentine policy.

Confusingly, but predictably, as the volume of intelligence reports increased, some officials expressed alarm at these developments while others suggested that no use of force was contemplated. Typically, the material which corresponded with established expectations was accepted, whereas that which appeared alarmist, such as the warnings given by the Captain of HMS *Endurance*, seems to have been discounted as special pleading, or not sufficiently worrying to merit a formal revision of intelligence assumptions. All this is common in a developing crisis, which is why senior political supervision and coordination of policy by a small team of decision-makers is regarded as a vital requirement for successful crisis management.[47]

At the beginning of January 1982 one basic question concerned the British officials who were responsible for the Falklands. How long would Argentina remain content to engage in negotiations which had little purpose? One more round of negotiations was all that Ridley had expected in September 1981 and nobody expected them to outlast 1982. On 1 January of that year Britain's Ambassador to Argentina submitted his Annual Review for 1981 in which he expressed relief that Britain and Argentina had survived the year 'without a bust-up'. Foreign Office officials agreed that 'they would be fortunate to do so for a further year'.[48]

At the end of January the Governor of the Falkland Islands also submitted his Annual Review. He emphasised the hardening of Islander opinion against lease-back, which had been reflected in elections to the Legislative Council on 14 October.

Hunt also complained about a large number of Argentine actions. If diplomatic relations with Buenos Aires had deteriorated so had the Argentine arrangements for providing supplies and communications to the Falklands. Air services had been reduced at short notice and there had been six overflights by Argentine Airforce aircraft during the course of the year. On 31 December 1981 he had also objected to the unauthorised presence of the Argentine Naval ice-breaker

Almirante Irizar in Stromness Bay on South Georgia. Fearing a deliberate violation of British sovereignty, he recommended that proceedings be instituted against Davidoff, the Argentine business-man involved, and a strong protest lodged with the Argentine Government.[49]

From the Governor's comments the Foreign Office concluded that the Islanders were effectively espousing a Fortress Falklands policy and that it was left with no way 'to prevent the dispute moving sooner or later' to more open conflict. In their reply to his report, officials pointed out that 'we are now perilously near the inevitable move from dialogue to confrontation'.[50]

Shortly afterwards, and for the first time in the history of the dispute, Argentina set a time limit for its resolution. On 27 January 1982 the Argentine Ministry of Foreign Affairs delivered a *bout de papier* to the British Ambassador in Buenos Aires, setting out in detail and at length Argentina's claim to sovereignty. There was nothing surprising in this, but it concluded by proposing the establishment of a 'permanent negotiating commission' to meet in the first weeks of each month, alternating between London and Buenos Aires. Its task would be to resolve the dispute 'peacefully, definitively and rapidly'. The commission was to have a duration of one year and it would be 'open to denunciation by either side at any time without prior warning to the other side'.[51] Thus Argentina began the process of escalation at the beginning of 1982 and at the very most Britain had less than a year in which to mount an effective response.

There was, in addition to these developments, important corrobora-tive evidence from other sources of a significant shift in Argentine attitudes. The British Ambassador, for example, suspected that the period allowed for further negotiations might be related to the 150th anniversary (in January 1983) of the British occupation of the Islands. General Galtieri, Commander-in-Chief of the Argentine Army, had also replaced President Viola as head of the Junta on 22 December 1981. And Galtieri had close links with the Argentine Navy whose commander, Admiral Anaya, was a personal friend. The British Ambassador, analysing the implications of this change, emphasised once again that the Navy was the most bellicose of the three services and that it was playing a decisive role in the new Government. Later, on 3 February, he warned that Admiral Anaya 'probably with President Galtieri's full agreement' was now dictating Argentina's negotiating position and had been responsible for ruling that a test period be set to see if 'negotiations got anywhere'.[52]

Finally, Argentine press comment at the beginning of 1982 also indicated that relations were rapidly deteriorating and that some violent Argentine response was under official consideration. Within the JIC, however, these comments were discounted as merely attempts to exert diplomatic pressure, despite the precedent of the 1970s when such reports had been given serious consideration as a significant contributory indicator of the level of threat. Even the absence of such a press campaign in 1976, for example, had been taken as an important indication of Argentine intentions.[53]

In fact, throughout the first three months of 1982 the Argentine press was full of the most direct warnings that some military adventure was planned against the Falklands. An authoritative columnist for *la Prensa*, Jesus Iglesias Rouco, predicted in January (before the Foreign Ministry's *bout de papier* was delivered to the British Ambassador) that the Argentine Government would specify strict conditions and a time limit for the continuation of negotiations. These, he predicted, would be broken off if the conditions were not met. He anticipated wrongly, as did the Junta, that Argentina would receive the support of the United States. Nevertheless, according to his sources, 'the possibility that the Islands would be recovered in the course of the year by military action was virtually certain'.

Rouco followed these reports with two further articles in February, both of which argued that in the new circumstances an invasion of the Islands was justified and likely. This was not idle speculation. The British Embassy established that Rouco had particularly close connections with the Argentine Navy and Foreign Ministry and that an orchestrated press campaign was under way. There were similar reports in the English language *Buenos Aires Herald* and in the magazine *Siete Dias*. Furthermore, the journal *Latin American Weekly Report*, which closely monitored the development of Argentine policy and the political debates within the Junta, also predicted that an invasion attempt was imminent.[54] It appears in retrospect that the new Junta had taken a decision sometime in January 1982 to mount an invasion of the Islands; the final decision to go ahead with the attack was, however, precipitated by the course of the South Georgia incident rather than by the dictates of a carefully planned schedule.

More diplomatic talks were held in New York on 26 and 27 February. In a brief exchange between the Foreign Secretary and the Prime Minister, which preceded the talks, the gap between the lack of political urgency in London and the increasingly dangerous situation in the South Atlantic became quite apparent. Lord Carrington minuted the Prime Minister and other members of the Defence Committee on 15 February. He summarised the terms of Argentina's recent *bout de papier* and outlined the prospects for the New York meeting. There was no suggestion that there had been any significant increase in tension. Argentina's timetable was thought to be 'unrealistic', and it was accepted that Britain's options had narrowed still further. No early breakdown of negotiations was anticipated, despite Argentina's new position, but notice was given that a meeting of the Defence Committee in March might be necessary. In response the Prime Minister merely insisted that the Islanders' wishes were paramount and that this had to be made clear to Argentina.[55]

According to Franks, a small force, 'either overtly as a deterrent measure or covertly as a precautionary measure', might 'reasonably' have been deployed at this point to strengthen Britain's position at the New York talks, but the suggestion was not raised either by officials or by Ministers. Similar action had been taken in February 1976 and December 1977, but Franks concluded that, in view of the difference between the two periods, the circumstances of February 1982 'did not warrant a similar naval deployment'. Argentine military actions, it was argued, were more indirect and less threatening and Ambassadors had not been withdrawn.[56]

But in the 1970s the Government had not decided to abandon sovereignty negotiations. Furthermore, by February 1982, it was also known that Argentina had contingency plans for the invasion of the Islands; that a press campaign was under way in Buenos Aires heralding an invasion; that the most hawkish branch of the armed services was in the ascendancy in the Junta; and that formal notice had been given to Britain that Argentina would withdraw from diplomatic negotiations within the year if no progress was made. It is true that any military response by the United Kingdom would have required judicious handling to ensure that it did not precipitate an Argentine attack, but this had been equally true in 1976 or 1977. There is good reason, therefore, to take issue with Franks, especially when the developments on South Georgia are also taken into consideration. Eventually, such differences as there were between the two periods are not sufficient to explain why the Conservative administration failed to consider any military response at all until a matter of days before the invasion.

At the New York talks the British accepted the establishment of the permanent negotiating commission which Argentina had demanded in the *bout de papier* of 27 January. Details were also agreed specifying the task of the commission and the way in which it was to operate. However, in an informal working paper jointly drafted by the two delegations, Britain insisted that the work should be conducted without prejudice to the sovereignty position of either Government. The commission would operate for one year and during that time either party was at liberty to terminate the arrangement. None of this was to be made public but a joint communiqué for official release was agreed. This merely stated that: 'The meeting took place in a candid and positive spirit. The two sides reaffirmed their resolve to find a solution to the sovereignty dispute and considered in detail an Argentine proposal for procedures to make better progress in this sense.'[57]

In anticipation of another year of discussions, and reassured by reports from a variety of sources that an Argentine invasion was unlikely, the Foreign Office concluded that although time was running out there was no crisis. Yet the new negotiating commission could be terminated unilaterally at any time and the agreement to set it up was not a promise of another year's grace.

More importantly, the Junta's attitude to diplomatic discussions had always been regarded as a significant indication of Argentina's intentions. It had always been thought that any sign of a breakdown in communication between the Argentine negotiating team and decision makers in Buenos Aires would help to signal a much more dangerous and unpredictable situation, providing one of those specific indicators which policy makers require to help distinguish bluff from the real thing.[58]

An ominous development occurred, therefore, on the day that the joint communiqué was issued by the two negotiating teams in New York. Almost simultaneously the Argentine Foreign Ministry in Buenos Aires issued a unilateral communiqué which, contrary to the understanding reached in New York, disclosed the full scope of the discussions, declaring that 'Argentina reserves [the right] to terminate the working of this mechanism and to choose freely the procedure which best accords with her interests'.[59] This was followed by increased Argentine press speculation about a forthcoming invasion and a transfer of sovereignty before the 150th anniversary of Britain's occupation. Rouco suggested, in *la Prensa*, that the action would come between the middle and the end of the year.[60] On 3 March Britain's Uruguayan Ambassador also telegrammed to say that Uruguayan sources considered that Argentina was taking a much tougher stance on the Falklands.

The Foreign Office's response began to quicken at last and the United States was asked on 1 March to intervene by means of representations by the United States Assistant Secretary of State for Latin American Affairs (Thomas Enders), who was on a visit to Buenos Aires. Asked to advise Argentina 'to keep things cool', Enders is reported to have raised the issue for general discussion, both publicly and privately, although his mission was to cultivate relations with the Junta. On his return he advised London that Argentina was not about to 'do anything drastic'.[61]

At a short meeting in the Foreign and Commonwealth Office on 5 March Lord Carrington reviewed developments with the new Junior Minister, Richard Luce, together with the two Foreign Office officials directly concerned with the Falklands. They agreed on a package of diplomatic responses to the rising tension. Argentina was to be urged to return to the arrangements agreed in New York. The United States was to be asked to help again but this time at a more senior level. The Foreign Secretary was to approach Alexander Haig, the US Secretary of State, and ask for his assistance. A response for the United Nations was prepared and it was also agreed to draw up a draft paper for an early DOPC meeting. In addition the Foreign Secretary was informed that in November 1977 the previous Government had covertly sent a small naval task force to the area. Although Carrington was not formally advised to consider a similar move, the suggestion must have been implicit in the notification, but he did not pursue the matter when he learnt that Argentina had not been told about the deployment.[62]

Hence, early March was a second point at which some British military response to the deterioration of the dispute might have been given serious consideration. Nevertheless, the Foreign Secretary rejected the idea of a naval deployment at the beginning of March 1982 for much the same reasons as he had refused to support Ridley's draft DOPC paper in September 1981. Evidence about Argentine intentions was now growing and he was considering an early return to the DOPC, but he still judged that it was insufficiently compelling. With hindsight he wished that he had deployed a nuclear-powered submarine on 5 March, but at the time he decided that the circumstances did not merit such a move. 'Nothing', he was to argue later, 'would have been more likely to turn the Argentines away from the path of negotiations and toward that of military force' than moving ships into the area.[63]

Thus by the first week of March there was an urgent need for the British Cabinet to give direct consideration to three critical issues: the poverty of Britain's diplomatic position; the contingency planning initiated by officials; and the question of 'whether the potentially more threatening attitude by Argentina required some form of deterrent action'.[64] But the politics of the Thatcher Cabinet ensured that no such consideration took place.

During that week Downing Street did begin to respond to the turn of events. The Prime Minister attached a note to the British Ambassador's summary of Argentine press comments which had followed the unilateral communiqué issued by the Argentine Foreign Ministry at the end of the New York talks. It read, 'we must make contingency plans'.[65] Mrs Thatcher's Private Secretary also wrote to the Foreign Office on 8 March drawing attention to this note and asking for an account of contingency planning to be included in the annexes to the paper for the long awaited, but as yet still unscheduled, DOPC meeting on the Falklands. Such details had been available since 7 September 1981, in the annexes to Ridley's draft DOPC paper. No reply was, therefore, sent to the Private Secretary's letter because it was assumed that the matter would be quickly dealt with at that meeting. It was not the advice which was lacking so much as the political direction needed to call it to Cabinet attention and arrange for it to be acted upon.

The Prime Minister also asked the Secretary of State for Defence how quickly Royal Navy ships could be deployed to the Falklands. On 12 March she was told that a frigate would require Royal Fleet Auxiliary support and that the passage to the Falklands would take about 20 days.[66]

By the middle of March the Foreign Office's diplomatic reply to Argentina's unilateral communiqué was finally ready for despatch. There was now a definite but still unclear appreciation that some crisis was in the offing. Officials warned the Foreign Secretary on 18 March that his message to Argentina's Foreign Minister, Costa Mendez, would be rejected and that Argentina might then take retaliatory action. Intelligence by this time had also concluded that 'unless a satisfactory reply meeting Argentine conditions was received by the end of March 1982, at the latest, early action to withdraw Argentine services to the Islands might be taken'. As a consequence the Foreign Secretary was advised to ask the Secretary of Defence again to maintain HMS *Endurance* on station. In addition, it was also suggested that a paper prepared by officials, urgently requesting political and financial authority to implement contingency plans for the replacement of services to the Islands, should be circulated to the DOPC in advance of any meeting. Although delivered to Ministers in the Foreign Office on 19 March, that paper does not seem to have been given any wider circulation, and it was a week before Nott was asked to keep the ice-patrol ship in service.[67] By then, however, the South Georgia crisis was dictating the final descent into conflict.

Intelligence failures

The failure of British intelligence, and the inadequacy of its analysis, seem to have been attributable to a variety of complex factors in addition to the inertia of its well rehearsed but flawed interpretation of the nature of the military threat. Again there was no single reason for what went wrong. Instead, the challenge of the issue once more exposed the institutional and political weaknesses of the system.

Under the new Government JIC reviews were infrequent, and the political and diplomatic analysis which they provided was poor. Military surveillance of the South Atlantic is also said to have been limited. In addition problems arose of the sort which are often found in the context of high tension and crisis, including conflicting intelligence reports and the difficulties in distinguishing a bluff from real danger.

Between November 1975 and November 1977 the JIC reviewed the Falklands situation no less than eight times, but between November 1979 and 31 March 1982 it provided only three reappraisals of the Argentine threat.[68] The first was a standard briefing for the incoming Government. The second, on 9 July 1981, reviewed the threat following the collapse of Government policy after the abandonment of the lease-back initiative in January of that year. The final review was produced on 31 March 1982 in response to developments on South Georgia.[69]

The critical report was the middle one of the three (July 1981). According to Franks it had 'considerable influence on the thinking of Ministers and officials'.[70] Prepared in direct response to the Government's decision not to negotiate on sovereignty, it was also the one which might have been expected to pay particular attention to that decisive shift in British policy. But there was little to distinguish it from the other two reports, or indeed from those submitted to previous Cabinets. Essentially it restated the institutional wisdom which had remained substantially unrevised for over a decade.

Reviewing events since 1979, it considered the progress of British talks with Argentina, political and economic developments there, the progress of Buenos Aires' dispute with Chile, and the Junta's improving relations with the United States and Brazil. In addition it specified in some detail the pattern of escalation that might be expected if Argentina became impatient with diplomacy. As usual 'diplomatic and economic measures' were expected first, including the disruption of air and sea communications, the interruption of food and oil supplies and access to medical treatment. Next it was thought that there would be a 'distinct possibility' that Argentina might occupy one of the uninhabited Dependencies, as it did South Thule in 1976. Alternatively there was a risk that a military presence might be established on the Falklands themselves, somewhere remote from Port Stanley. Harassment or arrest of British shipping was not thought to be 'a likely option unless the Argentine Government felt themselves severely provoked'. Although use of force was considered to be Argentina's last resort, the review emphasised that sovereignty negotiations remained the critical factor. If there was no prospect of a peaceful transfer of sovereignty, there was a high risk of forcible measures and Argentina might then 'act swiftly and without warning'. None of this seems to have been specifically related to the ending of sovereignty talks.[71]

The South Georgia-inspired report (March 1982) has also been criticised for failing to attach 'sufficient weight to the possible effects on Argentine thinking of the various actions of the British Government'.[72] Equally it did not take 'fully into account both relevant diplomatic and political developments and foreign press treatment of sensitive foreign policy issues'. Although 'changes in the Argentine position were . . . more evident on the diplomatic front and in the associated press campaign', the JIC's assessments seem to have undervalued both.[73]

In terms of specific military intelligence the JIC itself is said to have been ill-served. Military movements in Argentina, for example, were apparently subject to almost no direct surveillance, and no additional resources were assigned to this task, although in October 1981, following a review of intelligence requirements in the Caribbean and Latin America, the JIC had 'notified the collecting agencies that . . . the requirement had increased for intelligence on Argentine intentions and policies' with respect to the Falklands. The defence attaché in Buenos Aires claimed that his section 'had neither the remit nor the capacity to attain detailed information' about military deployments. By the time the dispute had seriously deteriorated at the beginning of March it would have been difficult, in any event, to evaluate such information because of the lack of knowledge about 'the normal pattern of Argentine military activity'. According to Franks 'no advanced information was therefore available by these means about the composition and assembly of the Argentine naval force that eventually invaded the Falklands.' There was no intelligence 'from American sources or otherwise' to show that Argentine forces at sea were intended for invasion, and no satellite photography was available. The annual Uruguay/Argentine naval exercises, which were used to cloak the assembly and despatch of the invasion force, were monitored by the defence attaché 'mainly on the basis of Argentine press reports'.[74] The increase in radio traffic generated by these exercises was, however, picked up by HMS *Endurance* as well as by the CIA and the US National Security Agency, and fed into GCHQ Cheltenham.[75]

Apparently there was a lack of precise and detailed military intelligence. But Britain participates in a worldwide intelligence network with the United States, Canada and Australia. The Royal Navy routinely shares the data supplied by the Fleet Ocean Surveillance Information Centre (FOSIC) run by the United States Navy in London. A major source of FOSIC's information is the global ship radio monitoring system run by these four powers. In addition the US Navy's four Ocean Surveillance Satellites (OSUS), which use radar and infra-red cameras for ship detection, can also monitor radio and radar transmissions. Close-up photo reconnaissance can be provided, in addition, by SR 71 ('Blackbird' reconnaissance aircraft). Furthermore, it has been reported that the United States flew such a surveillance mission, in response to a British request, prior to the invasion taking place.[76] Rowlands, who was Junior Minister in charge of the Falklands under the Callaghan Government, also revealed on 3 April 1982 that Britain had been reading Argentine radio traffic for years, and there have been no reports that acquisition of intelligence information caused special problems during the war itself.[77] If there was a significant gap in the military information available to British analysts and decision makers, the causes of it have not been satisfactorily explained, at least in public.

As tension increased so the intelligence picture also became more confusing. On 2 March, for example, the British defence attaché in Buenos Aires submitted a report on the Argentine threat, following a private visit he had made to the Falklands. His letter, which was widely circulated within the Ministry of Defence, identified the Argentine Navy as the most serious danger. It warned that:

on the worst possible interpretation of developments an Army President, who had already demonstrated his lack of patience when frustrated over such issues, could give orders to the military to solve the Malvinas problem once and for all in the latter half of the year.[78]

If talks broke down, or continued to make no progress, he considered that a 'direct seizure of the Islands was an obvious alternative', noting also that 'in Argentina a military *coup* was a fairly well practiced art'. On 10 March, however, an officer in the Defence Intelligence Staff of the MOD circulated another analysis of the situation which took a quite different view of the Argentine Navy's role and influence.[79] The paper was also at odds with the British Ambassador's concern at the close links between Galtieri and Anaya, as well as his warning that the Admiral was dictating Falklands policy. By the beginning of March, therefore, the volume of reports from the South Atlantic had substantially increased and so had the uncertainty surrounding the intentions of the Junta. At issue, however, was not whether, but when and in what form, Argentina would take military action. As the threatening tone and mounting confusion of reports indicated, Anglo-Argentine relations were already acquiring that dangerous uncertainty and independent momentum which often precedes the outbreak of conflict.

Franks concluded that the main reasons for these shortcomings were: first, that 'the arrangements for bringing to the Joint Intelligence Organisation's attention information other than intelligence reports' were deficient; and, second, that the JIC required a full-time independent chairman, with more influence, as the Prime Minister's appointee and member of the Cabinet Office.[80] In addition, the report further criticised the JIC for being 'too passive in operation to respond quickly and critically to a rapidly changing situation which demanded urgent action'. In the final analysis, however, the presentation of intelligence information, as much as the formulation of policy advice, takes place within a climate of opinion created by political priorities and political direction. Not only were far fewer JIC reviews produced between 1979 and 1982 than in the relevant Callaghan years, but Franks offered no evidence that there was any particular demand for them either. It is not inconceivable, therefore, that political immobility also made its contribution to an intelligence picture which was distinguished by its lack of political awareness.

South Georgia

The South Georgia episode brought the dilemmas and confusion which surrounded British policy to a pitch of indecision and provided a classic example of one of the major threats to peace in the South Atlantic which British intelligence had long identified. Exercising an option to purchase and dispose of scrap metal at the disused whaling stations on South Georgia, Constantino Davidoff arrived at Leith, South Georgia, aboard the Argentine Naval ice-breaker *Almirante Irizar* on 20 December 1981. This was the visit which had prompted the Governor of the Falkland Islands to protest to London that Davidoff had not received proper authorisation to land. Although the British Ambassador in Buenos Aires was instructed to deliver a strong protest to the Argentine Foreign Ministry, his note was not finally delivered until 3 February 1982, because Argentina officially denied any knowledge of the incident and evidence corroborating the complaint had to be gathered before the protest was finally lodged.

On 23 February Davidoff requested permission to return to South Georgia and contritely asked for advice as to how to proceed without causing official complications. In a conciliatory gesture he also offered to transport supplies to the British Antarctic Survey base there, and to make available the services of the medical team travelling with his own party. However, he sailed aboard the Argentine Naval support vessel, *Bahia Buen Suceso*, before official authorisations had been made out. On 20 March the Governor of the Falkland Islands relayed the signal from the British Base Commander at Grytviken that the Argentine ship had arrived in Leith harbour, put a sizeable party of civilians and military personnel ashore, fired off shots, hoisted the Argentine flag, and 'defaced' a notice against unauthorised landings.[81]

From then on, in a series of exchanges between London, Buenos Aires, Port Stanley and South Georgia, the incident rapidly escalated. The Argentine Government, 'clearly intent on raising the temperature' according to Franks, rejected British protests, turned down opportunities to defuse the incident and finally exploited it to cover the assault on all British territory in the South Atlantic which was launched at the beginning of April.

Once news of the Argentine landing reached London 'Foreign and Commonwealth Office and Defence Ministers' decided that HMS *Endurance* should sail to South Georgia on 21 March with a party of marines, and the Governor of the Falklands was instructed to keep her destination confidential. On 22 March the Base Commander at Grytviken reported that the Argentine ship had left and that there was no sign of the shore party. Accordingly HMS *Endurance* was ordered to resume her normal duties. Later the same day news came from

Grytviken that there was an Argentine shore party at Leith, and Captain Barker of the *Endurance* argued that Davidoff and the Argentine Navy were in league. HMS *Endurance* was then ordered to continue to South Georgia and await further instructions, although the Falkland Islands' Governor wanted her to be ordered to remove the Argentines. On 23 March Captain Barker signalled again, arguing that Britain was faced with a planned military operation. By then Foreign Office officials had also concluded from intelligence sources that the Argentine Navy was deeply involved. Ministerial approval was thus given for the marines on HMS *Endurance* to remove the Argentine party and a statement was made in the House of Commons explaining that 'the intention was to conduct the operation correctly, peacefully and in as low a key as possible'.[82]

Meanwhile, through diplomatic exchanges in Buenos Aires, Argentine Foreign Minister Costa Mendez argued that British reactions would make it more difficult for him to restrain the Junta. The British Ambassador then advised London that care be taken not to damage Anglo-Argentine relations. As a consequence the first order to remove the Argentines from Leith (given to HMS *Endurance* on 23 March) was quickly countermanded by a second, when 'Foreign and Commonwealth Office Ministers' ordered her to anchor at Grytviken instead.[83]

The next day (24 March) the British defence attaché in Buenos Aires sent a telegram to the Ministry of Defence revising his earlier assessment of the Argentine threat. He judged that any attempt to remove the Argentines by the Royal Marines would be met by force 'either from a warship at sea or by a "rescue operation" at Port Stanley' should the Argentine party be removed and taken there. In this case, he argued, the operation could escalate 'into an occupation of the Falkland Islands'. Such an escalation would be favoured by the 'hawks' in the Argentine Government who already wanted to exploit the situation. Before HMS *Endurance* was committed he strongly advised that 'the increase in the threat to Port Stanley' be taken into account. His advice was corroborated by other intelligence reports which were then circulating within the Foreign Office and the MOD. According to these reports Admiral Anaya was behind the South Georgia enterprise and the Argentine Navy was planning to take military action if the negotiating commission, set up after the New York talks in February, did not produce progress within months. Anaya, it was confirmed, had been responsible for the increase in the tempo of the dispute throughout the year.[84]

At the beginning of 1982 the outstanding issue facing British decision-makers had been whether negotiations would last one more round of talks. On 24 March, in his penultimate Minute to the DOPC, Lord Carrington announced that negotiations were finally at an end. All that was at issue was how much hostility could be expected from Argentina, where and when it would come, what form it would take and what the United Kingdom could do about it. It was acknowledged that the situation on South Georgia had become grave. The incident was either a prelude to armed hostilities or provided a ready excuse to turn the Falklands dispute into a major crisis.[85] Carrington had finally concluded that the time was now ripe for an early meeting of the Defence Committee. But time, as Cornford once noted, 'is like the medlar; it has a trick of going rotten before it is ripe'.[86]

The Foreign Secretary outlined all the options Argentina might be expected to employ, including a campaign at the United Nations, diplomatic and commercial reprisals and, 'in the final analysis, military action against the Islands'. He also sought financial support from the Government's reserve for the civil contingency plans which had been drawn up in May 1981 to replace air and sea services to the Falklands. In a separate letter to Nott he asked once more that HMS *Endurance* be retained and suggested that the MOD circulate a paper on military contingency planning before the Defence Committee meeting which he had now asked the Prime Minister to convene.[87]

The following day, 25 March, London was informed that Argentine warships had been sent to stop HMS *Endurance* from evacuating the Argentine party at Leith and that other units had been deployed to intercept the British ship if necessary on the passage between South Georgia and Port Stanley. Captain Barker on *Endurance* reported that a second Argentine ship, the *Bahia Paraiso*, had arrived at Leith and was 'working cargo'. On the evening of the 25th he further reported that three landing craft and a military helicopter were operating between the ship and the jetty, and signalled that *Bahia Paraiso* was flying the pennant of the 'Argentine Navy's Senior Officer Antarctic Squadron'. The Foreign Office knew that the vessel belonged to the Argentine Navy but had thought it was an unarmed scientific ship. Its suspicion that the Argentine Navy was deeply implicated in the affair was now confirmed.[88]

Thus 24–25 March was the final opportunity for some action to be taken. In addition to all the other indications that the Government was beset by crisis, there had also been overflights of the Falklands by the Argentine Air Force and one of its Hercules C-130s had landed unannounced at Port Stanley, allegedly due to an emergency but probably to test the airfield.[89] Co-ordination at Prime Ministerial and Cabinet level was required, not because the Junta's precise intentions were known, but because there was every indication that Anglo-Argentine relations had surpassed 'normal strain' (to quote Coral Bell's classic study of crisis) and were clearly 'rising to breaking strain'.[90] Given the Junta's decision to intercept HMS *Endurance*, a fact known to the British Government, the crisis was only days away from a direct military confrontation.

On 25 March 1982 the DOPC was not to meet for another *week*. During that time conclusive evidence arrived showing that an Argentine invasion fleet was at sea. However, liaison between the Foreign Office, the MOD and Downing Street continued to be conducted through bilateral exchanges and *ad hoc* discussions, with Ministers acting on the basis of their own information and priorities rather than in concert with an up-to-date and commonly agreed course of action backed by a revised JIC assessment. Thatcher, Nott and Carrington each became increasingly concerned about the course of events but they failed collectively to consider policy or co-ordinate British actions. It was also clear by this time that they no longer had confidence in the current JIC assessment, but none of them called for a fresh report.

On the evening of 29 March the Prime Minister, 'prompted by the most recent telegram', despairingly demanded that something be done. The Foreign Office had asked US Secretary of State Haig to intervene but that had had no effect, and on the 31st, in a final impotent gesture, Mrs Thatcher asked President Reagan to try to stop Argentina's invasion. The MOD, stimulated by its own intelligence reports, alerted the Chiefs of Defence Staff, and began to review its military contingency plans as well as initiating military preparations for the despatch of forces to the South Atlantic.[91]

Yet even these measures appeared to be as confused and contradictory as the orders issued, rescinded, and reissued to HMS *Endurance*. Julian Thompson, for example, recorded that his force (3 Commando Brigade) had been alerted 'for possible operations in connection with the Falklands' early in the week before the invasion. By the evening of 1 April, however, 'the last of the sub-units tipped-off for possible operations had been stood down'![92]

As late as 26 March, although the MOD agreed to Carrington's request for the retention of HMS *Endurance*, it did so reluctantly and temporarily because it still 'could not justify paying for her retention'.

On 29 March the Chancellor of the Exchequer also rejected the Foreign Secretary's request for money from the contingency reserve to implement the civil contingency plans prepared by his officials in 1981. Finally, on 30 March, by which time intelligence had confirmed that a large Argentine task force was intent on attacking at least one of the Falkland islands, the MOD and the Foreign Office disagreed on how many nuclear submarines should be sent to the South Atlantic. The first had been instructed to sail the previous day, when the Prime Minister and the Foreign Secretary had discussed the situation *en route* to a Common Market meeting in Brussels. The despatch of a second was agreed at an inter-departmental meeting on the 30th and a third was earmarked for use but not ordered to sail because 'the Ministry of Defence took the view that there would be significant operational penalties elsewhere'.[93]

Although the Foreign Office, the Ministry of Defence and the Prime Minister all now recognised that they were in a crisis of some magnitude, Carrington went ahead with a scheduled visit to Israel. In the absence of the Foreign Secretary, Nott convened an emergency meeting in the Prime Minister's rooms in the House of Commons at 9 p.m. on 31 March to announce that an Argentine invasion of the Falklands was imminent. The long awaited Defence Committee discussion on the Falklands took place the next day, and Argentina occupied the Islands the day after that.[94]

CONCLUSION

Making no allowances for the Thatcher Government's conduct of Falklands policy would be unfair and unrealistic. But there was misjudgement rather than 'misperception' of Argentine intentions in the United Kingdom. Many factors contributed in one degree or another to the mutually reinforcing train of events which then followed. They included the low priority of the issue; the confusion and uncertainty which surrounded the development of the dispute; the preoccupation of Ministers with other more important problems; the influence of established expectations lodged deep in the intelligence advice available to Ministers; the political dilemmas caused by the strength of Parliamentary and Island opposition to a transfer of sovereignty; the military dilemmas involved in having to deter an opponent from 8000 miles away without provoking a pre-emptive strike; the financial difficulty involved in trying to justify the

expenditure of defence resources on a minor commitment at a time of
budgetary restraint; and the speed with which the Junta finally decided
to go ahead with the invasion.

The Franks Report, however, was intellectually dishonest in making
every political allowance for each mitigating factor. Its conclusion
provided a quite unwarranted apologia for Thatcher and Carrington,
totally unsupported by the evidence on which the Report itself was
based. The issue was never a very important one and, as we shall argue
later, Parliamentary and Island opposition need not have been
elevated into such an obstacle to progress. There was, moreover,
nothing new about the military dilemmas which the Government faced
and the experiences of the 1970s had demonstrated how vulnerable the
Islands were and how quickly the dispute could escalate. The evidence
contained in the Franks Report provides a damning indictment,
therefore, of the political management of British policy-making.

3 Falklands and Lobby Politics

As a microcosm of imperial retreat and colonial enterprise in decline the Falklands story is intriguing for many reasons, but our concern in this chapter is with matters directly concerned with policy formulation and implementation. What was the character of the community whose wishes and interests were paramount in the conduct of British policy? Through what kind of political processes were its views articulated? And, finally, how were those views relayed by the lobby which acted on behalf of the Islanders in London? Only by considering these matters can we say anything sensible about the contribution which the Islanders made to the debate about their future, how that contribution was formed, and ultimately whether the outcome could have been different. Examining these issues will also serve to reinforce the basic argument that the failure of Falklands policy before the war was essentially a political one, and that underlying this political failure were the complexities of a small but intricate political problem.

A CONFLICT OF VIEWS

Incorporating domestic interests successfully into the policy process has been identified as a particular difficulty in policy-making. On the one hand, isolated from the pressures and dynamics to which policy-makers are subject, it is maintained that domestic actors are likely to become opponents rather than allies of the policy community and so frustrate the designs of policy-makers. Alternatively, it can be argued, as it was about the Falklands, that irreconcilable conflicts of interest between domestic constituents are the cause of policy failure.[1] Either proposition may be true, but in this instance neither constitutes a sufficient explanation of the collapse of British policy.

The Foreign and Commonwealth Office did not exclude the Islanders or the Falklands lobby from the management of policy. On the contrary, both parties were included and joined in discussions about the future of the Islands. The Island councillors were consulted about sovereignty negotiations and attended several rounds of talks, while the Islanders as a body were canvassed directly during visits made by Foreign Office Ministers. It was not the absence of consultation, therefore, but what the Islanders took to be its patrician and niggardly style which, together with their innate suspicion of London, helped to obstruct political progress.[2]

Integral to the evolution of British policy since the mid-1960s was the argument not so much that the United Kingdom's claim to sovereignty was unassailable, although that position was formally maintained, but that Britain had legal, political and moral obligations to the Islanders in its role as the administering power for the territory (under Article 73 of the UN Charter) and in respect of the rights of the Falkland Islanders to self-determination (under Article 1 of the Charter). These obligations were translated into a commitment to respect the paramountcy of the Islanders' wishes, a formula invented in some haste in 1968 as a response to the hostile public reaction to Lord Chalfont's proposals to negotiate about sovereignty. Paramountcy combined some of the language of Article 73 (which requires that the 'interests' of the inhabitants of 'non-self-governing territories' should be paramount, and their political aspirations taken into account) with an extended guarantee which made the Islanders' 'wishes' decisive. In that way the commitment went far beyond what was required by international agreement.[3] As a political device designed to counter Parliamentary objections, however, the formula was an immediate success. It served equally well on other occasions, but it granted Ministers very little latitude in responding to the issue when dealing with all the principal actors involved: the Islanders, Cabinet, Parliament and Argentina. If progress was to be made in settling the sovereignty dispute, by revising the paramountcy formula or otherwise, the loosely allied opposition of Islands spokesmen, their Parliamentary sympathisers and the Falklands lobby had to be overcome by one political means or another. For reasons which we will examine later, Parliament and the lobby would not have presented any serious political problems had the Islanders been willing to accept a settlement. The official expression of Islands opinion consequently became decisive.

Thus the political weaknesses of Falklands policy cannot simply be attributed to the exclusion of the domestic clients most directly concerned. The Foreign Office may be accused of taking too much notice of the representations of the Islanders and their allies, or too little, depending upon one's sympathies. But this only serves to emphasise that the outcome of British policy depended as much on the position adopted in Port Stanley as that which was adopted in London.

Whether these positions were necessarily irreconcilable depended as much on the contribution which the Islanders made to the discourse about their future as that which was made by British Ministers and their officials. In the event, the Islanders' perspective differed significantly from that of the Foreign Office. And just as British policy was the outcome of Cabinet, Ministerial and bureaucratic politics, so that of the Islanders was a product of their own local political conditions. A crucial divergence of views on the British side of the sovereignty dispute, derived from different political appreciations of the nature of the Falklands problem, quickly became fixed conflicting views about what should be done, which only the skilful use of power and persuasion were able to reconcile.[4]

Moreover, just as the Foreign Office's interpretation of the dispute possessed its own deficiencies, that of the Islanders was also deeply flawed. The divisions, contradictions and ambivalence which were thus introduced into British policy pre-dated Argentina's military regime. The behaviour of the Junta exacerbated but did not cause these problems. They originated, instead, in the contributions which each of the three British participants (the Government, the Islanders and the Falklands lobby) made to the political debate about the issue.

The Foreign and Commonwealth Office regarded the Falklands as a diplomatic problem with, so to speak, a human face; one that had to be resolved in order to avoid gratuitous political or military conflict with Argentina. The savings to be made in withdrawing from the South Atlantic were, of course, quite small, and the Islanders seem to have found it difficult to understand why Britain should want to negotiate with Argentina on cost grounds alone.[5] In order to protect major programmes and concentrate its resources on what was judged most necessary for the defence of the United Kingdom, however, the MOD has traditionally saved money by incremental adaptation and piecemeal expenditure cuts. Small and anomalous commitments, therefore, were persistently vulnerable for budgetary as well as strategic reasons.[6] Nevertheless, it was the wider question of an international territorial dispute complicating Britain's relations with Latin America and threatening the security of the Islands, as well as an unwarranted military conflict with Argentina, which was the inescapable consideration for London.

As has been seen, the Foreign Office's advice was immobilised because it was politically undercapitalised. Without extra political resources, in the form of Ministerial attention and political authority, officials alone could not reconcile the conflict of priorities which

existed between the paramountcy accorded to the Islanders' wishes
and the United Kingdom's national interest in solving its territorial
dispute with Buenos Aires. Diplomacy without a secure domestic
base, to paraphrase Hastings and Jenkins, is ultimately impotent.[7] A
political strategy was thus required to complement the diplomatic one.
In the British context, however, and despite the Foreign Office's
custodial responsibility for the continuity of policy, the absence of such
a strategy revealed the limits of the bureaucratic remit in policy-
making more than the failure of officials to cultivate 'a constituency of
political opinion for a compromise over the Falklands'.[8]

British civil servants are different from their American counterparts, for example, in this regard. They operate within a more
restrictive institutional and political setting. Their capacity to generate
such political support, although not entirely absent, is nevertheless
much more limited in both style and scope. British Governments
might, therefore, have suspended negotiations in 1968, 1977 or 1981,
as some have argued, 'on the grounds that the principle of self
determination represented an impossible obstacle to progress'.[9] They
persisted not out of bureaucratic intrigue but in response to political
considerations. No Cabinet gave any indication that it was prepared to
tolerate the cost of the military precautions which abandonment of
negotiations would have required. Similarly, it may have been
astonishing that 'a succession of Foreign Office officials . . . managed
to sustain the momentum of negotiations at all'.[10] Nonetheless, that
was what their Ministers and successive Cabinets instructed them to
do, because the political superintendents of the policy process were
determined to avoid the difficult political and financial choices which
the question posed. While the tenacity of the Foreign Office's
commitment to diplomacy no doubt reflected its departmental ethos, it
was the only course of action open to officials in the absence of any
other political preferences, and in the light of successive Cabinet
reviews which consistently licensed negotiations.

Consequently, although the failure to develop a political strategy for
dealing with the domestic politics of the Falklands dispute was a fatal
weakness in the conduct of policy, the responsibility for that failure lay
more with the politicians who superintended the formulation and
implementation of policy than with the officials who were routinely
responsible for Falklands affairs. Without political support officials
found it difficult enough to secure Ministerial and Cabinet attention
for the issue. It is not surprising, therefore, that they did not develop
that broader constituency for compromise which was so desperately
required.

Despite such considerations, this failure must also be attributed in some degree to the complications of Falklands politics and the determination of most of the Islands' opinion leaders to escape the fundamental dilemma which cast its shadow over their future: namely, political accommodation of some kind over some period to Argentine sovereignty or else continuing decline and mounting insecurity.

The arguments which the Islanders were persuaded to adopt were quite different from those which guided British policy. They insisted, conversely, that talk about transferring sovereignty had been incited by the recent economic decline of the Islands and that it had also been encouraged by Britain's economic neglect as well as its pusillanimous political behaviour in the conduct of relations with Argentina.[11] Hence the Islanders proposed instead that there should be no negotiation about sovereignty and that British protection should be extended to them indefinitely. In effect they demanded that Britain defy Argentine claims in a way which was quite inconsistent with the United Kingdom's post-imperial interests. This position could only ensure, however, that the Islands' economic relations and communications with South America would suffer, and that commercial companies would remain reluctant to invest in an area of latent conflict. Such a view was, therefore, self-defeating because, as Shackleton's first report emphasised, it was bound to frustrate any serious attempt to revive the Islands' economy or preserve their settlements.[12] In the event it also made a direct contribution to the process by which the sovereignty dispute degenerated into military confrontation.

Argentina's claim to the Islands was not an instance of political opportunism. It was an important and integral part of Argentina's national myth. In Britain even the House of Commons Select Committee on Foreign Affairs became divided over the question. In one Parliament it maintained that:

Britain's title to the Islands on the basis of acquisitive prescription following the occupation of 1833 had considerable validity in view of Argentina's failure to protest during most of the period between 1849 and 1909.[13]

Yet in another, after specifying the nature and frequency of Argentine protests during this period, it concluded:

The historical and legal evidence demonstrates such areas of uncertainty that we are unable to reach a categorical conclusion on the legal validity of the historical claim of either country.[14]

The pursuit of Buenos Aires' claim was reasonably consistent following the British take-over of 1833, but it was also pressed as opportunity dictated. Hence Argentine policy depended as much on the development of Argentine politics, and the retraction of British global power, as it did on the developing crisis in the Falklands' economy. The United Kingdom's imperial retreat, for example, was bound to encourage Argentine designs on territory which Britain had wrested from Argentine occupation during a period of imperial expansion. The likelihood was increased as, with Britain's decline, Argentine military power in the region grew through the purchase of sophisticated military equipment from Europe and North America.[15] The eclipse of British power could no more be arrested by an act of political will than Argentina's claims could be ignored indefinitely. Each was a product of complex historical processes that created an increasingly dangerous reality in the South Atlantic which was made worse by nostalgia and by the presumption that matters could go on as they were. Neither, in the long run, was in the Islanders' interests. Yet it was ultimately these sentiments which prevailed in their response to the political and economic problems which they faced. In these respects the Falklanders' reluctance to entertain political change involving closer ties with Argentina was encouraged by the support of the Falklands lobby as well as of those Parliamentarians who, from both sides of the political spectrum and for their own quite disparate reasons, opposed sovereignty negotiations.

Naturally, flexibility and uncertainty are preconditions of political discourse. Had the Islanders' views been axiomatic and monolithic there would have been no prospect of progress. But by the end of the 1970s many of them had developed a reasonably well-informed and lively understanding of the dilemmas which they faced. Equally, they were aware of the principal deficiencies of the position which they officially supported. The Islanders were unsophisticated but they were not uninformed and neither were they incapable of judging for themselves that their situation was becoming increasingly untenable.[16] Quite the contrary. Falklands society has been misrepresented in the United Kingdom in many respects, both by those who supported the colony as well as by those who opposed it, and this was one of them.

THE FALKLAND ISLANDS

Perhaps the greatest difficulty which the Foreign Office faced was not so much the social cohesion of the Falklands, or the uniformity of the Islanders' views, but the variety of their socio-economic divisions, the diversity of their local jealousies and the strength with which many of them held contradictory opinions.[17] A Foreign Office official who had long experience in dealing with the Islands observed, for example: 'it has never been easy to take the views of the Islanders in a way which added up to a clear picture on things.'[18]

The Islands community was described by Shackleton as an extremely hierarchical 'fairly class-ridden society',[19] in which those who spoke out were outspoken, but in which many preferred to keep their opinions to themselves and harbour their resentments. Its tiny population had all the characteristics of a village. No one enjoyed 'the luxury of anonymity'.[20] Yet, because of these social and economic structures, the Islanders were deeply suspicious of the Island Government, and extremely resentful of the influence and privileges of what they regarded as a 'clique' of farm owners, managers and expatriate administrators centred upon Port Stanley. As a consequence, 'ordinary working people are extremely reluctant to express political and/or controversial opinions publicly, fearing retribution.'[21] In such a 'feudalistic' community, where ideas were communicated and issues debated through direct social and personal contact, strong social sanctions supported the economic pressure to conform. The low educational attainment of the bulk of the population also meant that they were reluctant to express themselves on paper. In any event, they believed that questionnaires were a waste of time because the Island Government would only use the answers to satisfy its own interests.[22]

All aspects of life in the Falkland Islands were dictated by economic dependence upon the Falkland Islands Company and political dependence upon a colonial form of Government. This complex and comprehensive pattern of dependency produced a declining and socially fragile collection of tiny settlements, the largest of which was the administrative and service centre of Port Stanley, whose problems were compounded by steady depopulation, unbalanced demographic structures and physical isolation.[23] It was the tension and conflicting pressures, generated by this dependent existence which determined the contribution that the Islanders made to the debate about their future. Their official position on sovereignty was the product, therefore, of colonial parish-pump politics. These in turn were dictated by the divided and dependent character of Falklands society. Moreover, their position was adopted only after acrimonious internal discussions that left critical questions, which the Islanders themselves had raised, unanswered, and important reservations, which many of them shared, unresolved.

According to the 1980 census, 1849 people lived on the Falkland Islands, as compared with 1957 in 1972. Population decline was continuous from the 1930s but, until recently, it was most marked in the countryside, or what the Islanders call the Camp: this lost 11 per cent of its population after 1967 in East Falkland, and 15 per cent in West Falkland. The population of Stanley has remained stable over the last 20 years at just over 1000 people.[24] According to Shackleton, the Islands had other important demographic problems. 'The age and structure of the Camp settlements remains abnormal with relatively few young people or old people. The dearth of young women is becoming still more acute.'[25] Emigration proceeded at the steady trickle of 1.5 per cent per annum with many other Islanders actively thinking of leaving.[26] In 1979 the number of births exceeded the number of deaths for the first time since records were kept at the turn of the century. Those actually born in the Falklands continued to decline as a proportion of the population, although in 1980 they still represented about three-quarters of the inhabitants.[27]

The economy of the Islands was almost totally dependent on the production of wool for export. Philately was the next largest income earner. Sale of Falkland Islands stamps in 1982 provided around £600 000 or nearly 14 per cent of its GNP.[28] In 1976 there were 36 farm units managed by about 25 farming enterprises. Fifteen of these enterprises were owned by companies and ten were partnerships or sole traders. Eight of the companies were registered in Britain, six in the Falkland Islands and one in Jersey. The partnerships and sole traders farmed the small units, often on the small Islands. The companies varied greatly in size but by far the largest was the Falkland Islands Company (FICo). In 1976 it owned nine separate farming units which comprised 46 per cent of the total area of the Falkland Islands, and owned about 44 per cent of the wool production.[29] By 1982 little had changed, despite the recommendations of the first Shackleton report that owner-occupied farms should be encouraged in order to give Islanders some stake in the Islands and increase their commitment to live there. The Falkland Islands Company now owns 43 per cent of the total farm land as a consequence of the sale of one large farm to the Government, in 1980, for sub-division into six smaller units which were then sold at subsidised prices under favourable financial terms to aspiring owner-occupiers. A second farm on West Falkland was also sold in 1981 for sub-division and resale on a similar basis. These were largely token gestures of land redistribution. In 1982 the total of farm units had risen to 41 and by 1984, with a more vigorous redistribution policy, there were 30 resident owner-occupiers and two tenant farmers.[30]

The Falkland Islands Company, in addition, provides the Islands' shipping services and owns the greater part of the wholesale and retail distribution of the wool. In this way it dominates the economic life of the owner-occupiers. It also provides banking services and markets the wool crop (although since the War a commercial bank has been opened in Stanley). With the exception of the owner-occupiers, the 57 per cent of land not controlled directly by the Company is owned by other farm companies, a large proportion of whose shareholders are not resident in the Falklands. All the companies appoint managers to run the sheep ranches. Of the very few registered in the Falklands most have shareholders who live abroad and so also run their farms as absentee landlords.[31] Nevertheless, as a consequence of its size and the range of irreplaceable services and communication facilities which it provides, the Falkland Islands Company is effectively in a monopoly position.

The FICo grew out of early attempts in the 19th century to settle what was a naval staging post. On 22 December 1851 a Royal Charter was granted to 'Samuel Fisher Lafone of Monte Video in South America' to buy land on East Falkland and to have sole rights over 'all wild horses, horned cattle, sheep, goats and swine upon the Falkland Islands'.[32] After a difficult start the Company began to acquire a dominant position in the Islands' economy. In 1902 it became a limited company, increased its capital by 50 per cent and began buying up land. It further extended its control by establishing linking directorships with other farming companies and by 1948 these extended to eight more such operations. Similarly, the FICo extended its control over the shipping, marketing, wholesale and resale distribution of the wool crop. The Company's shares had always been held predominantly by non-Islands shareholders but in the 1960s this pattern had become even more marked. By 1968 there were 800 shareholders in the UK and between 70 or 80 in the Falklands.[33]

As non-Islands interests dominated the affairs and the trading of the Company, a process of decapitalisation of the Islands took place. A very large proportion of profits was distributed as dividends to shareholders, 80 per cent in the 1960s and up to 96 per cent in the 1970s, while the rest was invested outside the Falklands. Although the FICo did not have the worst record, with respect to reinvestment in the

Islands, investment generally 'has not been sufficient on many farms to maintain existing assets' particularly on West Falkland.[34] Hence the capital stock of farm equipment declined and the output of wool fell by 60 per cent between 1976 and 1982.[35] All this was encouraged in addition by the declining profitability of the wool industry. Average profit margins in 1976 were 20p/kg, while in 1981 they were down to 4p/kg.[36] Hence by the early 1970s the FICo had accumulated a large cash balance and a valuable portfolio of investments in other companies. These assets, however, were not reflected in the value of its shares. Consequently it was taken over in 1972 by Dundee, Perth and London Securities, a subsidiary of Slater Walker Securities. £500 000 in cash, together with portfolio investments worth £489 607, were stripped from it and transferred to the new holding company before the FICo was quickly resold in 1973 to Charringtons.[37] At this time, when the Company was still trading at a comfortable profit in wool from the Falklands, the Communications Agreements were being negotiated with Argentina and a search was on to replace the vital shipping service to the Islands which the FICo claimed it had to withdraw for economic reasons. Charrington's also cashed in some of the Company's non-Falkland investments, at a profit of £220 000. In 1979 Charrington's itself was taken over by the Coalite Group and the Company then became part of an even larger conglomerate with correspondingly less direct concern for the social or economic development of the Islands. In 1980 it accounted for less than one per cent of its parent company's pre-tax profits and about two per cent of Coalite's turnover.[38]

On 26 February 1982 it was decided that the FICo would no longer be registered separately as a public limited company. This was the final move in a long drawn-out process by which the Islanders lost all prospect of exercising any influence in or control over the dominating economic force in their lives. At the outbreak of the War there were no Islanders represented either as shareholders or directors of the company currently controlling the FICo.[39]

The health of the Islands' economy was, of course, entirely dependent on the world prices for wool, and these fell by about 20 per cent in real terms between 1976 and 1982. At the same time local energy costs also rose by 20 per cent and the Islands' GDP fell by about 25 per cent.[40] By the end of the 1970s, according to the Islanders' own account, their economy was in deep crisis.[41]

Even in 1989 it remains so precariously balanced that the loss of a relatively small number of 10 to 20 shepherds would cripple the management of its large sheep farms.[42] Training and retraining an adequate supply of skilled shepherds was a vital requirement but their numbers were so low that the General Manager of the Falkland Islands Company expressed fears, after the War, about 'how in the next few years we will carry on with these large farms'.[43] Despite the large-scale injection of development aid after the war, the House of Commons Foreign Affairs Committee concluded in 1984 that 'All round the prospects for the Islanders appear to be unattractive and unpromising'.[44] As the chairman of one farm company summarised the position:

> The main problem in the Falkland Islands as pointed out by Lord Shackleton is the loss of population, particularly from the Camps . . . This is caused by the fact that people who are working for a Company farm and who have tied houses have very little future. When they retire where do they go? There is a drift of population away from the land and these skilled workers are not being replaced by the same number of young people. This is a desperate situation for the future. I can see the day coming when the sheep will not be gathered in and they will not be shorn . . . The other reason is a social one. There is a chronic shortage of women. There are only six unmarried women outside Stanley.[45]

In effect, the Islands have many vocal chiefs but too few skilled Indians, and the mono-crop agricultural economy, which was the basis of their community, is 'nearly at a non-sustainable level'.[46] In more recent years income earned from fishing licenses has, however, transformed the Islands' finances.

FALKLANDS POLITICS

The impact of this economic dependence and decline had important social and political repercussions. In 1978 a *Sunday Times* journalist visiting the Islands provided this vivid account of life in the countryside:

> The men of the Camp . . . live in tied Company houses on Company land. They shop in the Company store for goods delivered by Company ships, and have bills deducted from Company wages. Many of them use the Company as a bank, the wool they shear from

the Company sheep goes to Tilbury, again by Company ship, where it is unloaded at the Company wharf stored in the Company warehouse and sold on the Company wool exchange in Bradford. By means of directorships and shareholdings, and by owning the only means of transport and marketing, the Falkland Island Company extends its influence over the Island's few other landlords. For better or worse the Falklands are Company islands.[47]

The Shackleton Report of 1976 argued that the feudalistic social relations and divisions were benevolently paternalistic but warned that they offered 'no encouragement for engagement in economic, social or political development since scarcely any of them [that is, native-born Falkland Islanders] have a stake in the place'.[48]

In addition to the Islanders' honesty and endurance Shackleton also detected 'a lack of confidence and enterprise at the individual and community level which verges on apathy'.[49] Furthermore, 'the distinctly low educational standards in the Islands leave locally taught people at a disadvantage in dealing with farm managers/owners and UK recruited persons, heightening the sense of dependence and relative inferiority'.[50]

The Falkland Islands have a diverse society. It is composed of Government employees, expatriate contract employees, Falkland Islands Company employees, independent farmers, farm managers, service workers and various non-waged groups such as retired people. Each of these groups has its own distinctive interests. The comprehensive range of problems which they face was documented in Shackleton's first report and confirmed in his second. They include, in addition to the economic and political dependence of the population on the farm companies, owners and managers, and on the Governments in London and Port Stanley: the lack of opportunity, especially for young people, to acquire an independent investment in the Islands; and the problems of life in the Camp which include the tied-house system, unbalanced age and sex structure, and the inadequacies of educational, recreational, medical and geriatric services.[51] This deeply fragmented and fragile social structure was riven by local rivalries whose conflicts and resentments were directed at a number of pressure points.

Isolation, together with the effects of economic and political dependence, produced a suspicion of outsiders. This was directed, in particular, at the Foreign Office, but it was also focused to some degree on expatriates from Britain.[52] Their pay and conditions were determined by rates and standards obtaining in the UK, to which they returned, having for a time made a living in the Falklands. Consequently they were rather better-off than the local people. However, resentment was also directed at the farm owners and managers whose conditions were also much more privileged than those of most of the Islanders; because they were able, for example, to take holidays, visit the UK, and educate their children in Britain.

Hierarchy, together with poor educational standards and the village atmosphere of Island life, produced a willingness to accept the lead of vocal opinion leaders who were concentrated amongst the owners, managers and administrators, most of whom lived in Port Stanley.[53] Simultaneously these conditions also cultivated a very strong resentment of the same people. A sympathetic local historian recorded that these local jealousies created considerable internal problems:

> The Falklands became a community of two parts, Stanley and the Camp, the people of Stanley versus the Campers, the working class versus the Establishment, the under-privileged versus the over-privileged.[54]

Although the Islanders held strong political opinions, they were 'sensibly reluctant to open themselves up to strange persons of obviously high status who interrogated them in the homes of their bosses'.[55]

Since 1982, especially, the pressure to unite against outsiders and support existing orthodoxy has (according to a House of Commons Committee) encouraged 'circumspection and, on occasion, evasion'.[56] In sum, life on the Islands was 'dominated by intense sub-group loyalties (to the farm, the Company and the Islands) or by extreme inter-group rivalries (between the Falkland Islands Company and non-FICo farms, between Stanley and the Camp, and between West and East Falklands)'.[57]

The two factors which the Islanders shared in common, and about which they held typically strong feelings, were a dislike of Argentina and a strong attachment to their 'Britishness'. A strong local loyalism overlaid all the Islands' social divisions. Combined with the social pressures to conform, 'Britishness' was a bond which helped to avoid serious and continuing schism amongst the settlers. As it has done elsewhere, such loyalist politics provided vital symbolic cohesion for an otherwise fragmented and fearful community. It also became the basis upon which a political consensus opposed to sovereignty negotiations was constructed in the face of an increasingly threatened existence. Some Islanders felt that Argentina's designs on the Falklands were part of a wider policy of expansion into the Antarctic and the South Atlantic. Many, however, simply rejected Argentine legal claims out of hand: 'after all, whatever happened 150 years ago doesn't matter. We're here now, this is our home.'[58]

Naturally the Islanders disagreed about their future, and this disagreement extended to the political status of the colony because all these matters were intimately linked. By the 1970s the Falkland Islands urgently required political, social and economic change in order to survive. That change ultimately demanded a resolution of the sovereignty dispute which would, in addition, secure commercial communications with Latin America, encourage investment and remove the political uncertainty which frustrated social and economic progress. As Mary Cawkell pointed out, political relations with Argentina had long caused controversy between and within the various Falkland settlements. For example, she criticised Mr Ridley's visit in 1980 arguing that 'If, like Lord Chalfont before him [in 1968], the object of his visit had been to create divisiveness he succeeded. The people, families, were split.'[59] These splits were not caused by British Ministers, however, but by the way in which the political dilemma the Islanders faced had a direct impact upon their lives. British Ministers had a responsibility to put that dilemma before them, not least because it caused problems for Britain as well.

In such a small and varied community there were no simple correlations between age, sex, class, occupational group, or area of residence and political attitudes towards sovereignty negotiations. The young and those living on West Falkland, which had suffered more from the the Islands' economic decline, were inclined to be most flexible.[60] But, in general, the response from such a varied and conservative social mosaic was much more inchoate, and it was excited and mobilised through the local politics of the Falklands' colonial system of government. The outcome was a political defeat for British policy-makers. By cultivating populist political feeling, and arguing that the consequences of Argentine hostility could be avoided, local opinion leaders and councillors succeeded in mobilising a divided and uncertain population against the British Government's policy concerning the dispute and its proposal to negotiate.

As a colony the Falklands are administered by a Governor (for a period after the War called the Civil Commissioner) who presides over an Executive and a Legislative Council, respectively known in the

Islands as Exco and Legco. Exco has an unelected majority and consists of the Governor, two ex-officio members (the Chief Secretary and the Financial Secretary of the Islands), two members appointed by the Governor, and two nominated by the Legislative Council. Legco is a largely elected body which consists of the Governor, two ex-officio members and six Councillors elected by universal adult suffrage under a cumbersome two-round system of elections.[61] A vast range of decisions have to be referred to London, but since 1977, when the Legco first obtained a majority of elected members, there has been a slow progress towards a greater measure of local self-determination. Shackleton urged this in his first report and subsequently the Islands Legislative Council conducted an inquiry into constitutional reform.[62] There is considerable pressure to introduce political change, although the large majority do not think that full self-determination is feasible.[63] Current suggestions are also designed to simplify the election of councillors, ensure a more balanced representation of Islands opinion and provide for an elected majority on the Executive Council. Because of the dearth of local political talent and expertise it has also been suggested that civil servants be allowed to stand in elections.[64]

Despite their loyalism there was, nonetheless, a widespread feeling that both the British Government and the Falkland Islands Government have been consistently unresponsive to the Islanders' views. Two of the most distinctive features of Islands politics, therefore, have been the invidious position of the Governor and the quite ambivalent sentiments of the Islanders themselves, especially those more politically articulate members who aspire to greater political autonomy for the Falklands.

The Governor occupied the unenviable position of acting as the broker in Islands politics.[65] He was the hinge between the popularly elected Legislative Council and the metropolitan power represented by the Foreign and Commonwealth Office. To the extent that he discharged his responsibility as a British public servant for administering the colony, by implementing London's decisions and wishes, he was likely to arouse the opposition and hostility of the Islanders. Alternatively, if the Governor sided with the leaders of Islands opinion he compromised his position as a representative of Her Majesty's Government. He was also the butt of much social and political jealousy, because the social life of the Islands' dominant personalities revolved around Government House. For these reasons Governors were sometimes mistrusted figures in the Falklands.[66] One way out of the dilemma which the position imposed was to identify almost exclusively with the Islanders, a line which was adopted by Sir Rex Hunt.

As for the native-born Falkland Islanders, who constitute the bulk of the population, Shackleton noted that 'Apart from the right to vote for the small group of people who make up the Legislative Council . . . they have no real opportunity to influence decisions on public affairs'.[67] The Legislative Council is 'dominated, at least numerically, by farm owners and managers'.[68] Some of these, while economically dependent upon the Falkland Islands Company and fiercely loyal to their British identity, also saw themselves as subject to a colonial domination which denied them 'a right to feel free citizens in their own land'.[69] In a familiar way, they resented London's authority, while espousing loyalty to Britain, on which they had to rely for security and development. Exemplifying the frustrations of a distant dependent colonial outpost, their deep ambivalence found expression in the language of Islands politics. Self-determination and even political independence were advocated by some, but, living in an internationally disputed territory, the Islanders were incapable of finding guarantees for such an ambition.[70] Most simply wished to retain their current life-style while remaining insulated from international economic and political threats by the retention of British power in the South Atlantic.

'Britishness', therefore, was a political symbol designed to express and consolidate the Islanders' identity, not a formula for resolving their practical problems. Although it united a scattered and vulnerable group of settlements it failed to address the issue which was central to their future. If they were to continue to live peacefully and to prosper in the South Atlantic they had to establish politically secure relations with Argentina and, thereby, economically favourable relations with their South American neighbours. Without such arrangements the colony's decline was assured. Indeed, by the late 1970s, it was already well on the way to reaching the point where viable settlement could not be sustained on the Islands at all. It has to be emphasised, moreover, that the Islanders' demographic, economic and even, in certain respects, political problems were not altogether dissimilar to those experienced by similar mono-crop agricultural communities and colonial dependencies.[71] The dispute over legal title to the Islands did not cause these problems, but it did exacerbate them. An economical and enduring resolution of these problems, therefore, continues to remain dependent on an acceptable political settlement with the Argentine. The War has merely changed the context, extended the timescale and compounded the difficulties of reaching such a settlement. There was in fact an appreciation of much of this in the Islands. It emerged particularly in the debates which surrounded the initiatives of the first Thatcher Government in 1979–81 when the ambivalence and contradiction latent in the Islanders' views also surfaced.

Two related and highly divisive issues occupied these internal discussions. How hostile would Argentina's reaction be if there were no political negotiations, and could the Islanders avoid the consequences of a refusal to negotiate? Second, was there a viable alternative political future for the Islands and could they be revived economically without the links with Argentina which Shackleton had argued were necessary as long ago as 1976?

At the time of the Ridley mission, the manager of the Falklands Radio Station estimated that 50 per cent 'liked the idea of lease-back', although many did not want to come out and say so.[72] Feeling 'for' was strongest in West Falkland. The Sheep Owners' Association as well as the Employees' Union Representative were also reported to have favoured the idea.[73] Ridley's visit confirmed this judgement and members of the House of Commons Foreign Affairs Committee have concluded subsequently that despite the hostility to Argentina the solution might have been accepted if it had been presented more effectively.[74]

However, there were those in the Islands who flatly refused to consider that there was any international dimension to the dispute at all. The editor of the Islands' newspaper was representative of this point of view and he remained obdurate despite the experience of invasion: 'We do not recognise any problem and do not recognise that there is any legal dispute or any claim with Argentina. Why should we be trying to solve it?'[75] A decisive intervention in the 1980 debate was also made by an outspoken and respected councillor from San Carlos in a broadcast on New Year's Eve which claimed that lease-back was a trick, that Britain should and would defend the Islands and that the consequences of rejecting lease-back could be avoided.[76]

Opposition was strongest in Port Stanley, particularly amongst the leading members of the Falkland Islands Committee which was the local branch of the London-based United Kingdom Falkland Islands Committee that ran the Falklands lobby. Here, hostility to any Argentine links was uncompromising. The Committee claimed to represent the populist sentiment of 'the man in the street' and his desire to prevent anything that would 'woo the Islands away from the

Union Jack'.[77] It was also suspicious of the Islands' Executive Council because it was appointed, and of the Legislative Council because it was not fully elected and was dominated by the owner/managerial elite.[78]

In fact, of course, as the manager of the Radio Station admitted: 'Everybody realises there is a problem', but 'they prefer to think it does not exist' and that they can 'continue the same style of life as they had before 1970'.[79] The entire issue of relations with Argentina was treated with a pugnacious passivity which was best summarised, after the War, by a disillusioned but bluntly honest Islander:

> Nicholas Ridley said, 'You must have lease-back', and we said, 'Not on your Nellie', and he turned round and said, 'If you do not have it the Argentine Government will get upset', and we said, 'They have not invaded for 149 years and they will not do it now'. In fact they did, so I hope we will be more realistic now.[80]

Rejection of sovereignty negotiations did not merely express opposition to a political agreement with Argentina; it also disguised the Islanders' procrastination, division and fear over their future. The general feeling was that if Argentine sovereignty was recognised, depopulation of the Islands would accelerate because people would refuse to come to terms with the new arrangements, no matter what the attendant opportunities or risks might be. Resettlement and compensation was something that was actually considered, but only as a last resort. Right of abode in the United Kingdom, for example, was regarded as a prerequisite. Whereas in Britain resettlement was dismissed as morally reprehensible and politically explosive, in the Islands it was necessarily seen as divisive and self-destructive; something which would undermine the solidarity of their position and hence their prospect of resisting political change.[81] It was rather like advocating in a storm that the lifeboats be made available when the captain and his officers insisted that the ship was still quite safe, although, in fact, the structure of the vessel was unsound and its position increasingly perilous. Hence resettlement and compensation did not figure on the Islanders' political agenda either.

Opposition to lease-back satisfied populist political opinion in the Islands only because the Islanders were persuaded that they could avoid the consequences of such opposition. In this they were misled by those who insisted that there was a viable alternative political future and that the Islands could be revived without a settlement. Such arguments took no account of Britain's radically changed strategic and economic circumstances, and its reluctance to advance the Islanders' preferences at the expense of the political and commercial interests of the United Kingdom. As Argentina was taken over by the military, and its domestic politics became bloodier, the Islanders received more political sympathy in London. Although they were in consequence able to frustrate Foreign Office policy, their spokesmen could not persuade any British Government to accept the logic of the Islanders' position. That would have meant defying not only Argentina but also the twin pressures which had reduced the United Kingdom from an imperial to a regional power: a radically changed strategic environment and the continuing decline of its economic competitiveness. If Islands spokesmen failed to prevail over Britain's preoccupation with its own intractable social, economic and strategic problems that was no surprise. Their defiance for over 15 years was a tribute to their tenacious dislike of the alternative, which was increased by political irresolution in London.

Insofar as the argument for a settlement with Argentina was economic, the Islanders and their allies countered by exaggerating the prospect of economic gain, especially from the seas around the Falklands. Fishing and the exploitation of alginates were indeed commercial propositions, although the Islanders were themselves neither equipped for nor inclined to engage in them.[82] Exploitation for hydrocarbon deposits in the Malvinas basin and the extraction of oil was also advocated but that remains a much more problematic enterprise. Only preliminary seismic surveys have been made and these have merely established that there is a likelihood that the geological formations in the region are oil-bearing. Whether any deposits could be exploited commercially is an entirely different question. Their extraction would be technically difficult, economically costly and dependent upon the energy market.[83] In any event, it is more plausible to argue that a precondition for the development of oil prospecting is co-operation rather than conflict with Argentina.

Where the argument for a settlement was strategic, some of the Islanders and their supporters tried to counter with a variety of more or less crude strategic propositions. These included the vulnerability of the Panama Canal and the strategic significance of the Cape route; the importance of Antarctica and the Islands' strategic location with respect to its future; and the need to contain the expansion of Soviet power possibly through some southern version of NATO. None of these arguments were advanced with any conviction, and all were quite outside the immediate concerns and interests of the vast majority of the Islanders. They were improvised merely to strengthen the Islanders' case. In no instance would outright defiance of Argentina necessarily advance British interests with respect to Antarctica, promote the wilder idea of a Southern Atlantic alliance, or effectively contain the expansion of Soviet power. On the contrary, if any of these propositions were to be taken seriously (and the question of Antarctica is an increasingly important one), circumspect co-operation with Argentina would once again be a more persuasive argument than continuing conflict.[84]

Finally, where the argument for a settlement was political, the Islanders appealed to the principle of self-determination. Those who were determined to exercise self-determination, however, had no effective answer to the social, economic and international forces which were already threatening to destroy Islands life. Few of these forces were subject to the Islanders' influence or took much account of their wishes, not least where they concerned the affairs of the Falkland Islands Company. Although self-determination is a powerful, if problematical, ideal, it takes little account of the Islands' tiny population, inadequate administrative and political structures and critical economic condition, all of which necessarily entail outside involvement in the Islands' affairs merely to sustain life as it is on the Falklands. Equally, as an internationally disputed territory, there has to be international negotiations between the two states involved.

When confronted with the real hazards of self-determination, therefore, the Islanders chose continuing dependence upon the United Kingdom.[85] The whole debate thus came full circle. For most of the Islanders, opposition to sovereignty negotiations was a convenient way of shifting the burden of political choice back to Britain, although, perversely, they deeply resented London's attempts to do anything about it. Others advocated instead an alternative but implausible future whose prospects and practicality many Islanders also mistrusted.

Thus there was an important opportunity, as well as a political responsibility, for the British Government to develop and maintain a coalition of support amongst the Islanders in favour of negotiations. Political coalitions are not facts of life waiting to be discovered but, as the Islanders' opposition to negotiations demonstrated, political achievements which have to be constructed out of conflicting views through the twin processes of political discourse: power and persuasion. Consensus building is not an easy undertaking under any circumstances and in the Falklands there were special difficulties.

There was little doubt, for example, that the Islanders preferred to exclude Argentina from any political change which they might have to accept, but there is considerable doubt as to whether a majority of them could not have been persuaded, with sufficient guarantees and assurances, to support political negotiations. To claim that this was impossible assumes that the Islanders' views were uniformly hostile to sovereignty talks and that their society was monolithic, neither of which was true.

Such a political challenge was hardly unique, especially in British experience, and it was central to a peaceful resolution of the Falklands problem. Instead, the wholly anomalous and untenable proposition that the Falklands could survive and prosper in the teeth of Argentine hostility, relying on British protection indefinitely, prevailed. The Islanders were thus allowed to transfer the burden of the ambivalence of their position, and vulnerability of their status, back to London.

Just as the Foreign Office was immobilised by the conflict between paramountcy and national interest which successive Cabinets failed to resolve, so the Islanders' position was immobilised by a conflict between wishful thinking and the realities of their situation. Opposition to sovereignty negotiations became the political device by which a divided and fragile community conjured up the illusion of an escape from its predicament.

The vicious circle of an impoverished and inadequate political discourse over the Falklands was thus a tight and complete one. British Cabinets wanted the Islanders to solve the United Kingdom's political dilemmas, while the Falklanders demanded that Britain resolve those of the Islanders. Without Cabinet pressure the Islanders would not admit sovereignty negotiations to the political agenda but, without the Islanders' agreement, no Cabinet was willing to risk the political capital involved in a determined initiative to resolve the dispute. Neither side was capable of making progress without the other's help, but each found it impossible to accede to the other's preferred solution. The Islanders wanted as far as possible to be left alone. However, British Governments could not allow that because they had a responsibility not only to deal with the international and economic forces which threatened the colony's existence but also to reconcile those pressures with British interests. Similarly, the United Kingdom wanted to withdraw from the South Atlantic, but the Islanders could not bring themselves to facilitate that withdrawal by accepting an eventual transfer of sovereignty to Argentina. They were fearful of political and economic change and disagreed both about its character and its advisability. As a result they elected to oppose officially what they were almost persuaded to accept unofficially, in the vain hope that London would somehow find an acceptable and viable alternative. Although the exercise of a veto over London's plans was something of a political achievement for the Islanders, by exploiting the opportunity which Britain's political immobility allowed them they merely succeeded in contributing to that process by which the issue became militarised.

THE FALKLANDS LOBBY

A third voice in Britain's domestic debate about the future of the Falklands was the Falklands lobby. If the Islanders' views were determined by their divisions, dependent status, and local brand of loyalist colonial politics, those of the lobby were determined in addition by its peculiarly ambiguous position and its own internal differences of opinion.

The pressure group went through various names and forms of life in the course of its history, but it had no formally accredited status. It was neither elected nor appointed by the Islanders and hence there was always an implicit question about its mandate. Even the Islanders treated it with some reservations. They seem to have valued its support, while at the same time objecting to any suggestion that it was constituted to speak on their behalf.[86] As colonists their interests were represented by the Islands' Governor but he, of course, was also a Government official. The Islanders had no independent representation in London so the lobby attempted to fill this gap on an informal basis. Members of the lobby were consequently divided amongst themselves about what or whose interests they were supposed to be representing, and how best they should represent them.[87] The United Kingdom Falkland Islands Committee (UKFIC, or the Falkland Islands Emergency Committee, as originally called) reflected the divisions of the Falkland Islanders themselves, and these problems were compounded by its self-appointed and self-sustaining nature.

Members of the Committee were quite aware of the ambiguity of their position and appreciated its political weaknesses. Just as opposition to sovereignty negotiations was the Islanders' political common denominator so it also became that of the Falklands lobby. It was the core view of those Islanders who served on its sister committee in Port Stanley, and with whom the UKFIC liaised most closely. Some of the most influential members of the UKFIC were also instinctively opposed to an Argentine connection. Just as hostility to political negotiations with Argentina consolidated the relationship between the London and Stanley Committees, it also served to defuse political differences within the UK Committee. It also diverted the UKFIC's attention away from divisive social and economic issues. This was especially important because it was on these issues that the pressure group had least legitimate political standing, and was most compromised by its financial and organisational dependence upon the Falkland Islands Company as well as its association with other commercial enterprises that had interests in the region.[88]

In relaying opposition to sovereignty negotiations, therefore, the lobby amplified and simplified the views of the Islanders. The strength of that opposition in the Falklands was problematical and variable because the future it spelled out was thought to be so uncertain and unlikely. But these reservations were lost as the members of the UK Falkland Islands Committee (relying most on the populist loyalism of the Stanley Committee and the views of farm owners, managers and administrators) processed the message through its own internal politics, and then passed it on to Parliamentarians, Foreign Office officials and the press.

In evidence to the House of Commons Foreign Affairs Committee, for example, a member of the UKFIC explained that the lobby sought to represent the views of the population of the Islands and argued that these were not distinct from those of the Islands' Government:

> In terms of the size of the community I think one can draw an analogy with a parish council. The likelihood of the parish council being significantly out of line with the views of the people in the parish is so remote that the potential problem has not arisen.[89]

This account was quite at odds with the strong evidence of a widespread resentment of the 'clique' which was thought to run the Islands' affairs, the mistrust of the Islands' Government and the deep division that the lease-back discussions had revealed; but then, as the witness also explained, 'our prime line is with our sister committee in Stanley, and we also have links with the Government'.[90]

By that peculiar resonance which sometimes takes place in political discourse, those Falkland Islanders who adamantly opposed political negotiations with Argentina had their convictions reinforced by the response which they received from their allies in the United Kingdom.

Hence the Falklands lobby did not misrepresent Islands opinion but helped to exaggerate its uniformity, so that it appeared more united than it actually was. In doing so the UKFIC claimed that it was merely performing a service for the Islanders. It was at pains to argue, for example, that it was non-political, but many of its activists shared and encouraged the loyalist political sentiment of the Stanley Committee.[91] Moreover, in seeking to ensure that the Islanders' views were represented, the UKFIC necessarily became an integral part of the political processes by which the Falklands issue was managed in the Islands as well as in London. All this is illustrated by the history of the lobby.

In response to the concern caused by the sovereignty negotiations which took place at the end of the 1960s, a Falkland Islands Emergency Committee (FIEC) was established in London with the financial support of the Falkland Islands Company in March 1968.[92] It then successfully orchestrated Parliamentary opposition to those negotiations. With the abandonment of the Memorandum of Understanding upon which diplomatic talks were expected to proceed, a Government promise to respect the paramountcy of the Islanders' wishes and a decision instead to concentrate on improving the functional economic links between the Islands and Argentina, the Committee 'stood down' in 1970 with its immediate political task achieved.[93] By 1972, however, disenchantment with the Communications Agreements signed in 1971 and a revival of political concern over the future of the Islands caused the Committee to be re-formed in April 1973 under a new name, the Falkland Islands Committee. Later, since a liaison committee was established in 1976 in Port Stanley, the parent committee in London was referred to as the United Kingdom Falkland Islands Committee (UKFIC).[94]

In 1977, after the Foreign Office had extensively reviewed Falklands policy and the continuing economic decline of the Islands had raised the level of concern once more, the UK Committee set up the Falkland Islands Research and Development Association (FIRADA).[95] This was an incorporated company which operated as an umbrella organisation for those whose commercial interests had been stimulated by the Shackleton Report's proposals for large-scale development and investment in the Islands, as well as for those individuals who had a social or political interest in the Falklands. FIRADA's finances came from individual and corporate membership and these were used to equip a Falkland Islands Office with a full-time secretarial staff and a Director General, who was appointed in March

1978.[96] The Falkland Islands Company retained its interest, and retired company managers were active in the affairs of both the Committee and the Association but, with the prospect of exploiting the economic potential of the South Atlantic, other commercial enterprises and banks with Latin American connections also displayed an interest in FIRADA.[97] The Research and Development Association busied itself with various economic schemes and proposals, setting up the South Atlantic Fisheries Committee in 1978, for example, but none of these came to very much.[98] It nevertheless continued to supply the indispensable infrastructure support for the UK Falkland Islands Committee, through the provision of the Falkland Islands Office. There was, of course, a considerable degree of overlap between the membership of the Executive Committee of FIRADA and the UKFIC, whose affairs were largely dominated by an executive committee of four.[99] In 1981 FIRADA established the Falkland Islands Trust, as a registered charity to raise funds to meet social and educational needs in the Islands. After the invasion of 1982 the Association set up a Falkland Islands Appeal, which raised about £600 000 by public subscription. Finally, the Association took an active part in the formation of the Falkland Islands Foundation, which has recently been set up to promote wildlife protection, conservation measures and the protection of historic buildings and wrecks.[100]

In short, following its establishment in 1977, FIRADA engaged in a wide-ranging promotional effort to stimulate economic and social interest in the colony through channels quite independent of the Islands' Government and Executive Council, and in the absence of any High Commission arrangement in London.

Despite its co-operation with the Stanley Committee and the nomination of an Islands Legislative Councillor to liaise with the UK Committee, the UKFIC and the Falkland Islands Association were not creatures of the Islanders' wishes. Some Islanders regarded the early FIEC as 'a bit dictatorial' and considered FIRADA to be something of a 'fiddle' to finance and support the London-based Committee.[101] Neither the Association nor the UKFIC had any standing in the many rounds of diplomatic negotiations which were conducted between Britain and Argentina, and the Islanders' spokesmen were keen to have the Islands' interests presented directly by Islands representatives rather than through the pressure group, although the lobby was engaged in extensive discussions with the Foreign Office prior to the despatch of the Shackleton mission in 1976. Indeed the Islanders were sometimes inclined to regard any initiatives taken by the lobby as more interference or 'rule' from Britain.[102] As the Chairman of the UKFIC admitted, 'over the years there have been ups and downs' between the Islanders and the FIEC.[103]

Accordingly, the impetus and direction behind the pressure group derived from London rather than Port Stanley. Given the paternalistic style and political ethos of those who effectively ran both the Committee and the Association in London, the two organisations attempted to promote what is best described as broad interest in extending the colonisation of the Islands. This combination of social, economic and political interests, however, was to cause internal divisions of opinion within the lobby, raise some further suspicion in the Islands, and force attention back to the principal political objective of the pressure group.[104]

As a consequence of the War a Falkland Islands Government and Development Agency Office was established in London and, in September 1982, an Islander was appointed to act as the Representative to run it. This development meant that FIRADA no longer had a role to play and in December 1983 it was decided to replace the Company with an unincorporated association known as the Falkland Islands Association. FIRADA accordingly ceased trading in March 1984 and its membership was transferred to the new FIA.[105] To avoid confusion with the Falkland Islands Government Office, reference to the Falkland Islands Office financed by FIRADA has also ceased. Currently the pressure group goes under the two titles of the UK Falkland Islands Committee and the Falkland Islands Association. The Committee is supposed to decide on policy and the Association 'provides the facilities necessary to enable the policies to be carried out'.[106]

LOBBY POLITICS

The management and activities of the Falklands lobby were influenced by a variety of factors. The most important of these were the uncertainty surrounding the status of the UKFIC, and its members' reservations concerning FIRADA's commercial schemes and interests. These, in turn, threatened the lobby's influence and effectiveness. The original Falkland Islands Emergency Committee, for example, tended to be regarded by the Foreign Office as something of a front for the Falkland Islands Company.[107] If it was not to be ignored or compromised, therefore, the pressure group had to cultivate all its available links with the Falklands, and concentrate its attention on an attitude widely shared amongst both its own membership and the Islanders: opposition to a transfer of sovereignty to Argentina. This was the initial goal of the old FIEC and it was re-adopted by the re-formed UK Falkland Islands Committee which in 1973 declared its aim to be 'to assist the people of the Falkland Islands to decide their own future for themselves without being subjected to pressure direct or indirect'.[108]

Aware of their political vulnerability to the charge that they had no authority to meddle in Islands affairs, members of the UKFIC's Executive Committee betrayed their sensitivity to it in a variety of ways. First, they laboured the point that the original FIEC had been set up in response to the Islanders' own appeal when members of the Islands Executive Council had written to MPs, *The Times* and other interested parties, in February 1968, warning that the Islands might be handed over 'at any moment' to Argentina. This letter prompted William Hunter-Christie, a barrister and former diplomat in Buenos Aires, who had written about the politics of Antarctica and become a Falklands enthusiast, to secure the support of the Chairman of the Falkland Islands Company for the setting-up of the Emergency Committee. However, he seems to have undertaken this task as much on his own initiative, and in response to commercial and Parliamentary concern in London, as in response to the councillors' appeal.[109] The ambiguity of the lobby's position was evident from its inception, therefore, and in evidence which the UKFIC later gave to the House of Commons Foreign Affairs Committee, the origins of the Committee were carefully described in the following way:

> The public interest and support within the United Kingdom for the Islanders was such that, following the arrival in London of the senior signatory to the appeal, the Committee was formed.[110]

Second, the lobby was concerned to emphasise that its links with the Islands were regular and comprehensive:

> The UKFIC ascertains the views and wishes of the Islanders through regular postal and telex contacts with an elected local committee in Port Stanley and with members of the public throughout the Islands. There are also personal contacts made on both formal and informal basis with visiting Islanders with whom the Committee keeps in close touch.[111]

It also maintained that

> it cannot be emphasised too strongly that the Committee was
> formed at the behest of the Islanders. Throughout its existence the
> Committee has continued through the will of the Islanders to whom
> it has made it known that it would dissolve at any time should they so
> wish.[112]

Finally, the pressure group sought to gain some sort of official
standing and thereby remove any uncertainty about its role in
Falklands matters. It suggested, for example, that it be taken over by
the Falkland Islands Government but this was turned down. In 1975
the Foreign Office also rejected the proposal that it should have a
similar status to Argentina's Malvinas Institute, and be engaged in
close collaboration on all aspects of Falklands business. In an allied
suggestion the lobby proposed that it should assume a position
somewhat equivalent to the British Antarctic Survey.[113] Although its
complaint that the conduct of British policy was fragmented among
several Whitehall Departments was substantially correct, the lobby
failed to persuade either the Falklands Government or the British
Government to provide it with some accredited position in the process
of promoting British involvement in the South Atlantic. In short its
grander designs were frustrated by the reactions it received both from
London and Port Stanley. Whereas the pressure group sought
co-ordination and integration of policy-making, and a positive role for
itself in the further development of British interests in the region, the
Foreign Office by contrast was preoccupied with finding a way out of
existing commitments. In addition, the Falkland Islands Government,
as a colonial administration, was in no position to accord the lobby any
formal status in Island affairs and the legislative councillors were
inclined to be jealous of their own popularly elected position. Hence,
as the 1970s progressed, what had begun as a simple device to alert the
British Parliament and Press to Government policy, and stimulate
opposition to any transfer of sovereignty, developed into a more
complicated lobby with a much wider range of interests.

By the mid-1970s, for example, the UKFIC had concluded that
'much of the indirect pressure brought to bear on the Islanders to see
their future only as part of Argentina emphasised the vulnerability of
their economy, based as it was only on wool'.[114] The Committee
became heavily involved, therefore, in the discussion of social and
economic issues which led to the Shackleton survey. This diversifica-

tion of its interests was to raise a fundamental policy dispute within the organisation.

As the UKFIC observed, 'there was at that time enormous interest in investment in the Islands as well as a great deal of individual interest in supporting the freedom of the people of the Falklands'.[115] However, the two did not necessarily go together, as the colonial era in the Islands' history demonstrated, and the Committee had no formal standing with respect to either. Nevertheless, some of its members saw an opportunity to extend the Committee's activities in order to provide a clearing house for all Falklands-related business; commercial and economic, as well as social and political. The production of discussion papers and commercial proposals together with the internal disputes about policy brought about an administrative and political crisis within the group.[116]

In the first instance a small but full-time secretariat became necessary, and some institutional reorganisation was required to manage the increased work which the expansion of its interests had generated. The solidarity of its membership, however, was also at issue and resignations were threatened because some members had deep misgivings about any direct intrusion into the social and economic affairs of the Islands.[117] They were acutely aware that the Committee was a self-appointed body, membership of which was by invitation only.[118] They argued, therefore, that socio-economic issues were best addressed through the Falklands' own, albeit colonial, political processes. Otherwise they would trespass into the Islands' internal politics and prejudice the Committee's standing with respect to its promotion of the Islanders' cause.

The lobby, therefore, had sound political as well as practical reasons to diversify organisationally. Hence the tripartite arrangement of the UKFIC, the Falklands Islands Office and FIRADA was established. By this means the Committee was able to rationalise and strengthen its financial and secretarial support, preserve a common front, and protect itself from the charge that it was merely an agent for commercial interests in London, rather than a defender of the Islanders' liberties. The crisis passed but the episode demonstrated the ambiguity of the UKFIC's position, added another dimension to it and injected a further complication into its relationship with the Islanders.

In the event FIRADA was conspiciously unsuccessful in stimulating commercial and economic interest in the Falklands. Although the Foreign Office acknowledged that the UKFIC's political position on sovereignty was closely allied to that of the Islanders' spokesmen, and that the Committee was a formidable Parliamentary lobby, it discounted most of the activities of FIRADA as a device for independent commercial interests whose ambitious propositions could not be advanced in any event until there was a political settlement of the sovereignty dispute.[119] Nonetheless, FIRADA played an important role in providing the essential secretarial support which the UKFIC required. Ability to excite Parliamentary opposition on the sovereignty issue, therefore, remained the Committee's most distinctive contribution to the politics of the Falklands dispute.

The Parliamentary achievements of the UKFIC were partly related to the energy of the members of its executive and to the commercial and political contacts which they cultivated.[120] A degree of all-party political support from Members of Parliament, for example, was secured when the lobby was first established. A Labour MP, Clifford Kenyon, was persuaded to act as the FIEC's first secretary. The Commonwealth Parliamentary Association was also used to finance MPs' visits to the Islands.[121] From time to time a public relations firm was employed and an experienced lobbyist was eventually co-opted to serve on the Committee.[122] After the military coup in Argentina, on 23 March 1976, the Committee extended its political appeal amongst Liberal and Labour MPs. Parliamentary interventions which required a Ministerial response rose from one a year in the early 1970s to five in 1977, including two debates. When negotiations moved to New York, in December 1977, more than 150 MPs ranging all the way from the right of the Conservative Party, to Liberals, Labour Party Tribunites, Nationalist MPs and Ulster Unionists signed a motion urging the Government to declare unequivocally that the Islands would not be compelled into dependence upon Argentina.[123] The lobby was also involved in rallying opposition to Ridley's lease-back proposals.

However, even on the basic question of sovereignty the UKFIC found it difficult to maintain an entirely united front. The 1980 debate on lease-back, for example, was only settled after several meetings and with a bare majority, of one or two votes, in favour of recommending the Islanders to reject the proposal.[124] Sir Nigel Fisher, a former Conservative MP and a member of the UKFIC, has since argued that:

the last chance of a *modus vivendi* and avoiding a war was Mr. Ridley's proposal in 1980. I argued at the time that that should be favourably considered by the Islanders, but we do not and cannot dictate to them, and indeed, as you have already seen, our own Committee was divided on precisely what advice to give them . . . I still think that something on the lines of lease-back will have to be resurrected if there is to be long-term economic development of the Islands.[125]

Although the Committee's 'favoured solution' was supposed to be some variant of the constitutional position of Andorra, where nominal sovereignty is shared between France and Spain but the country has its own administration and Legislative Assembly, there were certain influential members of the UKFIC who had much wider ambitions and wished to see 'a nation . . . built in the Falkland Islands'.[126]

PARLIAMENT

Despite the lobby's political reputation it would be misleading to suggest that Parliament's response to the Falklands was entirely attributable to the Committee's lobbying activities. The tempo of Parliamentary interest was dictated more by the rhythm of Falklands policy, while its temper was determined by the peculiar mixture of political emotions which the issue aroused amongst some MPs. Most interventions came, of course, when the Government itself had to announce a new departure, such as the opening of fresh talks, the adoption of a new proposal or the despatch of a diplomatic reply to Argentina. This accounts for the intense interest in 1968–70, for example, when the issue first came to prominence after the war, and in the mid-1970s, when the deterioration of Anglo-Argentine relations again brought it to public attention. The UKFIC was principally concerned to alert Parliament and the press to such developments, but it was not exclusively responsible for inducing the degree of interest which MPs of such widely different political persuasions periodically displayed in the Falklands issue. Only the coincidence between the character of the issue and that of the House of Commons was capable of achieving this effect.

The future of the Falkland Islands was a small matter, well suited to the cosmological and symbolic rhetoric of much Parliamentary debate and questioning. An item with minimum relevance to British interests, the issue nevertheless had maximum symbolic and human appeal. MPs were otherwise largely ignorant of the details of the question, and carried no direct responsibility for justifying the cost of the commitment or the risks associated with it. Furthermore, not only did Falklands policy lack sustained Cabinet support; it also cut across established inter-party conflicts. Released from the traditional constraints of party Government, therefore, MPs from all sides of the House of Commons employed national rather than party rhetoric to attack proposals to negotiate; and in the process the lexicon of Britain's defence culture was ransacked for suitable ammunition. In such circumstances the largely formalised responsibilities and dignified procedures of the Commons assumed an effectiveness inversely proportional to the significance of the issue and Members' understanding of the historic, economic and strategic aspects of it. Routinely impotent in matters of policy, and prepared to get excited about the Falklands for many different reasons, back-bench MPs helped to undermine the uncertain resolution of successive Governments, and demolished that of the Conservative Cabinet altogether in December 1980 with the celebrated savaging of Mr Ridley.

Although, as recorded in the previous chapter, more than 150 MPs had signed a motion, in 1981, objecting to the planned withdrawal of HMS *Endurance*, Parliamentary opposition was no match then for the political priority accorded to the reduction of Government spending, as the Prime Minister made clear when she confirmed the decision on 9 February 1982.[127] In the final analysis, therefore, neither the power of the Falklands lobby, nor the constitutional prerogatives and political sentiments of the Commons were decisive in the collapse of Falklands policy. They were important but subsidiary factors which served to compound and disguise the absence of political conviction at Ministerial and Cabinet level.

CONCLUSION

In as much as they made demands and raised expectations which they could not reasonably have expected to satisfy in peacetime, the Islanders' spokesmen and the UKFIC shared an important measure of responsibility for frustrating the political, social and economic progress of the Islands. An Argentine invasion which threatened the credibility of the United Kingdom's international reputation as well as the survival of its Government, together with the casualties incurred in the war which followed, was required before the Islanders were able to secure the degree of British interest which their position demanded. Such a tragic outcome was not, of course, on the Islanders' agenda. It was nonetheless a measure of the high cost of their pretence that they could survive indefinitely and undisturbed without a resolution of the sovereignty dispute. It cannot be argued that British Cabinets were kept in ignorance of the price of their political immobility. It is unlikely that the Islanders were privy to any intelligence assessments but they were able to judge for themselves what isolation from the mainland was doing to their living standards and future prospects. Similarly, there was little to prevent those who took an active interest in public affairs from recognising that the unresolved claims to sovereignty over the Islands were an increasing source of international friction in the South Atlantic.

Nevertheless, the Falkland Islands were ultimately the responsibility of the British Government. The fundamental weakness in the conduct of British policy was not so much a failure to appreciate the political nature of the problem, but the inadequate political resources devoted to the domestic as much as the international politics upon which its resolution depended. Of all the British actors concerned only the Ministerial superintendents of Britain's foreign and defence policy-making community could make those critical resources available to meet the political challenges involved.

One of those challenges was the need to supply some effective political leadership in order to generate an informed debate about the future of the Islands. Power can stimulate as well as limit discourse. This was required in Port Stanley as much as it was in London. Here, as elsewhere, however, only spasmodic and politically unimpressive attempts were made. Almost by definition, it seems, a minor political problem involving disproportionately high political costs has very little claim on the political resources required for its solution. Hence the future of the Falklands became a politically underprivileged issue trapped in a cycle of political deprivation. In other circumstances 'benign neglect' might have solved Britain's dilemma as eventually, under the pressures of depopulation and economic decline, the small colonial venture might have come to a quiet and uncontentious end. But another state was involved. Argentina had its goals to pursue and the impetus behind them was dictated by the internal dynamics of Argentine politics as well as the political signals which Buenos Aires received from the conduct of British policy. Britain's position had, therefore, to be politically active rather than passive. At the very least it required the constant monitoring of Argentine actions and intentions, and the implementation of appropriate responses. Ultimately the Falklands was not one of those political problems which could be safely relied upon to resolve itself.

Ministers were also required to back officials up with sustained political support if the Foreign Office was to reconcile the fundamental conflict of priorities between the Islanders and the United Kingdom's interests. Instead, homogenised and intensified through the medium of the Falklands lobby in London, the Islanders' views were transformed into a simplified political demand which left the difficulties that they faced unresolved. In submitting to this demand, British policy-makers allowed national policy to be dictated by the colonial politics of the Islands, and the oligarchic politics of a pressure group which sustained itself largely through the financial support of the largest absentee landlord.

No simple technical miscalculation or vested bureaucratic interests adequately accounts, therefore, for the bankruptcy of British policy. Officials were subject to strategic, economic and international dynamics rather than some narrowly conceived departmental interest. In seeking to avoid political and military conflict with Argentina over a minor post-imperial anomaly, the Foreign Office was directed by strategic reality, national economic decline and political choice. It persisted in trying to negotiate a settlement because, in addition, the socio-economic life of the Islands was deteriorating to the point of collapse and the Islanders themselves were confused and divided over what to do about it. The successful implementation of a post-imperial policy for the Falklands was frustrated, as a consequence, by a failure of political management in the reconciliation of colonial and national politics, and by an allied failure of political judgement in allowing a gross inversion of national priorities to persist to the point of war.

The positions adopted by Britain and the Falkland Islanders were not given, or sacrosanct, but products of their respective political processes and they did not reflect much credit upon either. Just as there was no basic intellectual or political rejection entailed in dismantling the British Empire, so the United Kingdom's attempt to withdraw from the South Atlantic was made under pressure of economic and strategic factors which were grudgingly accepted rather than generally understood—except perhaps by the professionals in the policy community. As elsewhere, the post-imperial stage of the Falklands dispute revealed lingering and apparently intractable cultural weaknesses in the domestic politics of British foreign and defence policy-making. Just as each episode in imperial retreat was determined by its own particular circumstances, so a peaceful transfer of sovereignty over the Falkland Islands was prevented by the loyalist politics of the Islanders and the political cost of denying them their wish to remain dependents of the British Crown. As a result the United Kingdom drifted into war.

The Falklands conflict, therefore, was a classic illustration of the problems and politics associated with Britain's imperial dénouement; a process in which British decision-makers, burdened with an imperial heritage which they could no longer sustain, were often trapped by a defence culture imbued with nostalgia for the global age of British power. The problems were complicated in this instance by a handful of colonial settlers and lobbyists who fought tenaciously to resist the changes brought about by imperial recession. Whereas larger questions of decolonisation had allowed no escape from the stark reality of Britain's decline, ethnic ties and the triviality of the Falklands issue encouraged many in Port Stanley and London to defy its logic. The human and financial costs of doing so were to prove absurdly high.

4 The Structure of the Crisis

Crisis, crisis management and the relationship between force and bargaining, have been exhaustively studied in the literature of international relations. Much of the theoretical analysis of the dynamics of crisis, and the strength of the evidence from case studies, argues that miscalculation by decision-makers is common and that resort to force always threatens to develop a momentum which political leaders will find difficult if not impossible to control. From this perspective crises are defined as highly unstable states hovering between peace and war, while crisis management is regarded as a monumentally difficult task whose prospects of maintaining peace are severely constrained by the structure of the crisis and the stressful impact it has upon decision-making. The Falklands example confirms these arguments and provides yet another illustration of the power of the logic of conflict. There was little in the episode which would have surprised students of bargaining like Schelling or Young,[1] or analysts of the classic communication problems involved in international relations, such as Iklé, Wholstetter and Jervis.[2] A great deal of this literature, however, is concerned with superpower relations and the nuclear environment, and some of it makes quite unwarranted assumptions about the decision-maker's capacity to control the use of force.[3] Thus the Falklands also demonstrated just how little relevance rational models of the use of military power have to real crises, particularly when they involve conflicts between lesser states which are not inhibited by the common fear of escalation to nuclear war.[4]

Nevertheless, the language of flexible response, of escalation and the exemplary use of force, has gained common currency. It therefore became one of the idioms through which Britain responded to Argentina's attack. Just as the idiom of Churchillian rhetoric was widely used to express the values which the United Kingdom thought were at issue, with the new Foreign Secretary (Francis Pym) declaring that 'Britain did not appease dictators',[5] and the Prime Minister that 'freedom must be protected against dictatorship',[6] so the language of graduated response was used to describe Britain's resort to military force as 'measured and controlled'.[7]

Notwithstanding the rhetoric used, it would be misleading to classify the actions of the War Cabinet, which was quickly formed to manage Britain's response to Argentina's invasion, as an exercise in crisis management. By 2 April 1982 Britain's political leadership had lost the opportunity to engage in such an exercise. The preconditions for it no longer existed. A diplomatic crisis in Anglo-Argentine relations had existed since about Christmas 1981 and it continued to deepen throughout the early months of the new year. On 2 April it was succeeded by the invasion crisis that Argentina's seizure of the Islands precipitated. This second and more unmanageable crisis quickly degenerated into armed conflict as the British Task Force arrived in the South Atlantic and opened its campaign for the repossession of the Islands on 1 May. Because there had been no sustained political direction of Falklands policy, the defence community was rendered incapable not only of pursuing a political settlement to the Falklands dispute but also of recognising, much before Argentina's invasion, that there was a crisis in Anglo-Argentine relations requiring close political control. Although the passage of the Task Force to the South Atlantic was characterised by all the typical features of a crisis—including urgency and stress, small-group decision-making and intense critical appraisal of a narrow range of options conducted on the basis of intuition as much as deliberation—these were not the features which marked it out. It was distinguished instead by the following two factors: first, the strength of the impetus towards war; and, second, the success of the British War Cabinet in adjusting to that impetus, so ensuring that the military campaign against Argentina was not fatally compromised by political indecision at home or international interference. Hence the prospects of preventing war were minimal, once Argentina had seized the Falklands, and they were reduced still further as Britain's counter-invasion force advanced into the South Atlantic.

THE STRUCTURE OF THE INVASION CRISIS

Several preconditions are required if decision-makers are to control the dynamics of crisis and retain any prospect of preserving peace. In the first instance both sides must fear war and the loss of control over the situation more than they do the loss of whatever is at stake in their confrontation.[8] Clearly neither Argentina nor the United Kingdom subscribed to this condition. The leadership of both countries, backed by popular support, was prepared to risk the gamble of a military contest rather than accept the political and national humiliation of an unsatisfactory compromise. Neither party accepted an overriding responsibility to avoid conflict. On the contrary each accorded priority to the satisfaction of their respective national political values. Moreover, there was a decisive inducement to do so, because the survival of their respective Governments had become dependent upon the outcome of the crisis.

Second, crisis management also depends upon the operation of tacit norms and conventions that have been established between adversarial partners through a competition which has been conducted over a long period and a wide range of issues.[9] Such ground rules help to structure the crisis and make it more manageable. There was, however, no acknowledgement by Britain and Argentina of what Philip Williams has called 'the rules of the game which have played such an important part in resolving super-power confrontations'.[10] The Falklands dispute was a long-standing one, of course, and the British believed that the ground rules did exist and that they understood how they operated. In this, as we argued earlier, they were mistaken. After 1975 Argentina had progressively modified the conventions of the dispute but the British had failed to appreciate fully what was taking place and consequently misinterpreted Argentine actions.

While decision-makers in London continued to assume that their Argentine counterparts were engaged in the usual practice of diplomatic protest and hyperbole to support their claims to the Falklands, the Junta had decided to experiment with brinkmanship.[11] The dangers inherent in this new context were significantly greater than those of the past because brinkmanship increased the risks involved. It was designed to issue substantial military threats to test British resolve up to and including an attack upon the Islands themselves. In a way it was also a self-perpetuating procedure with a dangerous momentum of its own because each successful challenge to British sovereignty, such as that on South Thule, encouraged a further gamble. The only logical outcome was either a successful bid for the Falklands, when the circumstances seemed propitious, or a military confrontation. Consequently, for Argentina, the invasion of 2 April was the outcome of an exercise in brinkmanship to which Britain responded in the most dangerous way. This nationalist adventure had its immediate origins in the political and economic condition of the country, Galtieri's take-over and the Navy's role in bidding-up the Falklands issue. It began in earnest with the disavowal of the February

1982 talks in New York and went over the brink at the very end of March with a decision to launch an invasion which had been contemplated as far back as the mid-1970s. Alternatively, for Britain, the attack was a cynical rejection of what it thought the ground rules of the Falklands dispute were supposed to be. While Argentine policy-makers had recklessly gambled themselves into a position where they had everything to win, or everything to lose, British policy-makers suddenly discovered that their adversarial partner had changed the rules of the game and was, therefore, no longer to be trusted.

Trust is a third precondition of crisis management. It derives in the first place from the rules of adversarial diplomacy, but it also depends upon the integrity of communications, which become vital in a crisis. It is especially dangerous in such circumstances to compromise communications by increasing mistrust through lying or deception.[12] But in the Falklands example the integrity of communications was fundamentally compromised from the outset. Britain regarded Argentina's invasion as *prima facie* evidence that the Junta was unreliable and the experience of United States mediation seemed to confirm this judgement. Furthermore, given the structure of the crisis—the acceptability of conflict, the absence of ground rules and the initial lack of trust—each side was prepared to use force as an escape from the impasse into which it had blundered. Communication thus became the means by which Britain and Argentina signalled their determination not to flinch in what was a competition of resolve rather than an exercise in crisis control. As such it was of limited use as a device for discovering a way to avoid war.

A fourth precondition of crisis control is freedom of choice. Crisis always speeds up decision-making and rapidly closes down options. Decision-makers have to avoid being trapped in all-or-nothing positions if they are to remain in control of events. Courses of action must be chosen which as far as possible keep options open, allow conciliatory gestures to be made and explored, avoid accidental clashes and eschew deliberate violence.[13] Once more the capture of the Islands subverted this precondition because, by invading British sovereign territory, Argentina had taken the most decisive step of all; a step which even the absence of British casualties could not disguise. It had crossed the threshold of conflict.

Of all the conditions necessary for crisis management and the avoidance of war the threshold of violence is the decisive one.[14] Once that threshold is crossed all cost-benefit equations are transformed by what theorists of crises call value escalation.[15] By this they mean that the conflict itself transforms what is at stake in the issue. A whole 'new set of forces takes over' and the course of events becomes structured by 'a pattern of interaction with an "inner" logic of its own which tends to develop to its fullest extent more or less autonomously'.[16] That logic is the logic of conflict. It creates a new reality. New themes and new characters emerge and the nature of the issue is changed.[17] This was precisely what happened to Britain over the Falklands. Prior to 2 April 1982 the future of the Islands was a trivial matter. Argentina's invasion immediately transformed it into a challenge to the United Kingdom's national credibility. It also became the supreme test of the resilience and survivability of Britain's political leadership, and in particular the leadership of Mrs Thatcher, whose popular political standing at the time was the lowest of any Prime Minister this century.[18] Hence a final precondition of crisis management, asymmetry of interests, was also absent.[19]

Crisis diplomacy may also retain some prospect of preserving peace as long as one of the protagonists considers that no vital interests are threatened. The invasion of the Islands, however, simply raised Britain's stake in the issue to the same level of national symbolic importance which it had always possessed for Argentina. Moreover, once the British had committed their forces to the repossession of the territory, all previous proposals for a peaceful settlement were withdrawn. As Mr Whitelaw, the Home Secretary, explained towards the end of the war:

> since our landings on the Islands and the losses that we have incurred it is unthinkable to negotiate about the future of the Islands as if everything was still as it had been before.[20]

In short the time for crisis management of the Falklands dispute was January to April 1982; before, not after, Argentina's invasion. That was the period when Anglo-Argentine relations deteriorated to crisis point as London refused to discuss sovereignty and the Junta finally repudiated negotiations. At first British decision-makers did not acknowledge that there was a crisis. When they eventually did, it was too late to respond effectively to the dynamics or the immediacy of the dangers involved. As a result they missed the chance to engage in that effective crisis diplomacy which the Junta's display of brinkmanship, so widely publicised in Argentina, virtually invited. The Prime Minister, the Foreign Secretary and Secretary of State for Defence were simply overwhelmed by the momentum of events.

BRINKMANSHIP

Brinkmanship has been defined as a confrontation in which one state knowingly challenges an important commitment of another with the expectation that its adversary will retreat when challenged.[21] Such a gamble is usually encouraged by the twin beliefs that the opponent's commitment is weak and that a successful challenge to it will pay dividends in overcoming any domestic or international problems which the author of the challenge faces. All the evidence suggests that this was exactly how the Junta interpreted the situation, with the exception that it was encouraged to believe that the British Government did not value its commitment to the Falklands. Brinkmanship succeeds, however, only if it achieves its purpose without provoking war. Almost invariably those who gamble with it miscalculate the prospects of success. One of the most striking findings in a study of brinkmanship published in 1981, for example, was that in only 3 out of the 14 cases studied did the author of the challenge accurately estimate the resolve of its opponent. In all the other cases those who risked this competition of resolve had themselves to concede or go to war.[22]

Argentina's Junta appears to have had little intention of provoking a military conflict with Britain and it made no careful preparations to fight one. Instead, the military regime in Buenos Aires expected the British Government to accept a *fait accompli* which was designed to bring a swift and decisive end to the United Kingdom's politically uncertain, and increasingly untenable, commitment to sovereignty over the Falklands. Between January and March 1982 the Junta raised public expectations in Argentina, and tension in Anglo-Argentine relations, in order to coerce British decision-makers into making important concessions on sovereignty. It miscalculated on at least three basic counts. First, despite Argentine signals, London did not appreciate that Buenos Aires was already engaged in that escalation of the dispute which British intelligence had consistently warned would be the prelude to a serious military confrontation. Second, by exciting Argentine expectations, the Junta created a powerful internal momentum which carried it up to and over the brink of war. Third, by crossing the threshold of conflict it radically changed the context of the issue. This fatal step appears to have been taken for many domestic as well as international reasons, but not least because Britain's response to Argentina's challenge was so ill-directed. In a dangerous and rapidly developing crisis Mrs Thatcher's Cabinet offered neither conciliatory gestures sufficient to allow the Junta to claim a measure of satisfaction, nor counter-challenges strong enough to allow Argentina's military leaders to retreat without much loss of face.[23] By the time the British Government began to organise such a response Argentina had already gone over the brink, exercising the initiative which British policy-makers had conceded to it in January 1981.

At the end of March 1982 the Junta desperately needed to satisfy its own as well as its public's expectations about the Falklands. It had excited these in the face of economic conditions and a level of political disaffection which threatened to drive it from power. Hence its position was precarious in the extreme. It therefore decided to go for broke, bolstering its choice with the most optimistic interpretations of its strategic and international position, dismissing the intercessions of the United States and, once committed, discounting reports about the threat presented by Britain's mobilisation. After it had made its choice it had every inducement to treat British reactions as a bluff.

We have considered the reasons for the political immobility of Britain's policy community in some detail. Its failure to respond effectively to the deterioration of the dispute was deep-rooted in Cabinet politics, a failure of Prime Ministerial leadership and the routing of the Foreign Office between December 1980 and January 1981, with the collapse of the Ridley initiative. British Ministers then appear to have adopted an almost classic form of what Janis and Mann called 'defensive avoidance'.[24] This is a strategy which decision-makers are likely to adopt when confronted with a dilemma that entails high costs no matter which positive course of action they decide to take. As a result, despite their dissatisfaction with current policy, they decide not to look for a better alternative but simply to reduce their frustration. They do so by disregarding the 'fear-arousing warnings' which their predicament excites. Janis and Mann identified three forms of avoidance strategy—procrastination, shifting responsibility for the decision and bolstering. British policy-makers seem to have engaged in all three.

After the defeat of the lease-back initiative further talks with Argentina were designed simply to delay and, in doing so, they accurately signalled uncertainty and prevarication to the Junta. Such political immobility also led directly to a loss of political control because it shifted responsibility for decision-making from London to Port Stanley and Buenos Aires. Bolstering occurs when policy-makers, who chose to do nothing else, exaggerate the positive aspects of procrastination and minimise the negative ones.[25] This feature was illustrated by Richard Luce's optimistic report on the outcome of the February 1982 negotiations and his subsequent surprise when the Junta disavowed them. Bolstering may also lull the decision maker—as it did Lord Carrington when he refused to take the Falklands issue back to the Cabinet—'into believing that he has made a good decision when in fact he has avoided making a vigilant appraisal of the alternatives in order to escape from the conflict this [may] engender'.[26] In this respect, according to Lebow, Carrington was guilty of exactly the same error of judgement which Israel had committed prior to Egypt's surprise attack across the Suez Canal in 1973.[27] He, like Israeli intelligence then, had insisted upon near certain knowledge of an intention to attack before he would initiate suitable political and military responses. In 1976–77 the British Cabinet, directed by Mr Callaghan, was persuaded to reply to Argentine pressure with the conciliatory gesture of a recommitment to sovereignty negotiations and an unprovocative strengthening of Britain's military position. But in 1982 a similar response was prevented by the unsympathetic political climate which governed the issue.

The British intelligence community also seems to have been influenced by the debilitating effects of this aspect of 'defensive avoidance'. Not only did the JIC neglect to reconsider its own strategic interpretation of the dispute but in a similar bolstering fashion it appears consistently to have minimised the disturbing nature of some of the intelligence reports which it was receiving about the Falklands. The Director General of the Falkland Islands Office, for example, publicly complained that warnings given by the Islanders as early as September 1981, that a crisis was likely at the end of the year, were discounted.[28] Similarly, many newspaper reports have subsequently claimed that lower ranking intelligence officials thought their raw material was far more alarmist than the blander summaries which eventually reached Ministers.[29] This raises the suspicion that various officials may have 'shaded their evaluations to bring them in line as much as possible' with the 'defensive avoidance' strategy of their political superiors.[30] No doubt they committed their own specific errors of judgement but Falklands intellligence appears to have made an immediate and impressive recovery after Argentina's attack. It would be an exaggeration to suggest that this restoration of institutional effectiveness could have been entirely attributable to the concentration of intelligence resources on the South Atlantic after the invasion, or to the increased assistance which was subsequently

received from United States and other sources. Apparently the
intelligence community was not so demoralised by the débâcle of the
invasion, or so intrinsically inefficient, that it could not take maximum
advantage of the galvanising impact of the crisis. In its defence
Admiral Lewin, Chief of the Defence Staff at the time of the conflict,
paid this tribute to its war-time operations:

> the work of the defence intelligence staff during the campaign was
> outstanding. I have no knowledge of any hold-up of raw intelligence
> reaching the people who needed it . . . and the intelligence
> appreciations which were prepared were speedy and, with
> hindsight, were extremely accurate.[31]

It was the change of milieu which was decisive and milieu, when it is not
the product of a dramatic change in circumstances, as it was after 2
April, is ultimately the product of political judgement and political
leadership.

THE LOGIC OF CONFLICT

When the diplomatic crisis in Anglo-Argentine relations erupted with
Argentina's seizure of the Islands, therefore, the invasion crisis which
ensued was already deeply imbued with the logic of conflict and
Britain's alternatives were already severely curtailed. Ostensibly those
options included the moral and economic sanctions which could be
imposed by the international community, an air and naval blockade of
Argentine forces on the Falklands and, finally, the use of force to
repossess them. In the event only the last of these was thought to be
practicable. Even before Argentine forces had landed, the Prime
Minister and her senior Ministers had committed themselves to a
large-scale military response.[32] They did so in a reflex reaction to the
advanced stage of the crisis and on the basis of the military advice
which they received. Military exigency quickly reduced their
remaining military alternatives to a single option.

Neither moral condemnation nor economic sanctions has much of a
reputation for resolving international disputes, and there is little
evidence that the British War Cabinet considered that either of them
was a serious alternative to, rather than a subordinate part of, a
military campaign. They were enlisted instead as an important
subsidiary and rhetorical contribution to the exercise of force. On the

evening of 31 March, during the course of the Prime Minister's emergency meeting in the House of Commons with the Secretary of State for Defence, Admiral Sir Henry Leach (Chief of the Naval Staff) made the Navy's case for the very forces which his Secretary of State had decided to scrap in the 1981 Defence White Paper. A large Task Force could be made available in a matter of days and was capable of doing the Government's bidding. He advised the Prime Minister accordingly and that advice was taken.[33] The mobilisation of a Task Force was authorised and the final order for its despatch was given two days later, at 7.30 p.m. on 2 April, as Argentina seized the Falklands.[34] When the Chiefs of Staff subsequently provided Ministers with a more detailed briefing, towards the end of the first week of the invasion crisis, their principal concern was to specify whether the Islands could be recaptured and at what cost.[35] Given the geographical, operational and logistical circumstances, there seems to have been no confidence in the suggestion that a blockade was capable of effecting a rapid withdrawal of Argentine forces from the Islands. In short, within a matter of days, the military option seems to have resolved itself into a single objective—repossession of the Falklands through amphibious assault.[36] Thus the War Cabinet became critically reliant upon its military advisers, whose recommendations were transmitted to it via Admiral Lewin and a small committee of civil servants formed to review requests for changes in the Rules of Engagement.

British efforts to negotiate a peaceful solution were thus fatally compromised by the political failure of the Government's pre-invasion policy. Instead of having to persuade its adversary merely to refrain from an intended course of action the British War Cabinet had to coerce the Junta into giving up what it now possessed. Hence crisis diplomacy in the period following the capture of the Islands had to achieve far more, in the worst possible circumstances, if peace was to be restored.

Just as they had lost political control of the dispute after January 1981 so, as the Task Force sailed to the Falklands, British policy-makers remained hostage to Argentina's military regime. From 2 April onwards the War Cabinet was dependent upon the Junta's willingness to accept the maximum offer which the British were capable of making, and undertake an otherwise unconditional withdrawal of its forces from the Islands. That offer was a return to sovereignty negotiations without prejudice to either side's position together with some internationalisation of the dispute. The prospect of this being accepted was poor from the very beginning. For its own reasons the Junta was equally unable to resist the logic of conflict which its exercise in brinkmanship had introduced and it was just as subject to that process of value escalation which had so transformed the British commitment to the Falklands. Whereas the British offer would have been regarded as a significant achievement prior to the invasion, after 2 April it was no longer sufficient to satisfy the Junta's new investment in the conflict.

Two of the greatest threats to the maintenance of peace in a crisis are the deficiencies of the decision-making processes of the actors involved and the structure of the crisis itself.[37] Deep-seated weaknesses on the British side had been laid bare between January and April 1982. Thereafter a small group of crisis decision-makers was formed, thus centralising the management of British responses to the invasion and the conduct of the war which followed. Britain's War Cabinet was less concerned to control the crisis, however, than it was to prepare for war if Argentina refused to withdraw. Furthermore, the problem of containing the conflict was compounded by the absence of a similar body in Argentina. The deficiences of the Argentine Junta are not a particular object of analysis here, but it is evident from Argentine post-mortems that its military leadership also made fundamental miscalculations when precipitating the conflict. There is, in addition, considerable evidence to suggest that it remained divided throughout the confrontation, and that its structural weaknesses as an agent of executive decision-making seriously undermined its crisis diplomacy as well as its management of the war.[38] Each decision-making community contributed in its different ways, therefore, to a crisis the momentum of which it was found impossible to control.

After Argentina's occupation of the Islands, the demands of the invasion crisis quickly effected a radical revision of the British interpretation of the dispute and so of British policy. The British position quickly embraced the logic of conflict, which effectively determined the course of events thereafter, confirming Williams' conclusion that:

> whether or not a crisis is resolved peacefully, as well as the precise terms upon which it is ended, depends in large part on its basic structure and the setting within which the bargain moves are made.[39]

Both Britain and Argentina were reluctant to explore the limited scope for compromise which existed in their respective negotiating positions. Neither proved willing to place the best construction on the other's intentions in the search for a peaceful settlement. Each was disposed instead to be intransigent with regard to their basic demands. In such an inflexible context, where the few alternatives available disappeared with the progress of the British forces, both actors came to 'define the situation as one in which the options are reduced to war or humiliation with a crippling loss of face'.[40] The invasion crisis, therefore, was a prelude to war.

A RITE OF PASSAGE AND A TACIT ULTIMATUM

Thus the mobilisation and despatch of a British Task Force, composed of a Carrier Battle Group and an Amphibious Task Force, revealed more about how wars are entered into than it did about how crises are managed or mismanaged. The model, if there has to be one, was August 1914 rather than Cuba 1962, and British decision-makers appear to have been engaged in a much more traditional activity than crisis management. The old order of peace had been overturned by Argentina's invasion. The passage of the British Task Force to the South Atlantic, therefore, became a rite of passage to war—a war which was intended to restore the United Kingdom's credibility, nationally as well as internationally, and preserve its Government from the consequences of its incompetence before the war.

But, like all transitions, the invasion crisis was also a period of profound uncertainty and many contradictions. Just as soldiers, sailors and airmen embarked on the ships headed for the Falklands went through their own individual and service rituals, as it dawned upon them that they were not involved in another exercise, so their political leaders had to engage in the political rites of passage by which Britain's counter-attack was to be supported and legitimised should diplomatic mediation fail. Decision-making, therefore, was improvised within a policy framework set by the collapse of prewar policy and the War Cabinet's initial response to the capture of the Islands. It approximated neither to the rational ideal of crisis management nor the conspiracy thesis of war-mongering. Instead, a classic socio-political drama was in progress.

The profound ambiguity of the invasion crisis was revealed most of all in the War Cabinet's pursuit of a peaceful settlement while it simultaneously tried to maximise the Task Force's prospect of a military victory. Many have found it difficult to believe that the search for peace could have been genuine while the commitment to the Task

Force was so strong. What appeared to be logically inconsistent, however, was nonetheless both understandable and necessary. Suspended between peace and war Britain's crisis diplomacy served many functions including an attempt to avert armed conflict.

The ambiguity of the period was further illustrated by the confusion which still surrounds the question of whether, and to what extent, the War Cabinet entertained hopes of a peaceful solution. Here even the evidence concerning individual views is conflicting. Although the Prime Minister appears to have believed firmly that force would have to be used, Alexander Haig recalled:

> In these early hours of the crisis it was evident that Mrs Thatcher, though she was strongly backed by Nott and also by Admiral Lewin, did not enjoy the full support of other members of her Government. In the days that followed other doubts surfaced.[41]

On 3 April the Defence Secretary declared in the House of Commons, 'we intend to solve the problem and we shall try to solve it continuingly by diplomatic means, but if that fails, and it will probably do so, we shall have no choice but to press forward with our plans.'[42] However, in 1984 he maintained that, unlike Admiral Lewin, he 'had not personally given up hope of a peaceful solution' by the last week in April. The Foreign Secretary, Mr Pym, seems to have been no exception to this uncertainty:

> It was always possible that some chain of events in Argentina might conceivably lead to a settlement at the end of the day but I am bound to say that my hope was never very great because of the political circumstances in Argentina, the unstable regime and the extraordinary steps they had taken in invading the Islands. It did seem, on the face of it, rather difficult to visualise them doing what would amount to a complete somersault.[43]

It is also important to recall, with Sir Nicholas Henderson, who was Britain's Ambassador in Washington at the time, that a commitment to the use of force did not automatically involve a full appreciation of what was entailed: 'When the British Task Force was despatched to the South Atlantic few of those responsible for the decision had any idea how the Argentines were going to be ejected by force from the Islands.'[44] Nonetheless, the War Cabinet knew that without an Argentine withdrawal an amphibious assault would be required, and it was quickly apprised of the more detailed plans for such an operation which the Task Force Commanders were rapidly drawing up. Hence, although it was impossible to determine precisely 'what our casualties were likely to be, or how much British public opinion would tolerate in the way of losses',[45] British decision-makers had to come to terms with the logic of their response while simultaneously preparing their publics for a conflict which many of them seemed to have expected from the outset. As they did so, 'the strength of the desire for negotiation swung in Whitehall with the tide of war'.[46]

Rites of passage are specifically designed to conduct the participants successfully from one social or political status to another.[47] Ultimately, therefore, as the House of Commons investigation into the sinking of the *Belgrano* concluded, all 'the factual evidence suggests that both Governments were prepared to accept the inevitability of a military conflict from an early stage',[48] and they acted accordingly.

In these circumstances the military measures which Mrs Thatcher and her colleagues authorised in the last days of March 1982 did not herald a carefully staged exercise in crisis control. Neither was War Cabinet policy carefully planned in accordance with a strategy of flexible response. As Lawrence Freedman has observed, much of the contemporary theory of conflict assumes that military logic can readily be made 'subservient to a political logic'.[49] Political logic is then supposed to dictate 'a graduated response, with each escalation only justified if political remedies continue to be frustrated; and all action at the early stages is expected to be solely for defensive purposes.'[50] Such conditions seldom if ever apply in practice because wars cannot be fought 'according to political rules with only slight regard for the exigencies of the military situation'.[51] In any event Britain did not have the capability to implement such a strategy and the military context was to create its own urgent demands. Instead, the War Cabinet initiated a general mobilisation of almost all the naval and amphibious forces which Britain had at its disposal in order to assemble a fleet that was capable of recapturing the Islands. The British Task Force was not, therefore, a responsive instrument in an exercise in crisis diplomacy. It was a traditional if tacit ultimatum to Buenos Aires which was to expire when the Fleet entered Falklands' waters. In the interim it allowed a short time, and granted some limited prospect for negotiating a settlement under the duress of a military conflict.

Thus the use of the British Task Force was logically entailed in its mobilisation as well as operationally entailed in its despatch: logically, because the structure of the crisis left the British Government with little option other than to issue such an ultimatum, or suffer the consequences of its pre-invasion failures; logically, also, because there must be a determination to implement such an ultimatum if it is to have any chance of success, a point acknowledged by the Prime Minister when she informed the House of Commons that 'it would be totally inconsistent to support the despatch of the Task Force and yet be opposed to its use'.[52] Operationally, because the limited capabilities of the British force, combined with the operational circumstances of the sphere of conflict, appeared to dictate that the Task Force be used on arrival and in full strength or not at all. With the possible exception of the operation against South Georgia, it had very little to offer as a flexible instrument of coercive bargaining because the range of effective choice which it provided was minimal.

THE MILITARY DETERMINANTS

Although the War Cabinet immediately made it clear that it required the removal of all Argentine forces from the Islands, only the commitment of the Task Force to battle would make it equally clear whether Britain was capable of implementing its ultimatum. From Argentina's perspective the military sanction behind the ultimatum appeared to lack both credibility and capability until a very late stage in the campaign. It was not an immediate threat, its advance took some weeks and its commitment to battle was a three-staged affair. As all crisis literature argues, the odds against a peaceful settlement under such conditions are overwhelming.[53] The military schedule was thus the ultimate constraint on British decision-makers. It allowed time for negotiations but if no satisfactory settlement was achieved it also specified when diplomacy had to end, even if the diplomatic process had not been exhausted.

There is no better statement of this point than that provided by Admiral Lewin. In evidence to the House of Commons Foreign Affairs Committee which investigated the sinking of the *Belgrano*, he recalled in detail the military constraints involved in the Falklands operation and thereby provided a graphic illustration of how, in the form of the military advice available to the War Cabinet, it must have determined the responses of the Prime Minister and her colleagues.[54] The Task Force was to operate 8000 miles from its home base, with the nearest available dockyard, Gibraltar, 7000 miles away. It had the minimum of air cover and no long-range airborne early warning system to provide advanced notification of Argentine air attack. Military planners expected that with the onset of the Antarctic winter, which reaches its peak in July, the weather would be mainly bad with frequent gales. Aircraft carriers were crucial but there were only two of them. Furthermore, one, HMS *Invincible*, was a new ship whose operational endurance over a long period had not been tested. The carriers' aircraft, the Sea Harrier, was also unproven and there was in addition 'only a small margin for attrition'; and a 50 per cent attrition rate was apparently predicted in the first official briefing to the War Cabinet.[55] Twenty-two aircraft were embarked with the Task Force and only a further 14 aircraft were available as reinforcements or replacements. There were similar fears about the operational availability over a long period of the Type 22 Frigates and, to a lesser extent, of the Type 42 Destroyers. As Lewin explained:

> The best estimate that could be given to Ministers was that the Task Force could sustain operations for a maximum of six months from the time of sailing, and for the last two to three months of that time it would be likely to become increasingly less effective.[56]

Operational endurance was one set of considerations to be taken into account but the timing of a counter-attack narrowed the military option still further and this was the critical factor.

The amphibious forces took longer to prepare and load than the naval forces and their speed of advance was slower. Hence the earliest estimate of their arrival in the vicinity of the Falklands was about 20 May.[57] Common sense dictates that a large force cannot be embarked indefinitely without losing its fitness or morale and hence its military effectiveness. The military estimate was that after 'some three weeks' it would be necessary to withdraw to Ascension Island and disembark the force for further training.[58] Although South Georgia was nearer, its terrain was not considered suitable for the training required. As a consequence,

> if the landing could not be carried out in the week to ten days after 20 May, by the time the force had returned to Ascension, retrained and sailed again for the Falklands, the onset of winter weather would make the landing and subsequent operations impracticable. *If there was to be a landing, there was a window of about ten days from 20 May when it had to be carried out.* [Emphasis added][59]

Admiral Woodward, the Task Force's operational commander, was later to confirm that on the eve of the landings 'we could only poise for a maximum of seven days'.[60] Similarly, Major General Sir Jeremy Moore, Commander of the Land Forces in the Falklands, recalled:

> Our first calculations were that, provided the weather did not impose any delays—for instance to the arrival of the Carrier Battle Group in the operating area (and it did)—we would be able to effect a landing on 16 May.[61]

This estimate was quickly revised by more staff work and by delays to the progress of the Fleet to the night of 19–20 May. Moore concluded, 'I believe it is a token of good fortune as well as, dare I say it, good planning, that in the event the landing took place only 24 hours after that target.'[62]

As Woodward subsequently observed, 'above all, for everyone, the impetus had to be maintained.'[63] The military logic was irresistible, therefore, once the forces arrived within striking distance of the Islands. The Carrier Battle Group rendezvoused with the Amphibious Task Force on 18 May in favourable weather and, as Woodward recalled, 'the political go ahead was received to conduct the landing at the first available opportunity'.[64] British troops landed at San Carlos in the Falklands on May 20–21, only one day after that which the Government had been advised was the earliest date for an assault. Whatever faith members of the War Cabinet may have retained in the prospect of a negotiated settlement, negotiations in fact did little or nothing to moderate the momentum of the military advance. Weather, distance, insufficient airpower, limited operational endurance, the timing of an attack and the extreme hazards of a sea-borne landing all contributed to such an outcome.

Admiral Lewin also explained that once the landing had taken place 'the inhospitable terrain of the islands would make it virtually impossible to continue an active land campaign against an enemy who had had time to prepare defensive positions.'[65] If international mediation then succeeded in introducing a cease-fire there were two additional dangers to consider. The position of the British ground forces would become intolerable as the winter progressed and the entire campaign might also drag on 'beyond the limit of Task Force sustainability'.[66] He concluded: 'these factors argued that if there had to be military action to resolve the crisis, it should be commenced as soon as possible. Time was not on our side'.[67] As a result, once hostilities were opened, the British were also obliged to reject all proposals for a cease-fire which did not entail 'full withdrawal' of

Argentine forces from the Islands.[68] This appears to have been the substance of the detailed advice given by the Chiefs of Staff when they made their first formal presentation to the War Cabinet a week after the Task Force sailed.[69]

Consequently the British Government entered into what amounted to an irrevocable commitment. As Schelling observed, such a ploy can be extremely effective if it is attended by a common fear of war or by a huge power differential.[70] In the latter case it may nevertheless fail to work because the weaker power may chose to reject it in an act of stirring defiance. There was something of this sentiment in Argentina's response to the threat of the Task Force, once it was realised that the British were in earnest. But that response came late in the proceedings. In the early weeks of the invasion crisis Argentina had four basic reasons for treating Britain's ultimatum as an incredible threat. First, it had to discount the British response in order to bolster its own misconceived and equally irrevocable decision to invade. Second, Britain's military mobilisation appeared to be quite inconsistent with the pattern of its previous conduct. Third, the credibility of the threat was dependent upon the War Cabinet's willingness to implement it. There was, therefore, every incentive to test Mrs Thatcher's political determination. Finally, implementation of the ultimatum threatened its author with heavy casualties; casualities, moreover, which seemed to be quite out of proportion to its material (as opposed now to its symbolic) interests in the Falklands.

Once Argentina's military leaders did recognise that Britain was prepared to implement its ultimatum they also had every inducement to test the operational capability of the Task Force; for example, by using diplomacy to compound its operational and logistical problems. For those in the Argentine military regime determined to retain the Falklands, uncertainty and delay would undermine the military effectiveness of the British force. The War Cabinet was acutely aware of this danger not only because it had reason to mistrust the Junta but also because it was operating within extremely narrow time and operational constraints.

As the logic of conflict took hold, so politics was increasingly subordinated to operational requirements and the momentum of war. There seems to be no doubt that the British Government was prepared to resolve the issue by military force at the earliest opportunity should a settlement not have been reached by the time its forces arrived in the South Atlantic. There is little or no evidence to suggest, either, that the progress of the Fleet was determined by anything other than military and logistical considerations. The Secretary of State for Defence at the time conceded that the pace of advance 'has not been dictated wholly by our diplomatic efforts; it has been necessary as a consequence of the time needed for our forces to deploy to the South Atlantic from the United Kingdom'.[71] Similarly he assured the House of Commons '. . . that any period of delay has been caused not by doubts but by the movement of our forces to the area of potential conflict'.[72] And the commander of the Task force maintained that the Carrier Battle Group sailed from Ascension Island 'almost direct for reason of political expediency' to the Falklands.[73]

CRISIS DECISION-MAKING

It is taken as axiomatic that large bodies, or deliberative forums, cannot run wars or anything else which requires quick decision and close control. Typically crises are handled by small *ad hoc* groups of decision-makers formed for the specific purpose of responding to the situation.[74] The invasion crisis, at least on the British side, was no exception. In April 1982 the British Cabinet was composed of 22 members. Guided by the advice of a previous Prime Minister, Harold Macmillan, and the current Secretary to the Cabinet, Mrs Thatcher decided to establish what was initially referred to as an 'inner cabinet'.[75] This was defined in Whitehall terms as a sub-committee of the Defence and Overseas Policy Committee of the full Cabinet. Hence its official title was OD(SA) (Overseas and Defence (South Atlantic)). The BBC began referring to it as 'the War Cabinet' on 19 April and that became its popular title.[76] Its membership was determined by several factors. First, it had to include those Ministers whose departmental responsibilities were directly involved. Second, it had in addition to provide appropriate professional advice from military and civilian specialists. Consequently, the initial membership selected itself. Finally, other individuals were incorporated to provide a measure of political and professional balance. In the event it consisted of 11 members in all; five politicians and five professional specialists under the leadership of the Prime Minister (see Figure 4.1). Mr Pym and Mr Nott were included by virtue of their departmental responsibilities, and Sir Geoffrey Howe because, as Chancellor of the Exchequer, he was the Cabinet Minister responsible for finance and it would have not been prudent in either political or practical terms to exclude him. Mr Whitelaw was the elder statesman, essential in

```
                    PRIME MINISTER
                  MARGARET THATCHER

    FOREIGN SECRETARY          CHANCELLOR
       Francis Pym             Geoffrey Howe

    DEFENCE SECRETARY          PAYMASTER GENERAL, AND
       John Nott               CHAIRMAN OF THE
                               CONSERVATIVE PARTY
                                  Cecil Parkinson

    HOME SECRETARY
      William Whitelaw

                  PROFESSIONAL ADVISERS

    CABINET SECRETARY          PERMANENT SEC. FCO
    Sir Robert Armstrong       Sir Anthony Acland

    CHIEF DEFENCE STAFF        RETIRING PERMANENT
      Admiral Lewin            SECRETARY  FCO
                               Sir Michael Palliser

    PERMANENT SEC. MOD
      Sir Frank Cooper
```

FIGURE 4.1   *The Falklands War Cabinet (OD(SA))*

maintaining the support of the full Cabinet and in sustaining back-bench confidence. In terms of his low Cabinet status the inclusion of Mr Parkinson drew particular public comment and he was brought in at a later stage than the other Ministerial members of the group. His task was officially described as keeping the Conservative Party, as well as the public, in touch with Government policy.[77] But it was generally accepted that he was co-opted to provide Mrs Thatcher with an unswerving ally against Mr Pym, by no means a Thatcher loyalist, and Mr Whitelaw, who was thought to be dovish. Similarly the Cabinet Secretary, Heads of the Foreign Office and Ministry of Defence, and the Chief of the Defence Staff comprised a powerful professional team which represented the most senior professional figures of the defence community. Sir Michael Palliser was included to provide continuity, as his retirement from the Foreign Office coincided with the invasion. His task was also to balance professional advice on immediate concerns with papers on background issues and to keep other Whitehall departments informed of what was going on when they needed to know or were required to make a contribution.[78]

In addition to these permanent members and advisers, other Ministers and officials joined in the War Cabinet's discussions as needed. For example, John Biffen, as Minister for Trade and Industry, was involved in decisions over economic sanctions and the requisitioning of merchant shipping. Similarly, the Attorney General, Sir Michael Havers, and the Foreign Office legal adviser, Sir Ian Sinclair, provided legal advice on changes in the Rules of Engagement and the legal aspects of various peace proposals. On several occasions individual Chiefs of Staff attended its meetings to give advice on specific operations. The Chief of the Air Staff was involved when the War Cabinet decided to authorise the Vulcan bombing attack on the airfield at Port Stanley.[79]

The War Cabinet met daily throughout the invasion crisis and the subsequent Falklands campaign. The full Cabinet was briefed on a weekly basis. It is impossible to determine the nature of this consultation, but the available evidence suggests that full Cabinet meetings were 'stocktaking' episodes in which Ministers accepted the exigencies of crisis decision-making.[80] None of the arguments and discussions which took place in the War Cabinet seemed to have been carried over into the Cabinet itself, either for further discussion or resolution. In general it seems as if the Cabinet was kept informed of the general picture and 'ignorant of any information which if leaked would cost lives'.[81] Special sessions of the full Cabinet were summoned at Downing Street to endorse the War Cabinet decisions to despatch the Task Force, to approve the Peruvian peace proposals and to authorise the final assault on Port Stanley.[82]

The Task Force's military schedule was not only adhered to but the military commanders also subsequently paid tribute to the War Cabinet's resolve and acknowledged its contribution to the successful outcome of the campaign.[83] There was, however, no formal induction into war. War was never declared. Nevertheless, there were three formal stages at which the War Cabinet was able to reconsider its earlier decisions and to confirm or contest the logic of conflict. Its freedom of choice was, of course, always constrained by the basic knowledge that the Task Force was only favoured by a very narrow margin of time and capability.

Discounting the initial decision to send the Task Force, these three points were: first, the decision to order the Carrier Battle Group to sail from Ascension Island and engage Argentine forces in and around the

Falklands; second, the decision to send the Amphibious Task Force from Ascension in pursuit of the Carrier Group; and finally, the decision to launch the invasion when the two forces rendezvoused on 18 May. There seems to have been no significant pause at any of these three junctures. On the contrary, as each stage was reached the impetus of the campaign gathered momentum, foreclosing the very limited options which existed and increasing the penalties which would be incurred if the assault was delayed. Here, as in many other respects, the *Belgrano* affair has been misleading. Understandably the sinking of the ship, and the great loss of life which it caused, focused analysis upon that one episode. Subsequently, when the War Cabinet's initial account of the incident was discovered to be quite false, the argument that the outcome of the crisis turned on the attack was strengthened by further revelations and accusations about the War Cabinet's decision-making. All this diverted attention away from the powerful dynamics of the invasion crisis and the compelling operational circumstances which governed the entire South Atlantic campaign. The great weight of evidence now available indicates instead that the fail-safe point was the decision to order the Carrier Battle Group to sail from Ascension Island, and that the decisive stage of the invasion crisis was 23 April–22 May. *The logic of conflict culminated in the sinking of the* Belgrano, *it was not initiated by that attack.*

Popular views about the use of force persistently underrate the momentum of conflict and the difficulties involved in bending military power to political and diplomatic objectives. The War Cabinet's declarations about the minimum use of force only served to fuel this illusion, as did the Opposition's demand that the Government should integrate diplomacy with 'the presence and potential of the Task Force'. However, neither position had much relevance to the practical as opposed to the political circumstances of the crisis. As the Secretary of State for Defence concluded in his speech to the House of Commons on 3 April: '[We] shall have no choice but to press forward with our plans, retaining secrecy where necessary, and flexibility to act as circumstances demand.'[84]

During the last week of April, War Cabinet discussion centred not only upon the political and legal strengths of Britain's public warnings to Argentina but also upon the urgent need to extend the Rules of Engagement (ROE) for British forces operating in the South Atlantic. As the Carrier Battle Group sailed south from Ascension Island, circumstances demanded that British forces be given the license not merely to defend themselves from Argentine attack but also to carry out their mission, which was to prepare the way for an amphibious assault. Hence the widest possible public warning was given on 23 April, although the continuing reference to a Maritime and later a Total Exclusion Zone caused widespread confusion, and the ROE were progressively relaxed until, at lunch-time on 2 May, British commanders were allowed to attack all Argentine forces within 12 miles of the Argentine mainland.[85]

Thus the last week of April was critical. It was the impetus given by the decisions taken then which, via the attacks and counter-attacks of 1 May and the sinking of the Argentine cruiser the *General Belgrano* on 2 May, ultimately predetermined the formal decision to launch the invasion. The only thing that would have prevented the final assault at that late stage was an unambiguous agreement which would have secured the unconditional withdrawal of Argentine forces from the Islands.

As each new stage was reached, at the end of April and on the eve of the counter-invasion, so the War Cabinet adjusted its diplomatic and political stance to indicate that new developments were about to take place and that the campaign for the repossession of the Islands was progressing.[86] At each of these points it also announced its disillusion with negotiations and reaffirmed its mistrust of the Junta.[87] Orchestrating the domestic and international politics associated with its ultimatum, it successfully adjusted them to the military impetus and retained domestic and international support, with the exception, of course, of the sinking of the *Belgrano*, which was nevertheless balanced some days later by the loss of HMS *Sheffield*.

The task confronting British decision-makers at the beginning of the invasion crisis was the construction under great pressure and changing circumstances of a new and sustainable interpretation of the whole Falklands affair: an interpretation that would express the War Cabinet's appreciation of what was now at issue in the Falklands, mobilise the maximum amount of national and international support for the ultimatum it had issued, seek a diplomatic way out of that ultimatum if possible and govern its progressive implementation if Argentina refused to withdraw. As in all policy-making, the interpretation was created and edited as it was enacted. In the process it was subjected to constant minor revision in response to military and diplomatic developments. The circumstances of crisis, of course, radically increased the degree to which policy was improvised and thereby extended the likelihood of serious error. Just as it was distinguished by a variety of themes, many of them conflicting, so

British policy became the vehicle of many motives, not only, as some
have argued, the Prime Minister's determination to restore her injured
pride.[88]

If the Government's reputation was at issue so its interpretation of
Argentina's attack as a comprehensive assault on British values and an
intolerable breach of international order was also widely shared by the
British Parliament and public. In addition, the invasion was deplored
by a very large section of the international community, which
concurred with the British view that universally important issues of
principle were at stake.

Facing a monumental political crisis at home, and assailed by doubts
about the reliability and political intentions of the Junta, the War
Cabinet prepared for the probability that it would have to undertake
one of the most dangerous of military operations. Despite the dualism
of War Cabinet decision-making, Britain's political leadership was
ultimately concerned with the formulation and implementation of *war*
policy. In the process, the language and thus the character of the
Falklands issue was transformed into a great symbolic drama
composed of a wide variety of interweaving national themes, all of
which focused on the future of the Islands and the outcome of the
conflict. The Government's political will thus became closely
identified with the validation of the country's values and symbol
system.

One additional and important feature of the crisis for British
decision-makers, therefore, was the domestic response of the British
public to Argentina's attack. War Cabinet policy was addressed at
least as much to its domestic audience as it was to Buenos Aires,
Washington or New York.

PUBLIC OPINION

Public opinion, however, is not a single voice expressive of a general
will. It is composed of many publics who speak with many voices
through a variety of media; and the medium, of course, affects the
message. It is, therefore, an 'ever changing assemblage of voices, some
discordant and clamorous, others quiet and persistent'.[89]

The public response in Britain was recorded in a variety of opinion
polls conducted at the time. Many were individual polls which were not
followed up by subsequent questioning, such as the ORC poll taken for
the Independent Television News programme, *Weekend World*, which

was published on 9 May. Consequently two sets of polls are analysed here in order, first, to examine the development of specific views as the conflict progressed and, second, to relate these results to the general impact which the conflict had on the Government's electoral popularity. The results of this analysis do not conflict with the picture presented in other polls, such as the ORC poll, but they do provide a broader account of the nature of public views and how they changed during the course of the conflict.

The first set of polls was conducted by Marketing Opinion Research International (MORI) throughout April and May of 1982. Five polls were done for a weekly journal, *The Economist*, and a sixth was taken for an Independent Television programme. All six were specifically designed to sample public reactions to the Falklands issue, and their principal findings are recorded in the graphs included at the end of this chapter. A second survey group, The Gallup Research Organisation, conducts regular monthly polls to assess popular support for political parties and their leaders, as well as to measure the Government's electoral popularity. Those which Gallup took during 1981–83 are analysed to record the effect which the Falklands had on the Government's general political standing.[90]

It is important to remember, of course, that neither war nor diplomacy can be conducted according to opinion polls. Hence, although the Government was sensitive to the need to maintain public support, War Cabinet policy was determined by the circumstances in which it found itself and by the political instincts of its members rather than by a slavish response to public opinion. Britain's tacit ultimatum was issued just as the public first became aware of the crisis and, as we shall argue in more detail later, its implementation was governed by operational factors. Just as public opinion did not dictate War Cabinet policy so the War Cabinet was in no position to dictate public opinion, although there was extensive orchestration of the information which was issued through the public media. If the War Cabinet was engaged in a rite of passage to war the British public proved to be a willing initiate. The relationship between the two, therefore, was far more subtle than either democrats or conspiracy theorists would allow.[91]

All disputes have histories, and all public opinion has antecedents in the form of broader more deep-seated assumptions. With respect to defence these assumptions are part of what we have referred to as a defence culture. It is important to distinguish between such assumptions and the opinions which are expressed about a particular issue, such as the invasion crisis and the War which followed.

Assumptions are general and latent while opinions are specific and contingent. We all have to operate upon the basis of assumptions, but we do not have to have an opinion about everything. An opinion, therefore, is an assumption or set of assumptions provoked into comment on a particular subject. Neither is monolithic or fixed and neither determines policy.[92] But, 'taken together, such voices constitute the context of feelings and demands within which the politician has to act and to which he has to respond.'[93]

A defence culture might be described as a complex of symbols, legends and assumptions derived from history, and subject to the slow remedial change characteristic of the development of a political tradition. Within that tradition public opinion may appear to be ambivalent and fickle because so much depends upon the questions asked and the complexity of the circumstances to which they are addressed. But even so public opinion rarely changes 'in arbitrary and radical ways. This is because it is expressed within existing traditions which themselves define the outer limits of acceptable argument'.[94] Public responses to the Falklands reflected all these features. They were more diverse and ambiguous than the War Cabinet or its supporters proclaimed, yet more independently supportive of War Cabinet policy than its critics have been happy to accept.

Initially public and Parliamentary support was offered to the War Cabinet rather than solicited by it. Each, of course, reacted to the Government's conduct of the crisis and to the media's reporting of it, but each also responded independently on the basis of shared assumptions which had been aroused by Argentina's invasion. Neither, however, was offered unconditionally. Public and Parliamentary support were especially contingent upon the handling of the conflict, particularly as the despatch of the Task Force was consistently portrayed as a limited back-up to diplomacy rather than an ultimatum. It took time for people to realise and accept that war was likely. The Parliamentary Opposition, for example, insisted upon restraint and the maximum use of the United Nations, while the public was clearly looking to see British honour satisfied without bloodshed. Retention of public support by the War Cabinet was thus a consequence of a shared defence culture, the unifying effects of the crisis and the swiftness of the Task Force's military victory, as well as a conscious attempt to mobilise opinion. In this respect there is evidence to suggest also that press, television and radio selected their news coverage in response to several sets of related considerations, including their interpretation of the public's reactions and sensibilities, their view of the 'justness' of Britain's cause, and their recognition of the demands of security. For that reason they have been accused of being too submissive to the Government's view.[95]

However, to the extent that the domestic politics of the Falklands conflict revolved around the maintenance of public support, the Government's success had less to do with the simple manipulation of popular sentiment and more to do with the way that populist political instincts were excited by the War and skilfully exploited by the Government. The Prime Minister's populism in particular resonated with public reactions, as these were translated through the media and opinion polls, just as her political talents, and preference for dealing with issues in terms of moral and political certitudes, suited the demands of the gamble to which the failure of prewar policy had committed her. Hence public support was maintained despite the criticism of the War Cabinet's media policy.[96] There is no way of telling how long that support would have been maintained, or what level of casualties it would have tolerated, had the War gone badly for the Task Force.

Argentina's invasion of the Falkland Islands provoked such a wide range of national sentiments comprising so much of Britain's defence culture that what is best described as a drama of national credibility ensued. Although public opinion took a little time to coalesce, it expressed strong support for the Government from the beginning, and it hardened as the crisis progressed, providing a firm basis from which the War Cabinet could run the risks of its military adventure (see Figure 4.3). There was a significant minority opposed to the conflict, just as there was a significant minority in favour of more extreme military action than the War Cabinet was willing to threaten (such as the bombing of the Argentine mainland). Even at the moment of victory, however, opinion polls displayed important ambiguities in the public's views about the whole dispute.

The first MORI poll was conducted on Wednesday, 14 April. It showed that public reaction was generally favourable to the Government (see Figure 4.3)[97]: 60 per cent of respondents recorded their satisfaction, and 30 per cent their dissatisfaction, with the way the crisis was being managed. At this time Government policy combined diplomacy with preparations to use force but public opinion was somewhat ambivalent about these measures. Although 83 per cent of the poll favoured the decision to send the Task Force, only 52 per cent were prepared to countenance the sinking of Argentine ships in Falklands waters. Similarly, although 50 per cent expected that force would have to be used, and 67 per cent favoured a reinvasion of the Falklands, only 44 per cent thought that retaining British sovereignty over the Islands was important enough to justify the loss of British servicemen's lives. A larger proportion, at 49 per cent almost half of those polled, were against this sacrifice. Conversely, a minority (28 per cent) favoured direct military operations against the Argentine mainland by bombing Argentine military and naval bases. In short, as *The Economist* concluded: 'the public wants the Government to save its national pride, but has yet to adjust itself to the hostilities which it accepts might be necessary to achieve that end.'[98]

Such ambivalence confirms one of the basic arguments advanced throughout this analysis of the Falklands conflict. The Prime Minister did not deliberately incite the confrontation in order to revive her political fortunes and the War Cabinet had no pre-set game plan for the military humiliation of Argentina.[99] As ever in politics the issue was much more confused than that. Just as the outbreak of the crisis was a result of political misjudgement in London as much as political scheming in Buenos Aires, so its conduct was governed by the improvised responses of the political leaders on both sides.

By the time the second poll was conducted on 20–1 April[100] general support for the Government's position had risen to 68 per cent (see Figure 4.3) and commitment to the use of force had also increased. About the same proportion as in the first poll favoured the decision to despatch the Task Force (85 per cent) but there had been a marginal increase in support for sinking Argentine ships (up to 55 per cent). Support for a landing was firm (at 65 per cent) although it was also opposed by a quarter of the sample. More significantly, half the sample in the second poll were prepared to accept the loss of servicemen's lives to regain the Islands (50 per cent). The proportion of those opposed to such a risk had dropped to 42 per cent. Similarly the proportion prepared to accept an attack on the Argentine mainland had also increased (up to 34 per cent).

As diplomatic attempts to avert war failed and hostilities opened, on the weekend of 1–2 May, so the trend of opinion was confirmed by two further polls which were conducted on 27 April and 3–5 May.[101] The April poll recorded 76 per cent in favour of the Government's management of the crisis, the May poll 71 per cent. Both polls also showed significant increases in public support for military action. By 5 May 72 per cent were in favour of landing troops, 38 per cent favoured bombing mainland Argentine bases and 81 per cent supported the bombing of Port Stanley which began on 1 May. But some important reservations still remained with respect to whether the Falklands were actually worth any loss of life. Although the 27 April poll recorded 58 per cent prepared to accept casualties (a rise of 8 per cent on the previous poll), in the 5 May poll, conducted after the sinking of the *General Belgrano* and HMS *Sheffield*, this figure had dropped back to 53 per cent.

During the first seven weeks of the crisis, therefore, the opinion polls recorded the public's learning process. The country discovered the Falklands issue, became familiar with some of the background and began to adjust to the military implications of restoring Britain's credibility. Not surprisingly that learning process was partisan and it must have been influenced also by the Government's news management.

Although support for the Government was high, the early polls did indicate a significant measure of uncertainty also about how important the Falklands were and whether they justified the cost of their recapture. On 14 April, for example, unemployment and the Falklands ranked equally as the major political issues facing the country (each was identified as such by 39 per cent of the sample). By 5 May, 61 per cent thought the crisis was the most important national issue as opposed to 25 per cent who still rated unemployment more highly.[102]

As the Task Force was committed to battle so the public abandoned many of its earlier reservations. Polls conducted on 25–6 May showed a marked rise in support for military action as well as for the Government;[103] 84 per cent expressed satisfaction with the Government's management of the crisis while 89 per cent supported the amphibious assault which had taken place on 21 May. This mood was further reflected in the response to several other questions: 79 per cent favoured sinking Argentine ships; 62 per cent were prepared to accept loss of life; and 47 per cent were prepared to support an attack on Argentina's mainland bases. The crisis had evidently become a war, displacing all other political issues, and national opinion had become loyally committed to the support of British forces.

With respect to the military dimension of War Cabinet policy, therefore, public opinion consistently supported the Government and ultimately accepted the implications of its ultimatum, recording a very high measure of support for the campaign to regain the Islands. Opinion, however, was by no means uniformly jingoistic, despite the rhetoric of many national newspapers, although naturally it became increasingly committed as British forces engaged in battle and suffered casualties.[104]

If support for the despatch and use of the Task Force provided the War Cabinet with a reassuring degree of public confidence, the Government's insistence on Argentine withdrawal also received widespread public support. Although it was not without ambiguity, here as elsewhere, public sentiment favoured the Prime Minister's more rigid stance, and was less inclined to accept diplomatic concessions as a way of averting conflict. Lease-back, for example, proved to be a very unpopular suggestion. In the first MORI poll conducted on 14 April, 63 per cent rejected it while only 26 per cent favoured it.[105] In the last poll, conducted on 25–6 May, 74 per cent rejected the idea. Proposals for joint Anglo-Argentine administration of the Islands also found little favour; 54 per cent of the MORI poll's sample were against it while only 32 per cent favoured it. Instead restoration of the *status quo ante bellum* received by far the highest level of public support. The second poll, conducted on 20–1 April, recorded 77 per cent in favour of the principle of self-determination, allowing the Falkland Islanders a final say over the issue of sovereignty. On 26 May, after British forces had landed, 70 per cent favoured the retention of British sovereignty backed up by appropriate military and naval forces.[106]

Against the background of this support, however, there was an additional development which reflected the complexity of the public's response and perhaps the reliance of the War Cabinet's policy on UN resolution 502 and Article 51 of the UN Charter. Public support for a UN trusteeship increased throughout the crisis until, in the last poll conducted after the San Carlos landings, just over half the sample (51 per cent) expressed a willingness to accept UN administration of the territory, although the same poll favoured the retention of British sovereignty by some 60 per cent (see Table 4.1).[107] In this there may have been a restatement of earlier reservations about the relative

TABLE 4.1 *Support for UN Trusteeship of the Falklands*

Date	Percentage of Favourable Replies
April 14	45
April 20–1	42
May 3–5	49
May 25–6	51

SOURCE: MORI data published in *The Economist*.

worth of the Islands. If military casualties had to be endured in order to restore British credibility, a long-term economic and strategic commitment to a post-imperial encumbrance which had no material significance in either regard was another question. Thus even at the moment of military triumph there was significant evidence of an underlying uncertainty about the future implications of Fortress Falklands. The strength of support for UN involvement was reflected in other polls as well. On 9 May, for example, the ORC reported 76 per cent of their respondents favouring an interim UN administration while Britain and Argentina negotiated about the future of the Islands.[108]

If broad-based and extensive public support offered the War Cabinet a strong and unified basis from which to conduct an extremely risky military operation, it also allowed the Thatcher administration an opportunity to reap the advantages in terms of electoral popularity. Prior to April 1982 the Government's political position had been reduced to a reputation for fortitude and determination in pursuit of long-term political and economic goals which were designed to regenerate the British economy and transform British society. With little to show for its efforts it was deeply unpopular (see Figure 4.5), and the Prime Minister's reputation in particular had suffered severely (see Figure 4.4). A poll published in the *Daily Mail* on 6 April revealed that 80 per cent of the country blamed the Government for the invasion, 36 per cent blamed Mrs Thatcher herself and 26 per cent thought she should resign. On 14 April *The Times* featured a Gallup Report which indicated that the public thought Mrs Thatcher the worst Prime Minister in British history, topping the list with 48 per cent of responses and reducing Neville Chamberlain, who usually received the accolade, to 12 per cent.[109] Quite fortuitously the seizure of the Falkland Islands presented the Government with the opportunity to demonstrate that the political values it espoused could in fact be translated into political results. In this way the Falklands campaign appeared to confirm the Government's argument that resolution and single-mindedness were the highest of political virtues. Hence the 'Falklands Factor' in electoral politics was created.

Thus both the Prime Minister and the Conservative Party measurably improved their public standing and electoral popularity.[110] This was revealed most tellingly in the regular monthly Gallup Polls. During the early part of 1982 Gallup had revealed the deep depression in the Government's fortunes. Although its standing began to rise somewhat before the invasion, from April onwards the polls recorded a remarkable revival in its position. This was confirmed by the Conservative Party's performance in local elections in early May and the trend was sustained after the surrender of the Argentine forces on the Falkland Islands. Eventually it carried the Government through to a crushing political victory in the General Election of June 1983 (see Figures 4.4, 4.5 and 4.6).[111]

PARLIAMENT

Just as the War Cabinet enjoyed a large measure of public support, which in many respects was independent of Government actions, so it enjoyed the advantage of bipartisan political support from all sides in the House of Commons.[112] The support of the opposition parties, however, was at the same time provisional.[113] They had their own policy preferences and coalitions of forces to contend with, as internal dissent from the lead given by Michael Foot to the Labour Party's response to the conflict illustrated. On 6 April some members of Labour's National Executive Committee only narrowly failed to dissociate the Party completely from the Government's handling of the crisis. Tam Dalyell and Andrew Faulds were also dismissed from Labour's front-bench team for opposing the Shadow Cabinet's support for the Task Force.[114] Bipartisan support was contingent, therefore, upon the details of Government policy, public opinion, party considerations and last, but not least, the prospects for mounting a genuinely damaging attack upon the Government's reputation.

In a crisis there is little time for widespread canvassing of public and political views. Although policy-makers require public support more than ever at such times, they are isolated by the speed of events and the urgency of the situation. As a consequence the usual processes of debate and consultation are replaced by the improvised arrangements characteristic of crisis, and a peculiar communion seems to take place between political leaders and their peoples by means of the traditional institutions, the media and the political symbols which they share.

Indeed, one of the most distinguishing features of the Falklands conflict was the degree of national unity which was displayed in Britain. As with public opinion so in Parliament the War Cabinet was faced with a unity of response which it had not created but which it had to foster if it was to regain its political confidence, maintaining that unity was one of the War Cabinet's principal political goals. It attained its objective not simply through the management of opinion and information but by diplomatic and military policies which received widespread political support because they relied not only upon patriotism but also upon international legitimacy. Minimum use of force, reliance on the international legality of British actions and the skilful mobilisation of international support thus contributed to the War Cabinet's ability to maintain one of its most important political assets.[115] Broad-based Parliamentary support thus complemented public opinion and consolidated the War Cabinet's domestic base.

Bipartisanship in British politics usually means that the opposition refrains from pursuing tactics, such as votes of censure or outright rejection of Government policy, which would divide national opinion. It does not, however, grant the Government freedom from all criticism. Instead, it merely sets some more or less ill-defined boundaries to it; for which concession opposition leaders, as in the case of the Falklands, are sometimes made privy to confidential advice usually available only to the Government. On this occasion, only the leaders of the Liberal and Social Democratic parties took up the invitation. Labour's leader, Michael Foot, declined.

The Labour Party in particular insisted that its support for the Government was contingent upon the maximum use of the United Nations, the exercise of military restraint and a genuine search for a peaceful agreement.[116] All this suited the transitional circumstances of the invasion crisis as well as the divisions within the Party. The duality of War Cabinet policy also helped to satisfy Labour's demands sufficiently to blunt the effectiveness of its Parliamentary criticism. Compromised in any event by the leadership's endorsement of the despatch of the Task Force, Labour's reservations appeared carping and irresolute. Since the war went well, the Labour Party began to suffer the political consequences of poor political leadership and a policy posture which also appeared to offer no moral or practicable alternative to that of the War Cabinet. Favoured by the success of its military gamble, Mrs Thatcher's Government ultimately enhanced its reputation enormously against divided and ineffectual opposition.

THE MEDIA

Finally, the relationship between the Government and the media also became an issue in the domestic politics of the Falklands conflict.[117] British newspapers, with the exception of the *Financial Times*, the *Guardian* and the *Daily Mirror*, were enthusiastically in favour of war.

The temper of political opinion thus helped to circumscribe political debate about the causes of the crisis and the wisdom of the Government's response. As tension mounted during the early stages of the conflict, for example, BBC Television's attempt to maintain a neutral reporting posture provoked an angry reaction from the Government and its back-bench supporters.[118] The War Cabinet's ability to exercise extensive influence over the reporting of the War was also greatly facilitated by permitting few correspondents to sail with the Task Force, the remoteness of the Islands, and the reliance of the media on Government and Service communications to transmit their reports.[119] Unlike Vietnam and other modern wars, media reporting of the Falklands campaign was extremely limited and carefully controlled. This revived the debate about whether the United States had lost in Vietnam as a consequence of the media coverage of the war there, and subsequently raised the argument that censorship and media manipulation played an important part in Britain's victory. Despite the information management involved in the Falklands conflict, however, such a conclusion would grossly misrepresent the complex relationship which obtains between Government, media and opinion. It would also take little account of the operational circumstances of the conflict. There is no denying that media manipulation by the Government and news manipulation by the media were features of the conflict—as they are in all conflicts. But it is difficult to determine precisely what contribution they made to public reactions already excited by Argentina's attack, beyond that of confirming and reinforcing the sentiments involved, particularly as the Government's handling of information was so widely attacked and deplored at the time.

The Government's media policy caused conflict and dispute from the very beginning of the crisis. In retrospect tempers cooled, more circumspect judgements were made and the subsequent Parliamentary inquiry into Press and public relations concluded, somewhat complacently perhaps, that 'in the main . . . the credibility of the information issued by the Ministry of Defence was sustained throughout the campaign'.[120] At the time the Government did appear to come close to losing its credibility as well as the propaganda debate. It was also accused of inconsistent and unnecessarily strict censorship which caused gratuitous delay in the reporting of events. In addition it was charged with managing the news and disseminating misinformation about operational matters.[121]

Some of these charges can be explained by reference to the

confusion of the period, the operational need for secrecy and the inevitable conflict of interest between those who wanted to report the news and those who wished to manage it. There is no simple way of reconciling the independence of the media, the public's right to know and the need for a critical appraisal of policy with the secrecy required for 'national security'; although in Britain the emphasis is always towards secrecy, it was seldom stronger than during and after the Falklands campaign. The basic dilemmas caused by these conflicting considerations were all highlighted during the invasion crisis and intensified by the ambiguity which characterised it. The War Cabinet's failures here reflected the general confusion in Government thinking about the handling of the media in wartime, the Navy's particular antipathy to having its operations reported (together with its general inexperience in dealing with the media) and the practical difficulties associated with the Falklands operation. Nonetheless, despite the MOD's pedantic reply to the criticisms levelled against it, the Defence Committee of the House of Commons was to conclude that many of the charges had considerable substance.[122] By sponsoring studies of the whole experience once the war was over, the MOD also tacitly admitted that its media dealings had left a lot to be desired.[123]

Despite the threatened breakdown in its relations with the press and television, and the total absence of any foreign correspondents with the Task Force, the Government nevertheless survived the mounting loss of domestic and international media confidence which its handling of communications began to cause. In the short term, close control of reporting from the South Atlantic eased the War Cabinet's political task but only the long term would have shown how damaging its communications policy failure might have been. Here again Mrs Thatcher and her Ministers owed their military forces an enormous political debt. As the Task Force delivered a swift and unconditional victory, it relieved the country's political leadership of many hazardous political difficulties in explaining and justifying the Government's conduct. In this, as in so many other respects, the War Cabinet's performance was flattered by the speed and decisiveness of Argentina's defeat.

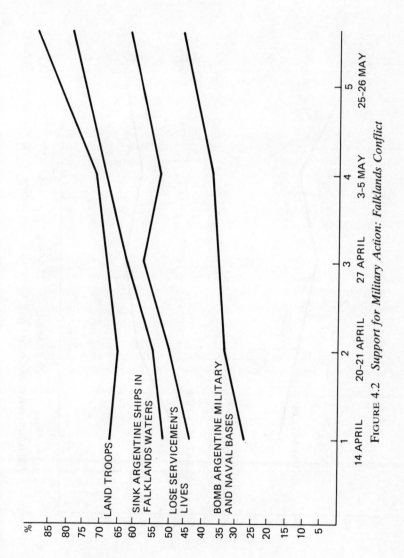

FIGURE 4.2 *Support for Military Action: Falklands Conflict*

126

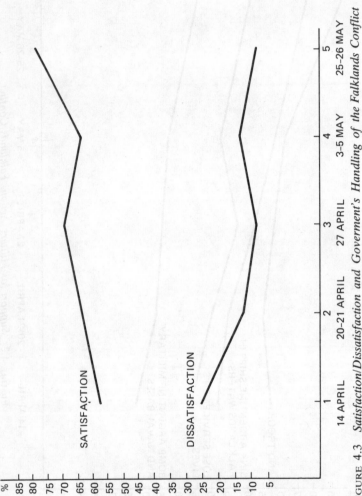

FIGURE 4.3 *Satisfaction/Dissatisfaction and Goverment's Handling of the Falklands Conflict*

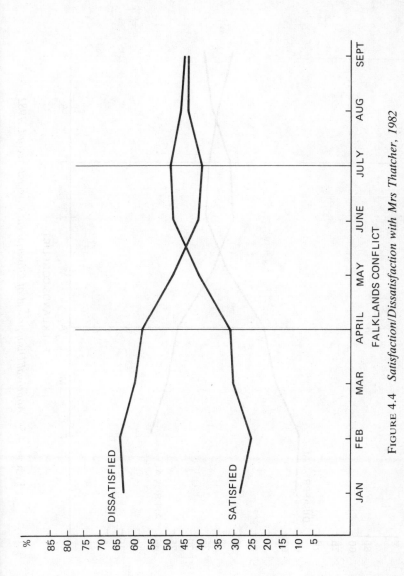

FIGURE 4.4 *Satisfaction/Dissatisfaction with Mrs Thatcher, 1982*

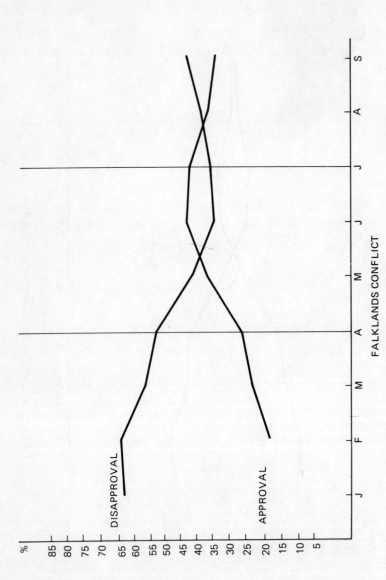

FIGURE 4.5   *Approval/Disapproval of Government's overall record, 1982*

129

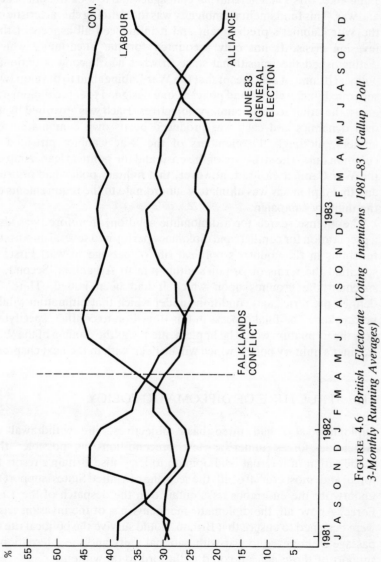

FIGURE 4.6 *British Electorate Voting Intentions 1981–83 (Gallup Poll 3-Monthly Running Averages)*

5 War Cabinet Diplomacy

Janus-like, Mrs Thatcher and her colleagues had to look to both peace and war. This fundamental ambiguity was the defining characteristic of the War Cabinet's predicament and it influenced all aspects of the invasion crisis. It not only accounted for the uncertainty which distinguished the transitional stage in what had become a national political drama, it also meant that the War Cabinet had to develop two separate but closely related policies, one designed to serve diplomatic goals, the other to serve military objectives. Each was governed by its own dynamics and each was produced by its own combination of authors, although the members of the War Cabinet provided a common link. The structure of the crisis and the political leadership of the War Cabinet ensured, however, that military policy had priority and that diplomacy was ultimately subordinate to the requirements of the military campaign.

The intense search for a diplomatic solution, therefore, was also a preparation for conflict, and diplomacy performed several important functions in the country's political rite of passage to war. First, it specified the terms of Britain's ultimatum to Argentina. Second, it specified the grounds upon which it had been issued. Third, it defined the terms and conditions under which that ultimatum would be revoked. The final process in this transition to conflict, specifying how the ultimatum would be implemented, was the domain of the War Cabinet's military policy, which will be dealt with in the next chapter.

THE STRUCTURE OF DIPLOMATIC POLICY

Diplomacy also had three basic objectives: the withdrawal of Argentine forces under as few preconditions as possible; the mobilisation of international opinion to legitimise Britain's resort to force; and, most crucial of all, the securing of United States' support to underwrite the enormous risks entailed in the despatch of the Task Force. Above all, the diplomatic manoeuvrings of the invasion crisis were designed to ensure that Britain should survive the political rite of passage from peace to war with national unity and the international support of those allies it could not afford to do without.

Mrs Thatcher announced in the House of Commons emergency debate on Saturday 3 April: 'It is the Government's objective to see that the Islands are freed from occupation and are returned to British administration at the earliest possible moment.'[1] In a further Parliamentary debate, on 7 April, the Prime Minister removed any ambiguity surrounding the phrase 'British administration' by making it clear that this meant British sovereignty.[2]

Although most politicians and political commentators at the time thought that Britain's military response would be confined to a show of force, there were others who clearly recognised what the War Cabinet's position implied. For example, Mr Callaghan declared bluntly:

> We have given ourselves a self-imposed ultimatum of a fortnight. It is a fortnight before the Fleet arrives at the Falkland Islands. It will not get there, turn round and come back if there has been no settlement . . . [3]

He was a little optimistic about the speed of the Task Force's advance, and indeed about the scale of the operation upon which it was engaged, but he was entirely accurate about the logic of events.

The Prime Minister's Parliamentary statement secured domestic political endorsement but this was an international as well as a domestic crisis. Consequently, the Government's objective required some form of international standing if it was to be the basis of a comprehensive and effective political position. It was given international expression, therefore, through the agency of the United Nations. Hence it was in New York that the terms of Britain's ultimatum were actually specified, through UN Resolution 502.

Specifying the ultimatum: UN 502

Once it had been informed that an Argentine invasion of the Falklands was imminent, the British delegation at the UN drafted a resolution for immediate submission to an emergency session of the Security Council. It also persuaded the current President of the Council to issue a call for both sides to show restraint. The draft resolution was confirmed with London on 2 April and adopted by the Security Council on 3 April, with only one vote against (Panama) and four abstentions (China, Spain, Poland and the Soviet Union). The resolution was mandatory and read as follows: 'Determining that there exists a breach of the peace in the region of the Falkland Islands (Islas Malvinas)', the Security Council

1. Demands an immediate cessation of hostilities,
2. Demands an immediate withdrawal of all Argentine forces from the Falkland Islands (Islas Malvinas),
3. Calls on the Governments of Argentina and the United Kingdom to seek a diplomatic solution to their differences and to respect fully the purpose and principles of the Charter of the United Nations.[4]

The text of the resolution had been carefully drafted to attract maximum support. In particular it specified a 'breach of the peace', as referred to in Article 39 of the UN Charter, but not an 'act of aggression' as specified in the terms of the same article. Similarly, it called upon both parties to return to negotiations. Such distinctions were important also when it came to efforts to reach a settlement.[5]

Britain's UN delegation thus won an important and surprising diplomatic victory ensuring that the Falklands was classified as an issue of international order rather than a question of decolonisation. As a consequence, the international discourse about the invasion crisis considerably favoured the British position. Even at the Organisation of American STates (OAS), which was backed by the 1947 Inter-American Treaty of Mutual Assistance, under which members agreed to support each other against extra-continental threats, Argentina failed to gain effective international endorsement of its cause. The OAS did not finally vote on a Falklands resolution until 28 April, and then it merely advocated a truce, recommending compliance with the Security Council resolution.[6]

As Sir Anthony Parsons, Britain's Permanent Representative in New York at the time, concluded:

the overt and the less overt support which we secured through the crisis from the non-aligned movement states as a whole owed itself to the fact that Argentina had launched a surprise attack, that they had broken all the rules of the Charter, and that this did not affect the view of many, many states in and out of Latin America that the Argentinian claim to sovereignty was well-founded.[7]

Argentina never escaped from the taint of aggression and its diplomatic position remained as weak as Britain's was strong on this point, at least until the sinking of the *Belgrano* reduced international support for the United Kingdom.

The international support which Britain received was a valuable asset not only as a means of isolating and stigmatising Argentina, but also in securing military support for the Task Force, while denying the Junta access to the arms supplies which might enable it to defeat the British forces. Although the United States was the critical actor here, Britain's European allies (especially France and Germany) were also significant. The ties of alliance might have secured the support of these states in any event but the strength of the British case made the diplomatic task of securing it that much easier. Moreover, just as the resolution contributed to Britain's diplomatic campaign so it also provided the basis of a secure bipartisan approach to the crisis in the British Parliament.

Resolution 502 was, therefore, much more than a valuable diplomatic advantage. By effecting a strong and enduring alliance between what the War Cabinet proposed to do as a matter of national necessity, and what it was licensed to do as a matter of international law, it served to integrate the military and diplomatic aspects of the British position and turn the War Cabinet's policy into a co-ordinated and effective political instrument. It was the basis upon which international mediation could be accepted, in a desperate effort to avert war, but closely monitored so that it did not end in a British humiliation. Similarly, it helped to legitimise a resort to force if mediation failed. Until Argentina complied with the resolution the United Kingdom was able to resist any proposal that would affect its title to sovereignty. In addition, the War Cabinet consistently refused to offer any concessions which might prejudice future negotiations on that issue. Instead Mrs Thatcher and her colleagues were able to insist that failure to comply with Resolution 502 granted Britain the right to enforce it by using the Task Force to expel the Argentine garrison from the Falklands if need be. In this way the War Cabinet satisfied the following indispensable and related policy requirements: the maintenance of its own internal cohesion, national unity, and international support. Finally, once the British counter-attack began, pressure for a ceasefire was resisted on the grounds that the terms of the resolution had to be satisfied first.

As Philip Windsor has observed, there was a price to be paid for this political and diplomatic success because 'in this way, Britain had accepted the need for an international jurisdiction over the issues, even while gaining a considerable diplomatic victory'.[8] The repercussions became evident first in the terms Britain was willing to grant in order to get an Argentine withdrawal and, later, in its attempt to conduct a national war under international expectations about the use and control of force. There were also those domestic critics, like Mr

Enoch Powell, who objected to what they regarded as over-reliance upon the United Nations.[9] But, in the event, despite the suggestion that seeking to comply with international law was irksome and unnecessary, the advantages heavily outweighed the disadvantages. UN Resolution 502 made a vital contribution, therefore, to the War Cabinet's success in avoiding many of the domestic as well as the international threats to its unity and support, as it prepared itself and the country for conflict.

Defence of the Ultimatum: Symbols and Rhetoric

If the War Cabinet had to specify the terms of its ultimatum in order to make its main political objective clear, it had, in addition, to explain the reasons why the ultimatum had been issued. To do this it had to give a detailed account, for domestic as well as international consumption, of why the invasion had taken place and of what was now at stake. It did so in a variety of ways. First, it was maintained that negotiations had been under way prior to Argentina's attack, that Britain had been negotiating in good faith and that progress was being made. Second, it was noted that Argentina had made belligerent gestures before without resorting to such extreme measures. Finally, it was argued that the invasion was a totally unprovoked and unexpected act of aggression by a volatile and brutal regime.[10] Hence the responsibility for the failure of prewar policy was neatly shifted onto Argentina's Junta, while the question of the Government's responsibility was quickly displaced by the new and more threatening issues of national pride and international order.

An ultimatum which left little room for concessions or conciliatory gestures was a natural product of the structure of the crisis, and the War Cabinet quickly adapted itself to the dynamics of the circumstances involved. Trust and dialogue could only be re-established, it was argued, if Argentina returned to the old rules by complying with Resolution 502. Equally, as the War Cabinet dismissed the question of blame and justified its commitment to the military gamble entailed in the despatch of the Task force, it had to reinterpret the history of the dispute and elevate the issue into one of supreme national importance.[11] What followed was a perfect example of a radical change of political discourse being used not simply to reflect but also to effect a transformation in the character of a political issue. In the process there was a great deal of hypocrisy and mythologising in the metamorphosis of the Falklands from a failure of post-imperial politics into a test of freedom, national credibility and international stability.

In explaining the grounds upon which the ultimatum had been issued, the War Cabinet invoked as well as exploited the central symbolic themes which distinguished British reactions to the invasion. If it was impossible to maintain that national survival was at issue, it was evident to most that its symbolic surrogate, national identity, certainly was. The credibility of Britain's entire defence culture seemed to have been challenged and the dangers appeared to be incalculable. The Prime Minister, for example, declared in the Commons on 8 April that: 'I took a decision immediately and said that the future of freedom and the reputation of Britain were at stake. We cannot therefore look at it on the basis of precisely how much it will cost'.[12]

Foreign Office 'appeasement' was also blamed for a crisis in which Britain's entire international status was now believed to be threatened. If a firm stand was not taken, it was argued, how could Britain deal resolutely with other post-imperial problems like Belize or Gibraltar—or indeed with more mundane NATO and Common Market issues such as 'fishing disputes, budgetary debates, defence contributions and the like?'[13] More generally, what credibility would Britain's deterrent defence posture retain if the Government proved 'weak and irresolute' over an issue which involved sovereign territory, the lives of British citizens and the future of its colonial dependants?[14] It was widely believed that if Argentina was not forced to evacuate the Islands, national interests and international order would both suffer.

Domestically, the crisis was also embraced as an agent of national renewal in a political culture where talk of political and economic revival had been a staple of political discourse for decades. As *The Economist* stated in one of its editorials, 'Britain has long needed its own sort of cultural revolution'.[15] A Conservative back-bencher went a little further. 'I believe', he declared, 'that this is the last chance, the very last chance, for us to redeem much of our history over the past 25 years, of which we may be ashamed and from which we may have averted our gaze'.[16] Such hyperbolic responses reflected the deep national frustrations which the invasion had excited. These resonated in turn with the Government's political ambition to restore the country's economic and political fortunes through assertive national leadership. Britain's resurgence and the restoration of the Falkland Islands, therefore, drew upon similar political sentiments. In the process the 'Falklands spirit' was born, with the Prime Minister leading and profiting from the mood. Professing to see 'this ancient country rising as one nation', she declared: 'Too long submerged, too often denigrated, too easily forgotten, the springs of pride in Britain flow again.'[17]

In sum the inversion of national priorities which had always dogged Falklands policy, so compromising the progress of imperial retreat from the South Atlantic, quickly assumed epic Churchillian proportions as Britain's political leaders, themselves responding to deep cultural instincts, exploited the United Kingdom's defence culture in formulating their response to the invasion.[18]

Nevertheless, the War Cabinet was not alone in agreeing with the Prime Minister that 'the future of freedom and the reputation of Britain were at stake'. It was joined also by the bulk of Parliamentary opinion. There were voices from both sides of the House of Commons which urged caution and there were some who flatly opposed the Government and its interpretation of events.[19] However, they were few and ineffective. The public reaction, as we have argued, was somewhat more circumspect but it too was heavily in favour of the War Cabinet's response to the attack.

These domestic reactions were instinctive rather than considered. Some, like Raymond Whitney on the Conservative side, warned that a national tragedy rather than a national humiliation was in prospect if the Task Force had to conduct a sea-borne assault upon the Islands.[20] Others, like Tony Benn and Tam Dalyell from the Labour Party, condemned the military action as fundamentally wrong and misconceived, and they remonstrated against it.[21] But George Foulkes, although a Labour MP and a dissenter from the Government's decisions, gave expression to the dominant sentiment: 'My gut reaction is to use force. Our country has been humiliated.'[22]

Despite the strength of feeling exhibited in the House of Commons, however, the Falklands conflict was not Parliament's war.[23] It was the War Cabinet which had first issued the demand for Argentina to withdraw its forces or have them expelled by force. Only luck or consummate political skill would have extracted it from that predicament without a military conflict or a major political defeat. But, in an act of political solidarity, Parliament echoed and amplified this response making it clear that, if the War Cabinet policy did not succeed, the Prime Minister and her colleagues would not be allowed to escape from the political consequences of the Government's failure. 'Unless firm and effective action is taken within a reasonable period of time to remove the invaders and to restore the Islanders to British sovereignty,' a Conservative back-bencher warned, 'the effect on the Government's standing will be dire.'[24] The fate of Neville Chamberlain, as well as the rhetoric of Winston Churchill, pervaded the atmosphere of Westminster in the immediate aftermath of Argentina's attack.

Because all international conflicts take place at the interface between international and domestic affairs, no state has a conception of its national interest which does not simultaneously and implicitly favour some related conception of how the international system ought to be organised. The United Kingdom's attitude derives, of course, from many sources. But its reliance upon the liberal tradition of the rule of law, in particular, received added emphasis from a long imperial retreat which was concerned to maintain international stability as a means also of retaining British influence. Thus the whole question of the international system, together with the rights of self-defence and self-determination as well as the peaceful resolution of disputes, was also at issue in the domestic debate which was provoked by the invasion. The Foreign Secretary, for example, insisted: 'We are dealing with the fundamental question of international order and how countries order their affairs.'[25]

Britain's position, therefore, also depended upon Article 51 of the United Nations Charter, which stipulates the right of self-defence, and upon various resolutions and declarations in which the UN has affirmed its support for self-determination.[26] These points, too, were not simply ornamental in War Cabinet policy but an integral part of it. Once again a fusion of themes was achieved with international order and British interests closely interwoven into a tightly integrated diplomatic policy that appealed to the broadest collection of political sympathies and constituencies. As a result it was capable of meeting objections from national or international sources and of uniting a wide body of opinion. But, as with all policies, British diplomacy also contained important ambiguities which became evident as the invasion crisis propelled its participants towards war.

Terms for rescinding the ultimatum

Finally, as the War Cabinet had to define its ultimatum, and defend its reasons for taking such a decision, it also had to explain under what terms and conditions it would refrain from the use of force. In one sense the answer to this question was simple. The only condition which would apparently satisfy the War Cabinet seemed to be the implementation of Resolution 502. That, however, still left at issue Argentina's historical claim to the Islands. Additionally, despite the

British insistence that military withdrawal was a prerequisite of renewed discussions, Resolution 502 also called on both parties 'to seek a diplomatic solution to their differences'. Thus, while the War Cabinet insisted on its right and its resolve to use force, Britain's negotiating position was a little more flexible and rather more familiar in practice than its rhetoric implied. Argentina's aggression was not to be rewarded, so no concessions could be made which would prejudice the Islands' future. Nonetheless, in a move uncommonly like the sovereignty umbrella employed in the 1970s, a return to sovereignty negotiations was offered without prejudice to either side's claims. In addition the terms of an interim peace agreement were also specified. Here, too, there was room for negotiation and for compromise. Hence the War Cabinet sought to use international mediation to secure a peaceful dénouement to the crisis on limited but negotiable terms. While it did so, it simultaneously maintained that Argentine withdrawal was a precondition of any settlement. Only that would satisfy British honour and the principle that international disputes had to be decided by negotiation. Moreover, the Task Force could not be restrained if Argentina did not comply by the time the Fleet was in a position to carry out its mission.

For a period, therefore, the demand for Argentine withdrawal was accompanied by some small but important concessions. Prior to the invasion these might have satisfied Argentina's goal of achieving material progress in the satisfaction of its claim to the Falklands. Explored through international mediation in the month following the attack, they were unable to satisfy the inflated political price set by Argentina's *coup de main*. That price was increased still further by the outbreak of undeclared war on 1 May when the Task Force's Carrier Battle Group began the campaign to recapture the Islands. The conduct of these negotiations was to dominate the War Cabinet's diplomacy in the days that followed the capture of the Islands, and through them British policy-makers also dealt successfully with a wide variety of additional political considerations, all of which had an important bearing on the outcome of the invasion crisis.

Unity of the War Cabinet

As the War Cabinet employed these devices to guide the country through the transition from peace to war, and as it revised them in response first to political and then to military developments, so its unity and resolve were tested. Naturally the fault line which threatened to divide its members was located at the junction of its military and diplomatic policies. Strong circumstantial evidence suggests also that this fault line lay between the Foreign Secretary and the Prime Minister. It was Pym's responsibility in any event to pursue a diplomatic settlement as best he could, and this was reflected in his public statements. His diplomatic responsibilities, therefore, were bound to bring him into conflict with his Premier who had overall responsibility for both aspects of War Cabinet policy.[27]

The public unity of the War Cabinet, however, was vital and it was maintained. Although Pym's studious use of diplomatic language was clearly designed to keep options open, whereas Mrs Thatcher's rhetoric was much more uncompromising, the Foreign Secretary never departed from the War Cabinet line. Indeed, when there was any suggestion of a rift he was quick to reaffirm his commitment to the lead given by the Prime Minister. For example, on 21 April he returned to the House of Commons (after issuing a formal statement in which he had maintained that he would seek to exclude the use of force 'as long as negotiations are in play') to insist 'that however hard I was trying to achieve a peaceful settlement, the use of force could not at any stage be ruled out. If there was any misunderstanding I want to clear it up'.[28] Similarly, he confirmed after the War that he felt bound by collective responsibility to support any changes in the Rules of Engagement (ROE) which the War Cabinet had to make in his absence: 'a change in the rules of engagement . . . was a reasonably routine practice' and that of 2 May, in particular, 'was one of many changes made in the course of the war and one that, in my absence, I would certainly support the War Cabinet in making'.[29] Once more Resolution 502 was the instrument which united both policy and policy-makers. It was the first step, as the major protagonists within the Cabinet both insisted, 'a prerequisite of any further progress'.[30]

PEACE NEGOTIATIONS

There were two stages to the peace negotiations which were central to the War Cabinet's diplomacy:(1 ttempts to bring about an Argentine withdrawal before full-scale hostilities opened with the arrival of British forces in Falklands v aters; and (2) attempts to negotiate a ceasefire once the British Task Force began its counter-attack on the Islands.

United States mediation dominated the first stage of these

negotiations. Peru's initiative came at the junction of the two stages and was markedly affected by the transition. United Nations intercession originated at the same time as Peru's but was subordinate to President Belaunde's intervention for a short while. It was then almost exclusively concerned with attempts to bring about a ceasefire. Although all these discussions proceeded up to and beyond the opening of Britain's counter-attack, they did not all have an equal chance of success and they did not contain exactly the same balance of considerations. It was clear, nonetheless, that War Cabinet diplomacy was governed by a basic strategy, derived from the Security Council resolution.

Initially the United Kingdom seems to have been engaged in a genuine exercise in dual diplomacy, designed to explore the opportunities for a peaceful solution without prejudicing the prospects of the Task Force.[31] Once the military schedule had caught up with diplomatic developments at the end of April, however, the subordination of diplomacy to the demands of military policy became irresistible. Thereafter, in support of the Task Force's counter-invasion, diplomacy was devoted to resisting any ceasefire proposals which did not amount to the unconditional surrender and eviction of all Argentine forces from the Falklands.

Haig's mediation

London had sought Washington's help from as far back as the beginning of March 1982 when Richard Luce, as we have seen, had asked Mr Thomas Enders 'to encourage the Argentines to "keep things cool" '. On 8 March the Foreign Secretary had apprised Haig of Britain's growing fears and 'expressed the hope that the Government could count on Mr Haig's help in ensuring that the issue was settled peacefully and in accordance with the democratically expressd wishes of the inhabitants of the Islands'.[32] Ultimately the Prime Minister herself had sought the President's intervention on the eve of the invasion. Each request was an indication of the growth of British alarm and thus United States mediation was a natural progression in the development of British reactions to the escalation of the dispute. Furthermore, it seemed that Argentina was more likely to respond to pressure from Washington than from any other quarter. Close ties had been developed between the Junta and the Reagan administration, and Argentina valued US economic and military aid.[33]

From the British perspective, however, if the United States was to make it clear that it would support the United Kingdom, the Junta might accept that its defeat was inevitable. Thus securing United States diplomatic and military help became one of the War Cabinet's principal diplomatic concerns because it was critical to the success of its overall policy. As Sir Nicholas Henderson, Britain's Ambassador in Washington at the time, observed: 'From my discussions with service leaders since the events, I conclude that it is difficult to exaggerate the difference that American support made to the military outcome.'[34]

If there was to be a peaceful outcome to the crisis, on terms which were acceptable to the War Cabinet, United States mediation might achieve it. If not, United States military aid could make all the difference to the balance of forces in the South Atlantic. Conversely, should the United States oppose the British, as it had done during the Suez crisis, the outcome was likely to be disastrous.[35] Just as United States intervention offered the best prospect of restoring peace, so its support offered Britain the best prospect of securing military victory. Neither object could be achieved, however, if Britain refused to engage in negotiations. Only by accepting mediation could the War Cabinet seek a diplomatic escape from war. Similarly, only by accepting mediation could it demonstrate its reasonableness, so encouraging the United States to make its assistance available at a speed and to a degree that would ensure the success of the Task Force. Finally, only if Britain engaged in negotiations could the United States resolve its own political dilemma and offer the support which Britain demanded.

American support for the British was not automatic. Henderson, for example, concluded: 'American support was not something that was inevitable. It could not have been taken for granted and could have been lost at any time had we shown complete intransigence in negotiation.'[36] Despite considerable public and Congressional sympathy for Britain's position, the United States Government was divided. As part of its hemispheric policy the Reagan administration had cultivated Argentina and extended support to the Junta. Its dilemma, therefore, was quite clear. If the United States supported Britain not only would it lose a valuable hemispheric ally, it would also damage its general political standing in Latin America. While the Secretary of State 'saw how close a bearing the crisis had on the future of the Atlantic Alliance', and 'was determined, as was the President, to do everything conceivable to help the British Government',[37] there were American interests to be considered and domestic opposition to be managed. Some in the administration doubted that Britain could achieve its ends by military means if diplomacy failed. Others, more sympathetic to Argentina and more concerned with the future of hemispheric relations and the geostrategic dangers of Soviet involvement, wanted the United States to achieve a diplomatic settlement by acting impartially. Haig has indicated that at one point he was almost alone in the State Department in thinking that the British could achieve their political objective.[38] Although the Department of Defense was already giving the United Kingdom 'a great deal of support',[39] there were those in the State Department and the President's entourage who either had to be convinced that the British could achieve their goal or outmanoeuvred because they were not in sympathy with the British cause.

In response to these considerations the US administration did not initially take sides and it continued to refrain from expressing a view on the issue of sovereignty. Nevertheless, the Secretary of State had assured the British Ambassador ('in the early days') that

> the United States was not at heart impartial, that HMG had always supported the Reagan administration in foreign policy, and that America could not privately be even-handed in anything involving its closest ally . . . notwithstanding the public stance, the President was our staunch supporter.[40]

Mediation offered Haig two ways of extracting the US from its predicament. Ideally a peaceful settlement would obviate the need to chose between the two allies, while denying the Soviet Union any chance of establishing influence with a South American regime. Should mediation fail, however, Haig would be better placed to overcome those who prized hemispheric goals above Alliance solidarity. The administration could then be united in support of its most important ally, as well as in defence of principles which it had always professed. Finally, and again from the British perspective, if negotiations failed to find a solution they might nevertheless stigmatise the Junta further by exposing its intransigence. This would help to sustain wider international support for the British position. It would also make a contribution to the important ancillary task of denying Argentina access to military and economic aid. Throughout this entire process British policy had to signal the War Cabinet's resolve by specifying clearly the limits of its position. Simultaneously it had to identify what the Secretary of State called 'constructive ambiguities' which might offer some prospect of a settlement.[41]

Haig's mission began on 8 April, when he flew to London to consult the War Cabinet, and all accounts maintain that he left impressed by the Prime Minister's resolve. On his arrival in Argentina he is reported to have emphasised Britain's willingness to use force as well as its superior strength. As a result there was a body of opinion in Buenos Aires which regarded him as Britain's ally rather than a mediator. Equally, but conversely, there also seems to have been a strong conviction in Buenos Aires that the United States would not side with Britain, an assessment encouraged by the factors we have just considered.[42]

It was quickly established that any settlement would have to deal in some way with three basic points: the withdrawal of military forces; the terms of an interim agreement; and the framework of negotiations for some long-term settlement of the dispute. All three categories were covered by the Security Council Resolution. Military withdrawal had been demanded by the Resolution and so had a return to negotiations. An interim arrangement was the corollary of these two points. The details, however, had to be negotiated and each side had to specify its respective positions. Britain emphasised withdrawal as a precondition of a settlement and insisted that any interim arrangements should not prejudice the framework for longer-term negotiations. Argentina was concerned most with the framework for the longer-term discussions, and tried to use its bargaining position to ensure that the final outcome would be a transfer of sovereignty.

Haig made his final suggestions on 27 April although, according to one report, his dealings with the Junta had led him to conclude as early as 19 April 'that he was dealing with a regime quite unable to take coherent decisions, let alone stick to them',[43] and he told the British so. The Secretary of State proposed a phased military withdrawal by both sides, the termination of sanctions and an interim agreement based upon a tripartite United States, British and Argentine authority, to be composed of one representative from each party supported by a staff of no more than ten advisors. The 'traditional local administration' of the Falkland Islands' Executive and Legislative Councils was to be retained but with important modifications. Their decisions would effectively be supervised by the tripartite authority. Argentina was also to be allowed two representatives on the Executive Council. Finally, the Falklands' small Argentine population was to receive proportional representation on both Councils in accordance with the rights of representation which the Islanders enjoyed. Other items in the Haig plan included proposals for restoring communications and for protecting the Islanders' existing rights 'relating to freedom of opinion, religion, expression, teaching, movement, property, employment, family, customs, and cultural ties with countries of origin'.[44]

The interim agreement was to last until 31 December 1982. By that time the tripartite authority, in consultation with the Executive Council, was to make specific proposals and recommendations to facilitate a long-term solution by specifying how 'the wishes and interests of the Islanders' were to be taken into account.[45] It was to do this by taking 'a sounding of the opinion of the inhabitants'. In addition it was to offer recommendations on the development of the Islands, the future of the Falkland Islands Company and compensation claims from the Islanders.[46]

Haig's proposals also stipulated that by the end of the interim period 'the two Governments shall complete negotiations on removal of the Islands from the list of Non-Self-Governing territories under Chapter XI of the United Nations Charter and on mutually agreed conditions for their definitive status'.[47] This long-term agreement was to include 'due regard for the rights of the inhabitants and for the principle of territorial integrity'. Such a formula attempted to combine the chief concerns of the two disputants, but it did not set a deadline for the negotiation of the settlement. The penultimate paragraph of the proposals stated that 'should the Governments nonetheless be unable to conclude the negotiations by 31 December, 1982' the United States would be prepared to seek a solution within six months of a request by both parties for its mediation. Britain and Argentina had to respond to any such proposals within a month. All this was designed to satisfy Argentina's concern that discussions would drag on endlessly as they had done in the past. Equally, it was also designed to satisfy the United Kingdom's determination not to be fixed to any deadline.

Haig's suggestions failed to satisfy Argentina for several reasons. The interim arrangements did not allow Buenos Aires sufficient involvement in Islands affairs to be able to determine the final outcome of the dispute—by out-voting the Islanders, for example, or expanding the Argentine population on the Islands. Inevitably, by making provision for the canvassing of Islands opinion, the proposals also weakened Argentina's position. Limited participation in the interim administration of the Islands might have been acceptable, the Junta argued, 'if it were clear that Argentina's sovereignty would be recognised in the end'. In those circumstances Argentina could have been 'more flexible regarding the matter of temporary administration'. Instead it demanded 'a fixed term', greater participation in the interim administration or, alternatively, 'provisions . . . precise enough to offer security for recognition of Argentina's rights within a specified period'.[48] For these reasons the Junta rejected the proposals and asked for other formulas to be found. In contrast, the British indicated that they were prepared to consider them as a basis for negotiations, although there is some dispute about whether they would have proved acceptable as grounds for a settlement. Admiral Lewin, for example, later told the House of Commons Foreign Affairs Committee that they were a long way short of being acceptable:

> The War Cabinet had with great reluctance agreed that he [Haig] should put them to Galtieri, but without commitment of the British Government. Those proposals would indeed I think have been very difficult for the War Cabinet or the British Government of all parties to accept.[49]

There was nothing in Haig's proposals which ensured progress towards a transfer of sovereignty, and Argentina had every reason to fear that the Islanders would be more rather than less hostile to it in future. However, had Argentina accepted Haig's proposals, and so tested the War Cabinet's willingness to make some limited but important concessions, it might have advanced its claim to the Falklands more than at any time since the early 1970s, by securing a return to sovereignty negotiations, some internationalisation of the dispute and Argentine involvement in the government of the Islands. At least, it might have caused diplomatic embarrassment to the War Cabinet.

If no fixed date was set for a settlement both the Islanders and the British Government (notwithstanding the impact of the invasion) would have found themselves more constrained to reach a solution than in the past. Moreover, the Foreign Secretary had insisted that 'I have an open mind about the way in which the long-term solution can, in due course, be achieved'.[50] He also intimated that Britain might now be willing to accept the jurisdiction of the International Court with respect not only to the Dependencies but also to the Islands. Pym's 'open-mindedness' was, of course, combined with the insistence that the Falklands remained sovereign British territory and that the wishes of the Islanders were paramount. Thus the Junta had an opportunity to exploit the divisions latent within the War Cabinet and expose the limits of its willingness to settle for a peaceful solution. But, given its own internal divisions and ineffectiveness, it was not capable of doing so.

Although it failed to produce a settlement the diplomatic exercise had nevertheless been important so far as the British were concerned. Most of all it had enabled the US to escape from its dilemma. On 29 April the United States Senate passed a resolution endorsing the United Kingdom's position by 79 votes to 1,[51] and the following day Haig announced that 'in light of Argentina's failure to accept a compromise, we must take concrete steps to underscore that the United States cannot and will not condone the use of unlawful force to resolve disputes'.[52] Accordingly US military and economic sanctions were imposed upon Argentina and, although British forces were already receiving United States military aid, military assistance was granted the authority of a Presidential directive.[53]

Second, the 'diplomatic vacuum' between the despatch and arrival of the Task Force having been filled, the British position had been consolidated and Argentina blamed for the collapse of the negotiations.[54] Whatever the merits of Haig's proposals, it was the Junta, and not the War Cabinet, which had actually refused to proceed with them. Finally, the experience seems to have resolved any doubts the War Cabinet may have had about the need to use force. The talks had been fruitless and the British appear to have confirmed to their own satisfaction that Argentina was a totally unreliable negotiating partner.[55]

Britain's War Cabinet was improvising its response to a fast-developing crisis on the basis of decisions taken at the end of March and the beginning of April. In addition, it was seeking to influence several separate and independent decision centres simultaneously. Thus it was hardly in full control of events, though the US 'tilt' in favour of Britain coincided with the arrival of the Carrier Battle Group off the Falklands and the initiation of the British campaign for the repossession of the Islands. That coincidence, however, was not fortuitous, but the outcome of an intense diplomatic campaign, conducted through the British Embassy in Washington, which was governed by the following objectives.[56]

The first of these was to set the terms of the issue emphasising the undemocratic nature of the Argentine regime, the right of self-determination of the Islanders, and the inadmissibility of using force to settle territorial disputes, especially in an area of many unresolved territorial conflicts. The second was to reinforce existing pro-British sentiment by the careful handling of crisis information and by exposing the excesses of Argentine reports. Extensive lobbying of certain target groups was required, including the major newspapers and networks as well as political institutions, particularly the Senate and its Committee leaders. The British Ambassador, for example, appeared 73 times on US television throughout the course of the conflict and visited Congress every day.[57] The third objective was to acquire military aid without advertising its scale. This was achieved by activating the deep bureaucratic structures of the Anglo-American relationship, including the large military mission attached to the British Embassy in Washington and the extensive socio-professional network that exists between senior members of the British and United States defence establishments.[58]

The final objective was that which distinguished British policy throughout the invasion crisis, to establish the reasonableness of the United Kingdom while emphasising its determination and its ability to use force. As one report recalled, the campaign 'succeeded in unlocking ancient, almost atavistic, emotions tying Britain to America'[59] and, on 30 April, the War Cabinet achieved its most desired diplomatic victory. United States support was secured, backed by Presidential direction, and subsequently nothing 'within reason' was refused.

The timing of the US 'tilt' was vital because the War Cabinet had become increasingly preoccupied with meeting the demands of the Task Force, once the Carrier Battle Group had sailed from Ascension Island and approached the Falklands. As the military advance overhauled the diplomatic negotiations, military exigency began to override all other considerations. Thus, although the War Cabinet's frustration with Argentina was no doubt genuine it was also timely. Similarly, although the failure of Haig's mission was a consequence of the Junta's inability (or unwillingness) to accept terms which it was unlikely to see bettered, his mediation was only just concluded in time for Britain to proceed with its military campaign backed by the public assurance of United States support. If this outcome was one that the British had striven very hard to achieve, the timing of it barely satisfied the War Cabinet's basic requirements. It is not difficult to imagine, therefore, the degree of strain on Anglo-American relations towards the end of April 1982. However, the civilities appear to have been maintained, at least publicly, and the goods were delivered both in diplomatic and military terms.[60]

The US attempt at mediation was succeeded by two further initiatives, one from the President of Peru and one from the Secretary General of the United Nations. Controversy has surrounded the Peruvian initiative, with various charges made with respect to the

Peruvian proposals and the War Cabinet's decision-making over the weekend of 1–2 May.[61] There are, essentially, two related aspects to this dispute. One concerns the diplomatic side of War Cabinet policy, in particular the status of the Peruvian proposals, and that will be dealt with here. The other concerns the War Cabinet's military plans and that will be dealt with in the next chapter, although the intimate link between the two will not be overlooked.

Peruvian mediation

The Peruvian initiative seems to have begun some time on 30 April when the Peruvian Foreign Minister contacted the US Ambassador in Lima.[62] It gathered momentum on 1 May when Peru's President, Belaunde Terry, accepted a seven-point peace plan proposed by Alexander Haig, which Belaunde was then to put to Galtieri. Simultaneously, in New York, the Secretary General was also confidently expected to mediate.[63] Arrangements were made, therefore, for the British Foreign Secretary to travel to Washington on 1 May to consult with Haig, and then to fly to New York on the afternoon of 2 May to discuss the Secretary General's proposals for a settlement.[64]

As these diplomatic developments took place, Britain's Carrier Battle Group was also committed to attack against Argentine forces on and around the Falklands. These operations necessarily exposed the British ships to Argentine counter-attack but that was part of the Task Force's strategic design to test the Islands' defences and establish local superiority in preparation for the amphibious assault.[65] From 23 April onwards the safety and success of the Task Force became the War Cabinet's immediate and paramount consideration. The evidence from Parliamentary debates, public announcements and subsequent inquiries into changes in the Rules of Engagement authorised at this time, all indicate that the War Cabinet finally committed itself to the implementation of its ultimatum in the last week of April. Indeed by rejecting Haig's proposals the Junta had allowed the British to escape from a difficult political dilemma. Amongst other reasons, the War Cabinet had been reluctant to use force while United States mediation was in progress, although the decision to recapture South Georgia risked such diplomatic embarrassment and could have incurred much higher British or Argentine casualties. But as the Carrier Group advanced on the Falklands, it was increasingly likely to have to engage in a large-scale use of force. Argentina's announcement, therefore, enabled the War Cabinet to commit the Carrier Group to battle without disrupting the Task Force's tight military schedule, or incurring blame for taking major military measures while its principal ally was preoccupied with a search for peace.[66]

The fate of Peru's proposals has to be considered in the context of these important diplomatic and military developments. Lack of time, conflicting interpretations, narrowing of options and reliance on basic convictions are four of the most distinctive features of crisis. All four factors were acutely evident on both sides throughout the conflict and by the end of April they had coalesced into a very powerful conjunction of forces.

The advance of the Task Force had allowed a breathing space of about three weeks. During that time the conflicting demands of Britain's converging diplomatic and military schedules were reconciled, at least publicly, until they met on 1–2 May. Then they exposed the War Cabinet's fundamental reliance upon military expediency. War was always highly probable, unless the prospects for a settlement somehow improved dramatically and unexpectedly. And in the aftermath of Haig's failure that did not look likely. Despite the many charges which have been levelled against the War Cabinet, and despite the way in which the British Government revised its various accounts of the sinking of the *Belgrano*, causing suspicion and confusion, the weight of published evidence suggests that there was no conspiracy to reject the Peruvian proposals. What took place appears to have been instead a consequence of many of the standard features of crisis decision-making, the stage which this particular crisis had reached and the force of the military logic which obtained in the South Atlantic. In short, the British ultimatum had expired with the arrival of the Carrier Group and there appeared to be no good diplomatic reasons for the War Cabinet delaying its use. Had it done so, it would have compounded the problems of Admiral Woodward's Force, further endangering his ships which had already engaged Argentine air and naval forces in the Total Exclusion Zone. British policy at this time was going through a final transition during which the military imperatives initiated by Argentina's brinkmanship and the British Government's pre-invasion failures largely determined the War Cabinet's actions. Consequently, at lunch-time on 2 May a general extension of the British Rules of Engagement was granted, which *inter alia* allowed the *Belgrano* to be sunk.

Peru's intervention, therefore, emerged out of the loss of diplomatic momentum which surrounded the conclusion of Haig's mediation and the outbreak of fighting which followed the commitment of British and Argentine forces to battle. At the same time, the UN Secretary General, Perez de Cuellar, was also preparing to take up where Haig had left off. With these international and military developments either in process or in the offing, Britain's diplomatic policy had to be substantially revised, not only because its initial commitment to seeking a peaceful outcome via US mediation had failed but also because its other objective, securing US support, had succeeded. The Foreign Secretary's visit to the United States over the weekend of 1–2 May was part of that process of adjustment. It was designed 'to take stock', consolidate US support, and explore with the UN Secretary General how he might mediate in the dispute. It was also undertaken in the knowledge that hostilities were imminent.[67] Presumably the Foreign Secretary recognised not only that his diplomatic brief needed to be modified but also that its status within the overall context of British policy had itself been signficantly reduced both by the advance of the Task Force and by the changes to its Rules of Engagement which had been agreed on 23 and 30 April.[68]

A shift from Haig's individual mediation to more complicated multi-intermediary diplomacy, via Haig and Belaunde, was also taking place. There was, in addition, a change of peace proposals in prospect. All this had to offer more than the diplomatic process which had just failed for the War Cabinet to forgo the use of the Task Force. Evidently Pym was in the United States to explore these and other questions. Absent once more from the War Cabinet, as he had been on 23 April when an earlier change in the Task Force's ROE had been agreed, he was not on hand to contest the decisive shift to general naval warfare in the South Atlantic which his colleagues were about to sanction. Indeed, there is no evidence to suggest that he would have done so. On the contrary, as we shall see in the next chapter, he argued for an additional and more specific public warning to Argentina but he did not dissent from the War Cabinet's actions.

As a result of decisions taken on 23 and 30 April the Carrier Battle Group had arrived in the vicinity of the Falklands supported by the widest possible public warning (issued on 23 April) that it would attack any Argentine forces seeking to interfere with its 'mission',[69] but with only limited military authorisation to open its campaign for their repossession. At this crucial point in the transition of the invasion crisis to war, accounts of what then took place diverge significantly, particularly with respect to three basic questions which have been raised about the Peruvian proposals. Did the War Cabinet know about

Belaunde's plan before it decided to change the ROE on 2 May? Ought it to have known, or was some diplomatic failure responsible for not relaying the details back to London? Were the proposals on the brink of success?

It is now evident that for Peru, Argentina and the United States, President Belaunde's initiative was the immediate focus of a highly intensive effort to revive diplomatic mediation. Belaunde was to present his seven-point proposal (later reduced to five) to Galtieri, because Peru had supported Argentina's position and its intercession was likely to be received sympathetically. It is equally evident that both Haig and Belaunde believed that the War Cabinet knew about the proposals, and assumed that it was being kept informed of their progress. According to Rice and Gavshon, Belaunde was convinced that he was close to a settlement, and Haig maintained in his memoirs that the Peruvian President had 'gained acceptance in principle from both parties'. In almost every other respect, including questions of fact as well as interpretation, these accounts conflict directly with the official British view.[70]

All the leading participants on the British side agree that nothing was known about the Peruvian plan until 2 May. They also maintain that there had been no British participation in the discussions between Haig and Belaunde, over 30 April–1 May, during which the proposals had been drawn up. Equally, they reject the suggestion that the plan represented a major new initiative which was close to success.[71]

There were three principal sources from which the War Cabinet might have received advance notification about the Peruvian plan. One was Francis Pym, who would have learnt about it from Alexander Haig. Another was the British Ambassador in Peru. And, arguably, a third might have been British intelligence sources in Argentina. Throughout, it has to be remembered that the War Cabinet changed the Rules of Engagement shortly after 12.00 BST (British Summer Time) on 2 May, and that the *Belgrano* was sunk at approximately 20.00 BST.[72]

Pym arrived in Washington on the evening of 1 May. There was some suggestion that he was in telephone conversation with Haig that evening but Pym categorically denied this, and Haig did not refer to any such call in his memoirs.[73] The Foreign Secretary maintains that he learnt nothing about the proposals until his discussion with Haig on the morning of 2 May, and that the proposals were only discussed then in the most general terms.[74] The details, such as they were, were duly reported back to London by diplomatic telegram after Pym had left

Washington for New York on the afternoon of 2 May. They were despatched from Washington after 5.00 p.m. local time (17.00 BST) and received by the Foreign Office at 23.15 BST; apparently this was the War Cabinet's first official notification of them.[75] The speed of their despatch would have depended upon two factors: when the proposals were first discussed and what significance they were accorded. In this respect, no special priority above and beyond what must have been attached to all diplomatic communications between Washington and London at this time seems to have been given to the news. Anyway, the time of the despatch shows that it was sent several hours after the War Cabinet had changed the Rules of Engagement and the proposals were received some time after the *Belgrano* had been sunk. In fact, while Pym and Haig were holding their discussions between 10 and 12 a.m. in Washington on the morning of 2 May the War Cabinet had already made its decision (Washington being five hours behind London time).

In short, only if the Foreign Secretary had known about the Peruvian proposals on the evening of 1 May, or in the early hours of 2 May, and only if they had seemed very likely to be the basis of a settlement, could it reasonably be expected that the War Cabinet would have learnt of them from this source. The evidence available, despite certain reports to the contrary, does not support such a suggestion, either with respect to timing or with respect to the status of the proposals.

Britain's Ambassador in Peru, Mr Wallace, similarly rejected the suggestion that he knew about the Peruvian plan on 1 May and that he was deeply involved in all the exchanges which took place between Lima, Buenos Aires and Washington. In his evidence to the House of Commons Foreign Affairs Committee, he maintained that in response to a request from Francis Pym he held a meeting with Peru's Foreign Minister, Dr Arias Stella, on the morning of 1 May to restate Britain's position, now that US mediation had ended and hostilities were impending. During the meeting Haig's 'tilt' statement was also discussed. In addition Wallace recalled that 'Dr Arias asked me if I thought there were any ways in which the Peruvians could help to break the diplomatic deadlock . . . I said I had no instruction to convey any specific suggestions to him'.[76]

After further general discussion, in which the Ambassador reiterated Britain's insistence on the implementation of Resolution 502 and expressed the belief that Peru could exert its influence on Argentina to comply with the resolution, the meeting ended. Wallace insisted: 'I was given no indication that any new initiative was being considered'. Subsequently he sent a telegram to the Foreign Office 'reporting my conversation in the terms that I have described . . . without any reference to any new proposals because no such proposals had been mentioned to me'.[77] This report, of what in the circumstances appeared to have been a relatively routine diplomatic exchange, was not forwarded to the War Cabinet.[78] On the morning of 2 May, Wallace received a summons to attend a meeting in Peru's Foreign Ministry at 18.30 local time. As he was driving to that meeting he heard Belaunde's public announcement of Peru's peace initiative broadcast on the car radio. In discussion with Arias Stella shortly afterwards he eventually received details of the peace proposals. London time was Lima plus 5 hours GMT (BST is GMT plus one hour).[79] Thus, unless the British Embassy in Lima received the telephone call arranging the Ambassador's 18.30 meeting with the Foreign Minister before 7 a.m. in the morning Lima time, there was no possibility that the War Cabinet could have received notification from that source of some diplomatic development which might have had a bearing upon its decision to change the Rules of Engagement. The Wallace-Stella meeting took place at 00.30 BST, hours after the War Cabinet session and the sinking of the *Belgrano*, and a summary of it was received in London about an hour and a half after the conversation had taken place (that is, at 02.00 BST 3 May).[80]

One possibility remains, however. If one discounts the evidence of the British parties involved, the War Cabinet might have received some informal or unofficial indication that a Peruvian scheme for a settlement was under active consideration. Perhaps Pym did get wind of it on 1 May, or perhaps Britain's Ambassador in Peru did receive some indication at his first meeting with Arias Stella.[81] Alternatively, British intelligence may have provided some privileged information. Gavshon and Rice, for instance, report that Belaunde, Costa Mendez, Haig and Stella all assumed that the British were closely involved throughout 1–2 May, even if 'Nothing from British sources . . . suggests that this was in fact the case'.[82]

These reports, and the speculation to which they have given rise, turn attention to the third question raised about the Peruvian proposals and to the charge that the War Cabinet ordered the sinking of the *Belgrano* to ruin the chance of a negotiated settlement.[83] The evidence, however, does not support the contention that the proposals represented a detailed plan which was close to being accepted.

When the particulars of Belaunde's intervention became known, all the British sources claim that the proposals were 'skeletal' and that

they contained a number of outstanding difficulties which required
further discussion and analysis.[84] In fact, whether the War Cabinet
knew about the initiative on 1 May or not, the claim that by 1–2 May
the Peruvian peace terms were broadly acceptable to both parties is
implausible for two additional sets of reasons.

First, both sides accept that in outline the proposals were similar to
Haig's plan, although simplified because the proposers knew that
there was little time left before fighting would begin (see Figure 5.1).
Mrs Jeanne Kirkpatrick, US Permanent Representative at the United
Nations, referred to it as 'a new Haig mission in disguise'.[85] But
Argentina had announced on 29 April that Haig's scheme could not be
accepted without significant revision, and there was no reliable
indication from Buenos Aires that it was now going to accept a
settlement on similar lines. On the contrary, although there seems to
have been a strong move amongst some senior members of the
Argentine armed forces to accept a settlement in the wake of the
British attacks of 1 May, the military Committee of the Junta had not
met to discuss the Peruvian proposals when the War Cabinet took its
decision around lunch-time on Sunday 2 May. Galtieri was reported to
be favourably disposed towards the Belaunde scheme, but he was still
discussing details by telephone with the Peruvian President at 14.00
BST on 2 May.[86]

To suggest, therefore, that there was not very much to discuss
because the proposals were derived from earlier mediation is to ignore
the fact that Argentina had found the earlier proposals profoundly
unsatisfactory on a number of crucial points only two days earlier.
Conversely, to suggest that the Junta was about to change its decision
because it had finally been persuaded to do so by its catalogue of
diplomatic failures, the mounting tension of the crisis, and British
attacks of 1 May, discounts the deep divisions which contributed to its
disastrous handling of the entire Falklands dispute.[87] Furthermore,
those divisions had not been reconciled in favour of peace at the time
the British War Cabinet took its decision. The Junta discussed the plan
on the afternoon of 2 May (evening London time) and news of the
sinking was announced while it was still in session.[88] If Peru's initiative
was a revised and disguised version of Haig's scheme, therefore, it was
reasonable for the British to require reliable evidence that Argentina
now found it more acceptable. None was available because the Junta
itself had come to no decision and there are good grounds for arguing
that it would not have accepted Belaunde's plan.[89]

Second, there were in fact some significant differences between the

1. Immediate ceasefire.

2. Simultaneous and mutual withdrawal of forces.

3. Third parties to govern the Islands, temporarily.

4. The two Governments would recognise the existence of conflicting viewpoints about the Islands.

5. The two governments would recognise the need to take the viewpoints and interests of the Islanders into account in the final solution.

6. The contact group which would start negotiating at once to implement this agreement would be Brazil, Peru, West Germany and the United States.

7. A final solution must be found by 30 April 1983 under the contact group's guarantee.

FIGURE 5.1 *The Peruvian Peace Proposals, 1 May 1982*

SOURCE: D. Rice and A. Gavshon *The Sinking of the Belgrano* (London: Secker & Warburg, 1984), p. 84

two sets of proposals, notably the exclusion of the two disputants from the interim administration of the Islands. And, in addition, there remained the problems of Argentina's objection to the inclusion of the United States in the contact group and insistence on a time-scale for a final agreement. Exclusion of the two disputants, although later to be conceded, was a new proposal. Moreover, Britain's negotiating position throughout the invasion crisis had always avoided making any commitment regarding the timing or the substance of a definitive resolution of the dispute. Finally, in discussion between Lima and Buenos Aires during 1–2 May, reference to the Islanders' wishes again became a problem, prompting a search for a formula based upon 'aspirations' rather than wishes.[90] To the extent, therefore, that Peru's initiative differed from Haig's and also left basic differences of view unresolved, so demanding clarification and amendment, the British did have grounds for arguing that when they learnt of the plans there were outstanding points requiring further discussion. Indeed, this was borne out by the subsequent amendment of the proposals.[91]

Instead, the evidence indicates that Peru thought that it had an agreement and that Britain's military pressure was having some effect in Buenos Aires. However, it does not demonstrate that the Junta as a whole was in any way committed to the Peruvian plan, or especially well disposed towards it, before the War Cabinet took its decision to attack the *Belgrano*. The War Cabinet was justifiably sceptical in any

event of the Junta's capacity to take decisions or to stick to them.
British Ministers and officials have claimed that getting agreement
with Buenos Aires on crucial points was made especially difficult by
divisions within the Argentine regime, and their arguments were
supported by independent Argentine sources which have subsequently
concluded that Galtieri would have found it politically impossible to
withdraw his forces from the Islands.[92] It is conceivable, although
there is no evidence to support the point, that the War Cabinet might
have had some tentative indication of the Peruvian initiative before
taking its decision on 2 May. However, this could hardly have
counterbalanced the dangerous and compelling circumstances then
faced by the Carrier Battle Group.

All the reports indicate, and not surprisingly, that the exchanges
over Belaunde's plan meant different things to different people. Each
participant viewed them from his own perspective and it is also evident
that the interchanges were significantly affected by the stress and
circumstances of the crisis. For example, there is every indication that
in the confusion of that weekend, the Peruvians exaggerated the
prospects of their own proposals. In addition, Haig has also proved
himself to be an unreliable rapporteur of the events which took place.
In his memoirs the Secretary of State recalled that Belaunde had
'gained acceptance in principle from both parties'.[93] But, in a letter
submitted to the House of Commons Foreign Affairs Committee on 14
February 1985, he maintained instead: 'At no time during that difficult
weekend of 1–2 May 1982 did I believe we were on the verge of a
settlement'.[94]

As in the children's game of whispers, the intelligibility of
communications seems to have suffered considerably as many actors
engaged in passing messages one to another. And Gavshon and Rice
effectively concede this point: 'nuances were lost, precision became
diluted, misperceptions or misunderstandings crept in, glosses were
added, hidden messages remained undetected.'[95]

Finally, there is every indication that the British were not, or at least
not formally, involved in this game until 2 May. At that point,
however, the War Cabinet had more pressing matters to occupy it. In
the operational circumstances of the South Atlantic the Prime Minister
and her colleagues had very few options. Their time as well as
Argentina's had run out.

On Sunday 2 May 1982 Mrs Thatcher and her colleagues were
conducting a war, and commanding a large military force 8000 miles
from its home base, which faced changing threats to its safety and the

success of its mission. Diplomacy required time, talk and a mutual willingness to compromise if a peaceful settlement was to be negotiated, but the War Cabinet's military plans required speed, decisiveness and force if military victory was to be achieved. John Nott has since acknowledged this 'inherent conflict' of interest between the two sides of British policy.[96] Unless the Junta was to display a surprising degree of diplomatic acumen, that conflict was always likely to be resolved in favour of the unleashing of the British forces and the achievement of their military objectives. Consequently, the War Cabinet allowed the Royal Navy to engage in general naval warfare in accordance with the operational plan for the recapture of the Islands.

Taken together, these considerations explain why Peru's initiative did not appear to be as promising to Britain as it apparently did to its sponsors, and why it probably had little direct influence over the decision to sink the *Belgrano*. But what they do not account for is precisely why the *Belgrano* itself was attacked. That can only be explained by reference to the specific circumstances of the time, the details of the War Cabinet's military plans and the practical requirements which governed them. These issues have to be considered in a separate chapter because they raise their own catalogue of issues and have their own, although related, log of events.

30 April, therefore, was the high-point of British diplomacy in the conduct of Falklands policy. After the sinking of the *Belgrano* the War Cabinet was forced onto the diplomatic defensive. Some of the political damage done by the attack had to be repaired and the legitimacy of Britain's position maintained. Furthermore, the scale of the casualties together with the loss of the British Type 42 Destroyer HMS *Sheffield*, on 4 May, restored some impetus to the search for a way of avoiding the hazards of a full-scale assault upon the Islands.[97]

A full Cabinet session on 5 May agreed in principle to accept a modified Belaunde plan, and the Prime Minister announced to the House of Commons on 6 May that the Government had made a 'very positive response' to it.[98] At that stage the British regarded the parallel UN proposals as too imprecise to form the basis of a settlement.[99] In her statement the Prime Minister insisted on an immediate cessation of hostilities and a mutual withdrawal without the reintroduction of forces. The ceasefire had to be precise as to timing, sequence of events and verification of the agreement. The contact group to govern the Islands was to be the four countries specified in the original Peruvian plan: namely, Peru, Brazil, the United States and the Federal

Republic of Germany. Britain had earlier expressed reservations about Peru but seemed willing to drop them. The contact group was to verify the withdrawal; administer the Islands during the interim period in consultation with the elected representatives of the Islanders; and, according to Mr Pym, 'perhaps help in negotiations for a definitive agreement on the status of the Islands without prejudice to our principles or the wishes of the Islanders'.[100] Finally, it was to ensure that all other terms of the agreement were respected. Provisions were also included for the lifting of the existing exclusion zones and of economic and military sanctions.

A very tight time-schedule was in fact specified: 24 hours for the instruction to go out ordering a ceasefire, and 48 hours for the representatives of the contact group to begin work in taking over the Islands. The Prime Minister nevertheless qualified the already guarded optimism which accompanied her announcement with the following warning:

> It would not be impossible—indeed it may well be likely—that the Argentines are concentrating on a ceasefire without withdrawal. That would be a very evident ploy to keep them in possession of their ill-gotten gains, and we are right to be very wary of it.[101]

According to the transcript of a telephone conversation which took place between Galtieri and Belaunde on 5 May, Galtieri objected in particular to the inclusion of the United States in the contact group and to the time-schedule. This discussion ended inconclusively with Argentina effectively rejecting terms which were perhaps slightly more advantageous to Buenos Aires than those offered by Haig, because they excluded both protagonists from the interim administration but included two Latin American powers.[102]

It has been suggested that the War Cabinet was persuaded to accept the Peruvian proposals because it calculated that Argentina would reject them and that Britain would thereby regain some of the diplomatic initiative it had recently lost.[103] Whether this is true or not, Argentina could still have gained some diplomatic advantage by accepting them. Under the terms of the proposals Argentina would have been able to keep the Falklands high on the agenda of international issues and might ultimately have worn down the British into further concessions with respect to a lasting solution. Certainly in any future negotiations the British Government would have found it much more difficult to retain the high degree of Cabinet unity, national resolve and political indignation which sustained its position throughout the conflict. By refusing to accept a proposal to which the British were prepared to be committed, and by switching its attention back to the UN in search of a better deal, the Junta continued to signal its willingness to run the risks of war and so confirmed the War Cabinet's mistrust. Argentina's postwar commission of inquiry was also to conclude that the most rational and productive course of action open to the Junta at this time would have been to accept the revised Peruvian plan. It was prevented from doing so by the escalation of the War, its own internal divisions and its domestic political circumstances.[104]

United Nations mediation

As Argentina's diplomacy shifted to the United Nations so did Britain's, but negotiations in New York never developed the momentum, matched the urgency or came as close to fruition as did those sponsored by Haig and Belaunde. Britain continued to insist on a ceasefire 'accompanied by a withdrawal to a specific timetable and in a comparatively short time'. Similarly, it continued to reject any conditions which would ensure that sovereignty would be ceded to Argentina, and the Islanders' wishes also remained prominent in its statements. However, despite maintaining these conditions, the War Cabinet remained willing to accept the internationalisation of the dispute. As late as 13 May, for example, the Foreign Secretary held out the prospect that negotiations on the long-term future of the Islands might be completed in 'a matter of months', and third-party involvement in an interim administration also remained acceptable, which significantly qualified Britain's declared objective of restoring the Falklands to British administration. In addition, a role for the United Nations was not ruled out.[105] Finally, and perhaps most important of all, the Foreign Secretary insisted that, although the Government had no reservations whatever about the British title to sovereignty,

> we did not, before the invasion, rule out discussion on sovereignty in negotiations with Argentina . . . We still remain willing to discuss it as one of the factors in negotiations about the long-term future.[106]
> [Emphasis added]

Over the weekend of 15–16 May, Britain's Ambassador to the

United States, Sir Nicholas Henderson, and its Permanent Representative to the United Nations, Sir Anthony Parsons, were recalled to London to attend an important War Cabinet meeting. Since the collapse of Haig's mediation the political exchanges over Peruvian and UN mediation had served to confuse the diplomatic aspects of the crisis and so, on the eve of the British counter-invasion, a final review of Britain's diplomatic position was conducted in preparation for the most dangerous phase of the entire conflict. The exercise was specifically designed to agree the final concessions which the War Cabinet was willing to offer in order to avoid the dangers of an amphibious operation. If they were acceptable war could be avoided. If they were not, the War Cabinet could not be accused of not having made a genuine effort to secure a peaceful settlement short of political humiliation. But the proposals necessarily reflected the peace bargaining of the previous weeks and the hardening of the War Cabinet's position.

This final offer was conveyed to Argentina through the United Nations on 17 May.[107] The following day the Prime Minister announced in the House of Commons that the country faced a 'critical week' and a Parliamentary debate was also scheduled for Thursday 20 May for a final mobilisation of domestic opinion on the day before the landings were scheduled to take place. The terms of the offer included the following proposals:

Withdrawal of forces
Mutual withdrawals were to be completed within 14 days, at the end of which period British ships were to remain at least 150 nautical miles from the Islands (by way of contrast Haig's proposals specified that all forces should return to their normal operation areas and bases within 15 days). The War Cabinet claimed that these new terms were reasonable, given the proximity of the Argentine mainland, but they also indicated its increased mistrust of the Junta.

Interim arrangements
A United Nations Administrator, appointed by the Secretary General and acceptable to both parties, would administer the Falklands' Government in the interim between cessation of hostilities and the conclusion of negotiations on a final agreement. He was to do so in accordance with the 'laws and practices' traditionally obtaining in the Islands, while consulting with the Executive and Legislative Councils. Each Council was now to include a representative (nominated by the

UN Administrator) of the 20 or 30 Argentines normally resident on the Falklands. There were to be no changes which would prejudge the outcome of the long-term negotiations, such as allowing an influx of Argentine settlers, for example, or changing the Islands' residence and property laws. The Administrator was also to verify the withdrawal of forces. Article 73 of the UN Charter, which refers to the paramountcy of the Islanders' interests rather than their wishes, was also incorporated into the interim arrangements. Finally, a small UN force was to be installed to prevent the reintroduction of the combatant forces and to assist the Administrator. The interim agreement was to remain in force until long-term negotiations were completed.

Long-term negotiations

These were to be conducted without preconditions and without prejudice to either party's claims or the outcome of talks. No time period was specified for their completion.[108]

Britain's Permanent Representative to the UN has since maintained that by the time these proposals were drawn up, Argentina had retreated from its insistence that an interim settlement should be the means of ensuring a transfer of sovereignty, but this was to make no difference to their fate. He was also to argue that the British package was 'an eminently reasonable basis for a peaceful solution', and recalled that he had thought at the time that the Junta 'would be mad' not to accept it. Although the proposals were more restrictive than either the Haig or the Peruvian plans, they still offered Galtieri a better opportunity to advance Argentina's claims by peaceful means than that which had existed prior to the invasion, as Britain's War Cabinet now had the support of the United States and its military campaign was well advanced. With Fleet Headquarters having already issued orders for the landing at San Carlos, Argentina was unlikely to get better terms without inflicting a military defeat on the British.[109]

In its reply on 19 May, however, Argentina objected to the exclusion, for the first time in the negotiations, of the Dependencies of South Georgia and the South Sandwich Islands, which the War Cabinet had omitted from its latest proposals on the grounds that Britain's title to them was a separate issue.[110] It also objected to the inclusion of Article 73 which it suspected would be used to strengthen Britain's argument in favour of the Islanders' right to self-determination, and demanded mutual withdrawal of all forces to their normal bases and operating areas, including the newly installed British garrison on South Georgia. In addition, Argentina counter-proposed that the interim administration should be the exclusive responsibility of the UN and its Administrator, to be advised by an equal number of British and Argentine residents of the Islands. Freedom of movement for Argentine nationals and equality of access with the Falkland Islanders to residence, property and work was also demanded. Finally a long-term solution was to be negotiated in accordance with the UN Charter and various resolutions of the General Assembly, which Argentina had always relied upon to support its case (notably 1514 XV and 2065 XX). If at the end of the period specified for these negotiations no agreement was reached, the General Assembly was to determine the basis of the final agreement.[111] In short, Argentina reverted to a formal statement of its major demands.

Arguing that Argentina's reply 'rejected virtually all the movement that their representatives had shown during the Secretary General's efforts to find a negotiated settlement' and accusing its leadership of 'obduracy and delay, deception and bad faith', the Prime Minister informed the House of Commons during the debate of 20 May that Britain was no longer committed to the proposals it had offered on 17 May: 'The proposals have been rejected. They are no longer on the table'. Naturally no specific military developments were signalled but in every other respect the Prime Minister's statement carried the gravest political warnings.

She began the debate by declaring: 'During the past 24 hours the crisis over the Falkland Islands has moved into a new and even more serious phase.' And in her conclusion she summarised the purpose of the entire transitional political exercise that had occupied the previous seven weeks:

> The gravity of the situation will be apparent to the House and the nation. Difficult days lie ahead, but Britain will face them in the conviction that our cause is just and the knowledge that we have been doing everything reasonable to secure a negotiated settlement.[112]

The following day British forces landed at San Carlos. From then on the political goal of 2 April was restated ('to return the Falklands to British administration') but now it was pursued without the qualifications and concessions which had characterised the transition to war and there was no disguising that it was to be attained by military means. It is impossible to be exact about when the War Cabinet actually decided that it would have to repossess the Falklands by force.

Much decision-making literature teaches, in any event, that it is difficult to isolate a point of decision.[113] Most likely, therefore, it was never decided as such. All the evidence strongly suggests, however, that the last week of April was the decisive period, the time when the War Cabinet's military and diplomatic schedules finally converged and its military priorities became irresistible. 20 May was simply the formal conclusion to Britain's rite of passage to war. In practical terms the War Cabinet's tacit ultimatum had expired long before then.

Once British forces were committed on land, diplomatic policy was directed at resisting all cease-fire proposals which did not amount to unconditional withdrawal of Argentine forces. Whereas in previous weeks the diplomatic exercise had served a number of divergent goals, it was now entirely subordinated to military policy. Although Government spokesmen denied that the objective of British forces was the unconditional surrender of the Argentine garrison on the Falklands, just as they had denied that any ultimatum had ever been issued, once more that in effect was what the exercise was about. On 27 May, for example, the Prime Minister revealed what her preferred interpretation of Security Council Resolution 502 had been: 'The essential feature of Resolution 502 is the unconditional demand for immediate withdrawal of all Argentine forces from the Falklands.' Similarly, she outlined her interpretation of War Cabinet policy:

> The objective of sending British forces and to try to retake by force what was taken from us by force is first, repossession, second, restoration of British administration and, third, reconstruction, followed by consultation with the Islanders—a true consultation with the Islanders—a true consultation about their wishes and interests in the future.[114]

If Mrs Thatcher's antipathy to compromise was revealed in these statements, as it was in many other Parliamentary and public speeches, the evidence does not support the argument that she cynically manipulated the diplomacy of the invasion crisis. If in the analysis of pre-invasion policy it was important to counter the argument that no personal responsibility was involved in the mismanagement of the Falklands dispute, it is equally necessary here to balance the suggestion that only Mrs Thatcher's judgement counted after 2 April. No one disputes that the Prime Minister's influence was one of the most distinctive features of the conflict. But her judgement was exercised within the very limited scope for choice presented by the invasion crisis and the operational conditions which obtained in the South Atlantic.

If the politics of advice within the War Cabinet clearly revolved around the worth of diplomatic negotiations and the extent of the concessions that could be tolerated, that debate also turned upon the politics of reputation which involved the Prime Minister and the Foreign Secretary. There is little to suggest, however, that its diplomacy was an entirely cynical, rather than a typically political, exercise. On the contrary, given the risks attached to the use of the Task Force, it is evident that Mrs Thatcher and her colleagues were persuaded that a diplomatic resolution had to be sought, and that some concessions had to be made to obtain it. The limits of these concessions expressed the political and operational constraints within which the War Cabinet was operating as well as the individual convictions of its members. Consequently it was the structure of the crisis as much as the instincts of the people concerned which ensured that these limits were narrow.

In the final stages of the War, British diplomacy continued to defend the legitimacy of British actions but it was also concerned to allay United States fears that Argentina's military defeat might have serious hemispheric and geostrategic repercussions. Equally, the new British position had to be made clear to Washington. So, under instructions from London, Ambassador Henderson informed Haig on 24 May that

> the establishment of the British bridgehead in the Falklands was bound to have a major effect on our diplomatic position. We could not in present circumstances consider the idea of British withdrawal from the Falklands or the establishment of an interim administration.[115]

Diplomatic efforts to effect a ceasefire did not cease, although the War Cabinet's attention was almost exclusively focused upon the recapture of the Islands. Had the land campaign run into serious military difficulties, however, there might have been some adjustment in British calculations, but the military objective was clear and while progress towards it was being achieved there was no incentive to revise the War Cabinet's priorities. Though this 'hardening' of the British position appeared to cause some concern in Washington, it was to cause no significant political difficulties.

On 26 May the Security Council unanimously adopted a new resolution on the Falklands calling for the Secretary General and the combatants to co-operate in negotiating a ceasefire.[116] By this stage the United Kingdom had lost a considerable amount of international support at the UN, but by the same token its diplomatic reversals in New York did not present any serious threat to the pursuit of the War Cabinet's military objective either. On 4 June, when a Security Council resolution drafted by Spain and Panama called for an immediate ceasefire, it was vetoed by the British and United States representatives. This was accompanied by profound confusion in the US delegation, whose Representative (Mrs Jeanne Kirkpatrick) later explained that the United States had intended to abstain.[117] Throughout the land campaign, therefore, Britain's diplomatic task was to field peace proposals and avoid any serious international embarrassments.

Europe

The success of the War Cabinet's diplomatic policy was also repeated in Europe, although slightly different political considerations obtained in the NATO and Common Market forums through which European support was enlisted.

The European Community's reactions to the invasion crisis were described as 'the fastest ever'.[118] They were also unusually united, at least in the beginning. In a communiqué issued by the ten Foreign Ministers on 2 April the EEC countries unanimously condemned the invasion and called for Argentina to comply with Resolution 502. An arms embargo was then imposed by means of co-ordinated national decisions, because the EEC has no defence responsibilities. Similar embargoes were announced by Canada on 5 April and New Zealand on 13 April, but the European embargo was particularly significant in the light of Argentina's reliance on French and West German arms supplies and spares. On 10 April Britain also succeeded in persuading its partners to assemble a package of economic sanctions imposing a ban on Argentine imports (not already in transit or contracted for prior to 14 April), until 17 May. Thus European support was a useful but qualified political achievement, particularly because Italy and Ireland had important reservations about the measures adopted.

As Britain's military actions eroded its support at the United Nations and placed its relations with the United States under some strain, so the sinking of the *Belgrano* also caused divisions in Europe's united front. Italy and Ireland sought to lift sanctions when they came up for renewal on 17 May. They failed, but the import ban was extended by only eight countries for a further seven days, and the two dissenters subsequently decided to lift their sanctions unilaterally, although they undertook not to undermine the embargo of the other states. When the Community decided to extend economic sanctions indefinitely, Denmark also decided to opt out of the Community framework.

The strain on European solidarity was evident in voting at the United Nations as well. At the time Ireland and Spain were also members of the Security Council. Spain had abstained on Resolution 502, although France and Ireland had voted in favour. On 4 June, however, Ireland reversed its position and voted with Spain for the ceasefire resolution which Britain and the United States vetoed. France abstained in this vote.

Diplomatic policy with respect to NATO was determined by different considerations, and elicited even more qualified public support, for two reasons. First, the Falklands conflict was outside the area defined in Article 6 of the North Atlantic Treaty, within which an armed attack on one ally is considered to be an attack against all. Argentina's invasion could have been construed as an attack upon the United Kingdom's territorial integrity, which under Article 4 of the Treaty is not geographically limited and is also a ground for invoking the Alliance. However, use of NATO for out-of-area activities is very severely constrained and governed by the understanding that it would only apply to threats to vital interests involving a risk of conflict with the Soviet Union and its allies. Accordingly, Britain's Permanent Representative to the North Atlantic Council was instructed to 'inform' the United Kingdom's allies rather than 'consult' them. The second consideration was that, from 2 April to 30 April, the United States was officially neutral and this necessarily limited NATO's official reactions to the crisis.

An emergency NATO Council meeting called by Britain on 2 April was convened shortly before Argentina's invasion was confirmed. Its communiqué, issued by NATO's Secretary General, merely noted that the members of the Council 'expressed deep concern' at the development of the dispute. By 5 May Britain had strengthened NATO's response, persuading its European members, meeting in the EUROGROUP, to condemn Argentina's attack. Subsequently the condemnation was endorsed by the NATO Defence Planning Committee on 7 May, but it was the middle of May before the United Kingdom finally secured NATO Council condemnation from the ministerial meeting, which was held in Luxembourg on 17–18 May. On

10 June, however, when the land campaign in the Falklands was at its height, a meeting in Bonn of NATO Heads of State and Government avoided all mention of the Falklands because for the first time the meeting was also attended by Spain.[119]

CONCLUSION

In sum, the outstanding achievement of British diplomacy was the contribution which it made to the War Cabinet's ability to steer a path through all the ambiguity and uncertainty of the invasion crisis. That, in its turn, was an achievement for which the War Cabinet deserved and received considerable political credit. As a result international support was obtained from where it was most required, the political unity of the Government was maintained and domestic support was consolidated on the basis of high moral principles as well as raw national sentiment. Diplomacy, nonetheless, was only one aspect of War Cabinet policy-making. From the outset Mrs Thatcher and her colleagues had also to determine how they were going to implement their ultimatum when the time came to do so, and for this they required a military policy to complement their diplomatic efforts.

6 War Cabinet Military Policy

The United Kingdom's military response to Argentina's seizure of the Falkland Islands could hardly have been so successful if the War Cabinet's military plans had not been as decisive as its diplomacy had been productively dualistic, But, although the twin dimensions of Cabinet policy complemented each other to some degree, they were ultimately governed by different considerations and designed to serve divergent objectives. Whereas diplomacy was working towards a peaceful outcome (to the extent that it was not also concerned to secure the best possible conditions for the use of the Task Force), military policy was designed to intimidate Argentina and repossess the Islands by force. The tension which thus arose between them was displayed when the *Belgrano* was sunk, but the underlying conflict was in evidence throughout the invasion crisis.

The War Cabinet's military policy had its origins in the emergency meeting which took place in the House of Commons between the Prime Minister and the Secretary of State for Defence on 31 March. This meeting was also attended by the Chief of Naval Staff, Admiral Leach. There, on the enthusiastic recommendation of Leach, it was decided to mobilise a Task Force. The advance elements of the force could be composed of serviceable ships from the Royal Navy's First Flotilla of destroyers and frigates which were then engaged in exercise 'Spring Train' off Gibraltar. On the basis of his discussion with Ministers, and in anticipation of Cabinet authorisation, Leach issued orders for these ships to head for the South Atlantic and for the rest of the Fleet to be made ready to sail.[1]

Mobilisation of the Task Force was based upon the military contingency planning which was first conducted under Callaghan's Government' in the 1970s.[2] Reviewed during Ridley's attempt to revive Falklands policy in 1980, these recommendations subsequently provided the British Fleet with an outline of the size of the force needed to repossess the Falkland Islands but they did not provide a blueprint for their recapture.[3] The contingency planning merely specified what was likely to be required in general terms. In particular it did not specify how British forces would be used or what further reinforcements they would require in order to defeat an Argentine occupation force. Quite simply, 'in the critical first days of April, there had been no hard-headed calculations about the difficulties of fighting a major war in the South Atlantic, far less of conducting an amphibious landing.' [4] At 7.30 p.m. on 2 May the full Cabinet met in Downing Street 'and agreed that the Task Force should sail'.[5] That decision was announced at the beginning of the emergency debate which was held in the House of Commons on the following day, although military preparations were by then well in train.

Hence the authors of military policy were the members of the War Cabinet and their military advisers, and the considerations which they had to take into account were necessarily quite different from those which concerned the crisis diplomacy that preoccupied the Foreign Office and the Diplomatic Service. Apart from the Prime Minister, most other senior decision-makers seem to have taken a little time to appreciate that they had in effect issued an ultimatum, and the pursuit of military, diplomatic and economic sanctions against Argentina allowed the War Cabinet to maintain that it was trying to resolve the crisis by a combination of equally balanced means. Admiral Lewin was later to argue, for example, that it was extremely difficult to determine when, and to what degree, the emphasis between sanctions, negotiations and military action shifted.[6] However, this seems to have been as idealised a version of War Cabinet decision making as the allied suggestion that military policy was a refined exercise in escalation management. Neither account fits the evidence but each was an important feature of the rhetoric of policy which was designed to satisfy domestic and international expectations about the control of military force. There was, instead, a hierarchy of means, with the War Cabinet's principal instrument, the Task Force, at the top, and the widely discredited instrument of economic sanctions at the bottom, included as much for symbolic as material reasons. Thus, the military command did not have to argue the merits of a military response in a bureaucratic debate about the management of the conflict. But, as will be seen, Lewin did have to lobby hard for the licence to use the Task Force to the greatest effect.

CIVIL-MILITARY RELATIONS

In modern times the military necessarily plays a direct and influential role in the making of national security policy, but the Falklands provided no simple illustration of political decision-makers 'captured' by their military commanders, or of military commanders operating beyond the control of political decision-makers.[7] Neither does it substantiate the opposite but equally inadequate model of deterministic civilian control. A complex symbiotic relationship exists in Western societies between the civil and military participants in defence decision making. That interdependence was heavily emphasised in the particular circumstances of the Falklands conflict, however, where Britain's military and political decision-makers were closely reliant upon each other to perform different functions in the management of policy.

By virtue of the failure of prewar policy, the British Government was left with little option but to gamble upon a military reply to Argentina's invasion. Hence the military objective, to recapture the Falkland Islands, was also a political necessity if diplomacy failed to remove Argentina by negotiation. Thus, if the military campaign was lost, everything was lost. Naturally, the Prime Minister and her colleagues were compelled to make sure that this did not happen, at least as a consequence of political decisions. Hence, political control necessarily involved specifying the conditions under which the Task Force would be used and when it would be unleashed. In this respect the War Cabinet was rather more concerned with calculating to best advantage the application of force than it was with restraining the urge to use it. British policy was ultimately subject, therefore, to the operational requirements of the Fleet and the decisions of the War Cabinet served military needs just as the operations of the Task Force served the War Cabinet's political purposes. The strength of this interdependence made a significant contribution to the success of the Falklands campaign.

The decision to assemble and despatch the Task Force appears to have been made without consulting the other Chiefs of Staff or giving any detailed consideration to what would ultimately be entailed by the mobilisation.[8] It was an instinctive reaction, driven by immediate political need rather than by forethought. And it came at the end of a week of increasing tension during which Britain's incremental military response, which had been chasing rather than dictating events, soon evolved into a large-scale mobilisation. Militarily, therefore, it was part of an attempt to make a belated reply to Argentina's military threats. Politically, it was motivated by the need to provide the Government with some defence against the widespread Parliamentary and public criticism which was naturally anticipated. It also seems to have reflected an optimism about British capabilities which was greatly encouraged by a considerable ignorance of Argentina's.[9] The momentum imparted to events by the force of these factors seems also to have been increased by the Chief of Naval Staff's determination to defend the reputation of his Service, as well as that of his country, in a time of adversity for both.[10] According to early reports, Ministers were consequently shielded from the reservations and fears which the mobilisation of the Task Force excited in other branches of the armed forces. These considerations aside, there was also a gut desire to strike back and repossess lost territory and people.

Thus, just as it short-circuited the regular processes of military consultation, so the invasion crisis also reduced the process of political accountability to its bare essentials. Had the Falklands War been a disaster, criticism would no doubt have focused more critically upon the political judgement of the Prime Minister and her immediate colleagues who, in addition to their contribution to the outbreak of the conflict, risked a substantial military defeat in the South Atlantic on narrowly based and operationally inadequate military advice. There was minimal information about Argentine forces and no detailed assessment of the hazards of the mission upon which the Task Force was embarked,[11] confirming the view that the wars which are fought are seldom the ones which are planned. It had become a matter of acting first and asking questions later, because the stakes in the conflict had suddenly become so symbolically important. By the time more detailed military assessments had been made, British decision-makers were already firmly in the grip of the logic of conflict.

As Mrs Thatcher had insisted from the beginning, the question of cost had little relevance. In addition to the circumstances of crisis, therefore, we have to add the force of political will together with the concentration of political authority as factors which helped to determine that Britain would fight for the Falklands. If Mrs Thatcher's leadership committed the War Cabinet to the use of the Task Force it also provided the political direction which war required. The deliberation associated with policy debate and the analysis of a wide range of options was conspicuous by its absence, but the decisiveness required for successful policy implementation was available to an unusual extent. Thus while Mrs Thatcher's resolution turned out to be an indispensable political asset, the concentration of decision-making allowed it full scope in the direction of British policy.

If the circumstances of the crisis made Britain's civil and military leadership especially reliant upon one another, that interdependence was further emphasised not only by the character of the individuals involved but also by the structure of decision-making within which they operated. Just as crisis had centralised political decision-making, so it also centralised the military channels through which the War Cabinet received its military advice. Both developments facilitated the process by which each side made their respective contributions to the other's needs.

While the centralisation of *political decision-making* was to protect the Task Force from the delays, divisions and uncertainties which would have resulted from more considered political debate, centralisation of *military decision-making*, especially during the early days, was to prevent Ministers from losing their nerve as the enormity of their gamble became apparent. As the Chief of Defence Staff guided the War Cabinet through the developments of the campaign and its changing military requirements, so the Prime Minister and her colleagues held the military objective constant. Whereas the War Cabinet preserved the Task Force from political indecision, and granted it the licence to proceed with its mission at each stage in the progress of its passage to the Falklands, so the Task Force Commanders displayed their professional skills in dealing with the problem that was set for them.

Thus each side in the decision-making process contributed what the other desired most, reinforcing the influence of the logic of conflict which already dominated the Task Force's passage to the Falklands. From political leaders the military received a clear goal and unswerving support. As a result the military staffs had an opportunity, almost unique in their post-1945 experience, to plan and execute a classic military operation without the usual complications of weak political leadership and confused objectives. From the military, political leaders received coherent and co-ordinated advice in a language which they could understand. Moreover, it was advice which reassured them that their immediate objective could be attained by military means. That itself was very unusual. Much of Britain's recent experience in the use of force, in Northern Ireland and elsewhere, has taught quite different lessons: notably that the most the military can do is to contain a situation, allowing political processes an opportunity to function and seek a political settlement.[12] Here, in the peculiar circumstances of the Falklands campaign, there was an unusual, and for those involved apparently satisfying, symmetry between political objectives and military means.

In short, to their mutual gratification, military and political decision-makers 'delivered the goods' which each required most but could not themselves produce, and upon which the success of the whole campaign to some extent relied.[13] According to the officer commanding 3 Commando Brigade, the military command at Naval Headquarters in Northwood, under the political direction of the Prime Minister and the War Cabinet, 'guarded our backs well and for that we were extremely grateful'.[14] Yet, like so many of the features which distinguished this conflict, the complementarity of political and military decision making was never seriously tested over time or by significant military setbacks. And it has to be accepted, in addition, that Britain's victory was heavily reliant upon the inadequacies of the Argentine command, the quality of the British forces and the considerable good fortune which they enjoyed.

Centralisation of military decision-making was facilitated, in addition, by a reform of the central institutions of defence which had been introduced shortly before the Islands were invaded. Since the Second World War the tripartite service structure of defence policy-making in Britain, with its partisan and pluralistic service rivalry, had been progressively replaced by a more centralised system. These changes were intended to simplify executive decision-making by requiring conflicting professional judgements to be reconciled before presentation to Ministers. From being the collective head of the Chiefs of Staff Committee, the Chief of Defence Staff, by degrees became the principal advisor to Ministers in the Cabinet.[15] Throughout the Falklands conflict, therefore, Admiral Lewin (Chief of the Defence Staff) was, in his own words 'responsible for seeking the advice of my colleagues, taking their views into account, then presenting my own view as the views of the department'.[16]

Just as this helped him to secure control over the politics of military advice to the War Cabinet so, together with the impact of crisis, it helped him to secure centralised operational control over the conduct of the military campaign. As a result the link between War Cabinet and Task Force was a short and uncomplicated one, dominated by the CDS, through which Lewin was able to retain the support of his political supervisors while moderating the impact of the inter-service conflict inherent in a tri-service operation. As he later explained:

I insisted that the only link with the Commander of the Task Force, Admiral Fieldhouse, who was Commander of all three services (he was a tri-service Commander) should be through me and my office . . . so that, if Ministers took a decision then I would translate that into an objective and pass it to Northwood.[17]

Operational command of the Task Force was exercised by Rear Admiral Woodward (Flag Officer, First Flotilla), while overall command lay with Admiral Fieldhouse at Royal Naval Headquarters in Northwood. In addition, close personal relationships consolidated what was, structurally, a tightly organised system of command and control.[18]

According to one report:

> The Chiefs of Staff met after Lewin returned from War Cabinet each morning, ran over its decisions and reviewed any strategic options outstanding. By then Lewin had already been in telephone communication with Fieldhouse . . . Not until late April for instance, did the army get a senior man, General Richard Trant, into Northwood.'[19]

Service Chiefs, however, did attend the War Cabinet on three or four occasions when matters concerning their individual services were discussed. All three Service Chiefs gave Cabinet briefings, with Lewin summarising the general picture, both at the end of the first week of the invasion crisis, when the War Cabinet was presented with its first overall operational assessment, and on the eve of the amphibious assault.[20] Formally speaking, the Chief of Defence Staff was not eligible to be a member of a Cabinet Committee. Hence his status in the War Cabinet was that of an official advisor. Nevertheless he attended all of its meetings and was popularly, if inaccurately, regarded as a member of it. Lewin was thus able to play a pivotal role not only in War Cabinet discussions, but also in the strategic direction of the Task Force, during this first and apparently successful test of the new command structure. Ultimately, however, responsibility for the conduct of policy lay with those Ministers who comprised Cabinet Committee OD(SA).

A 'ONE-SHOT OPERATION' AS THE 'MEASURED AND CONTROLLED' USE OF FORCE

In order to secure domestic and international support for the use of the Task Force the War Cabinet was obliged by its diplomatic and political objectives to conduct its military campaign according to international law and customary expectations about the control and limited use of force. Its military policy was, therefore, composed of three closely related elements: public statements which provided a political rationale that attempted to meet these expectations; detailed operational plans which specified the strategic design for the repossession of the Islands; and specific Rules of Engagement which operationalised those plans, granting British forces the license to undertake certain military actions.

Public rationale

Publicly the War Cabinet maintained that it was acting in accordance with Article 51 of the UN Charter, which specifies the right of self-defence. Action in support of self-defence is also governed by international legal requirements concerning the nature and the immediacy of the attack and the proportionality of the response to the seriousness of it. In particular Article 51 requires that 'Measures taken by members in the exercises of this right of self-defence will be immediately reported to the Security Council'.[21] Hence the public warnings which the War Cabinet issued in order to make Britain's intentions clear to both Argentina and the rest of the world, as well as to substantiate its claim to be in control of military developments, were also transmitted to the United Nations. These warnings included the announcement of a Maritime Exclusion Zone (MEZ) on 7 April, the issuing of a public warning on 23 April, the announcement of a Total Exclusion Zone on 28 April and a further public warning issued on 7 May, designed to clarify the British position in the confusion caused by the sinking of the *Belgrano* outside the Total Exclusion Zone.[22] In addition the War Cabinet also reported military actions such as the recapture of South Georgia to the Secretary General. At home the House of Commons was kept informed about the progress of the conflict in a series of statements, answers to Parliamentary questions and six full-scale Parliamentary debates.[23]

By claiming that it was acting with the minimum of force, the War Cabinet deliberately encouraged the suggestion that the exercise of military power would be a closely controlled process of escalation. Indeed, according to Hastings and Jenkins, while some military and political decision-makers thought that a mere demonstration of force might achieve the Government's purpose:

> Admiral Woodward and most of his Captains saw an obvious escalation of options at the disposal of the British Government: first, the mere advance into the South Atlantic; then the establishment of a blockade; the recapture of South Georgia; and thereafter an increasingly delicate stepladder of attacks on Argentine ships and aircraft until total war broke out.[24]

In retrospect it is now evident that this was the language of strategic theory rather than strategic reality, an ideal quite unrelated to the logistical and operational dynamics which governed the use of the Task Force. It also disguised the general character of the campaign just as it rationalised much of the reasoning that lay behind its specific military operations. There is little evidence to suggest that the military advice presented to the War Cabinet at the time bore much resemblance to such a model either.[25] Only a force capable of retaking the Islands would serve as an effective demonstration of strength and only a determination to use it would give effect to the Government's ultimatum. The mobilisation, despatch and employment of such a force created its own compelling category of needs from which the logic of conflict was derived. It was these rather than any abstract notion of flexible response which appears to have dictated how and when the Task Force would be employed.

Theories about the political control of escalation assume that the use of force can be proportional to political purpose, the principal concern of which is to achieve a satisfactory settlement at the lowest military price. Thus military force is supposed to be subject to political need. There are two standard objections to this idea. First, it is quite clear that the use of military force creates its own needs. Second, it is almost equally evident that these demands displace political goals, replacing them with military objectives. In the Falklands example military objectives were not in fact substituted for political goals because the War Cabinet's primary political concern had been reduced to a single military requirement by the failure of the Government's prewar policy. Nevertheless, the general impact on War Cabinet policy was much the same, and the Task Force was confronted with a very distinct military problem whose operational requirements quickly imposed themselves upon its commanders. If Britain was to achieve military victory in the Falklands, these operational requirements had to determine policy. Because of the identity of interest which existed between military and political leaders this consideration remained paramount.

Despite Clausewitz's dictum, war is not the extension of politics by other means.[26] Our experience of it suggests instead that it is a separate universe of moral and practical conduct with its own distinctive characteristics and dynamics, one, moreover, in which the practice of politics usually becomes subordinated to and transformed by military imperatives. In many respects war is a mirror image of the civil order it replaces: 'a world of permissions and prohibitions—a moral world therefore in the midst of hell'.[27]

As a social reality created by human conduct the practices of war change and the conventions which govern it, even in the so-called 'age of total war', are contingent and problematical. The Falklands campaign, therefore, was governed by military imperatives some of which, like secrecy, were derived from the general nature of war, but most of which were derived from the specific circumstances of the conflict.

Obviously the Falklands was not a 'total war'. It was limited in terms of geography, weapons used, military objectives and forces deployed. However, if limited war is defined in terms not only of limited means but also of the subjection of military force to rational political management, the Falklands illustrated the vanity as well as the inadequacy of that ideal, notwithstanding the limitation of each side's strategic objective to possession of the Islands. Once Argentina crossed the threshold of conflict, decision-makers found themselves in an entirely new 'ball-game' (in fact, language-game) in which the exigencies of conflict dominated the actions which they were obliged to take. Above all the Task Force was engaged in what the commander of 3 Commando Brigade graphically described as 'a one-shot operation': 'It couldn't be like Dieppe, where if we tried and it didn't work, we could make sure we did better next time. We had to get it right in one go.'[28]

In order to get it right first time the planning of the campaign seems to have been dictated by this one overriding consideration. Thus any suggestion that a dangerous amphibious landing was to be attempted only after proceeding up a ladder of escalation which would have threatened the operational endurance and survival of the forces required for that assault seems to have been fanciful.

In one sense the British Cabinet chose to interpret Argentine actions as a *casus belli* and to foster all the public sentiments that went with such an interpretation. But in another sense, because it was based upon assumptions and values which were taken for granted as part of the fabric of Britain's political culture, the Government's response appeared to be a natural one. No casualties had been inflicted by the Argentine invasion force upon the British garrison during the capture of the Islands and this fostered the illusion, particularly in Buenos Aires, that no significant threshold had been crossed.[29] Although there are good grounds for disputing whether the absence of casualties was a matter of luck rather than a product of Argentine planning, the point is that Argentina's attack breached a symbolic, not a material order; and ultimately thresholds are symbolic rather than physical entities, even when physical distinctions are involved as, for example, with nuclear weapons. Argentine decision-makers failed to anticipate the impact of their assault upon Britain's political culture, just as they underestimated the nationalism and political obduracy which had become the hallmarks of the Thatcher administration. The War Cabinet's diplomatic policy was determined by the structure of the crisis, the ambivalence of the rite of passage to war and ultimately by the dictates of the military schedule. Equally, its military plans were dictated by this fundamental operational requirement and the military problems to which it gave rise.

The strategic design

The Task Force did not possess the endurance or physical capability to mount a sustained blockade of the Islands and reportedly there was no enthusiasm amongst the military commanders for doing so: 'Lewin and his fellow service chiefs were unequivocal. The danger of attrition and enemy action put sustained blockade out of the question.'[30]

Although the British force was capable of mounting an amphibious assault it could only conduct such an operation within certain narrow constraints, including the short time-scale specified by Admiral Lewin, the limited capabilities of the Task Force and the physical conditions in the South Atlantic. In particular British forces were hampered by two outstanding operational deficiencies, in addition to their greatly extended lines of communication and support. First, the small number of Harrier aircraft embarked with the carriers provided only the minimum amount of air support. Second, the Task Force had no long-range airborne early warning system (AEW). Despite these limitations the British Fleet had to engage an opponent armed with modern naval equipment, some of it British and identical to that employed in the Task Force, supported by land-based as well as carrier-borne aircraft. In addition it would have to mount a sea-borne landing without one of the single most important requirements for such an operation—the benefit of air superiority.[31]

A sea-borne landing was in prospect from the moment Leach commended the use of a Task Force to the Prime Minister on 31 March, and the succeeding weeks were preoccupied with the detailed planning for it.[32] To some degree this was an example of a standardised military response to an anticipated policy problem: an Argentine invasion of the Falklands required an amphibious operation to repossess them. For the most part, after setting the basic parameters, the Navy's recommendation initiated a response which in all other respects was dictated by the limitations on the means available and the specific operational circumstance in which the campaign had to be conducted. By the same token issuance of the final orders for that assault had to await a suitable stage in the development of the international politics which occupied the duration of Britain's tacit ultimatum.[33] Thus, if an amphibious assault was the principal object of military policy then the imposition of a blockade or selective attacks upon Argentine shipping had to be dictated by the strategic design for that assault.

A sustained blockade of the Islands was not an option because it would place the British carriers at risk and tax their air strength. If a landing was to be attempted the carriers had to be protected and their aircraft conserved to support the amphibious assault. Similarly, if the strategic design for the recapture of the Islands dictated that British forces should seize the initiative at sea quickly, and gain some decisive military advantage over their enemy, then selective attacks against Argentine shipping were unlikely to be delicate affairs. In any event the destructive power of modern conventional weapons generally betrays such notions as surgical strike. What was required instead was an 'intimidatory', rather than 'exemplary', use of force so as to establish naval superiority in the battle zone. Whichever way the Task Force was used, therefore, its use had to be functional to its mission, and its mission was repossession of the Falklands. Time constraints, operational circumstances and the Task Force's limited capability appeared to allow no other effective option.

Implementation of the British ultimatum was, nonetheless, progressive, matching the arrival of different elements of the Task Force in the South Atlantic. This allowed the War Cabinet to maintain that the advance of the Fleet would signal Britain's resolve and possibly intimidate the Junta into a peaceful withdrawal. British decision makers were firmly trapped by the paucity of their alternatives, however, and the central dilemma associated with the use of force: although military action appeared to pressure the Junta into giving some serious consideration to negotiations, the progress of the British Fleet reduced the prospects for an agreement because it necessarily increased each party's commitment to conflict, in both military and political terms.

There were three stages to the Falklands campaign. The first was the mobilisation and build-up phase which began on 31 March and continued up to the end of April. During that time the original amphibious force of 3 Commando Brigade and the 3 Battalion of the

Parachute Regiment, together with support elements, was reinforced by 5 Brigade and the 2 Battalion of the Parachute Regiment.[34] The second stage was the battle to impose the Total Exclusion Zone which began on 1 May when the Carrier Battle Group attacked Argentine forces on and around the Falklands. Because of the strengths as well as the weaknesses of the Carrier Force, the intention of the Naval Staff at this stage seems to have been to establish surface superiority and, while protecting the Fleet from air attack, to contest the air space over the Islands.[35] The final stage was the land campaign which began on 21 May with the landings at San Carlos. Each of these stages was governed by its own particular military requirements.

The pace of the Task Force's progress was dictated by logistical factors, the speed of its fuel tankers, the scattered disposition of the different elements of the Force, and all the other myriad details associated with the confusion as well as the pace of its rapid mobilisation.[36] Speed was of the essence because the War Cabinet wished to establish a military presence in the South Atlantic as quickly as possible for political reasons and all those involved in the operation took pride in its despatch.[37] Enforcement of the Total Exclusion Zone did require the imposition of a form of blockade. However, that blockade was limited and its purpose was a military rather than a political one. It required the Carrier Battle Group to prepare the way for the sea-borne landings without exhausting the Fleet or losing the war. As Admiral Woodward recalled:

> First and fundamental to all other thought, it was very early appreciated that the loss of one, much less both, carriers would immediately and seriously prejudice the whole operation and probably kill any thought of longer term operations.[38]

With limited air strength there was little prospect of gaining complete control of the air but the Carrier Group, particularly in combination with the nuclear hunter-killer submarines, was nevertheless an extremely powerful naval force capable of establishing a large degree of maritime superiority over its Argentine opponents. The objective, therefore, was not so much to impose a total blockade of the Islands as to interdict supplies to the Argentine garrison while conducting all the other operations associated with reconnaissance and preparations for the landings. Time was at a premium here also. As the land force commander subsequently explained:

Timing did not really present any serious problems as far as the decision making was concerned, since it was in all our interests that we should land as soon as might be practicable, and that was largely a matter of mechanics, of speeds of advance and sailing times.[39]

Once the troops were ashore they had to defeat Argentina's garrison as quickly as possible because the Carrier Battle Group could only provide effective support for a limited period; the operational availability of its ships and aircraft would decline with use and the weather was also closing in.[40] In addition the War Cabinet required a quick victory. At no point during the course of any of these stages did the demands of diplomacy overrule those of military exigency.

Rules of Engagement

As units of the Task Force arrived in the South Atlantic, their Rules of Engagement had to be changed not only to satisfy their defensive requirements but also to operationalise the Fleet's strategic plan. ROE were not invented for the Falklands conflict. They are standard operating procedures which, for the Royal Navy, are contained in a manual entitled *Fleet Operation Tactical Instruction*. This is a technical and comprehensive text, specifying all the different procedures required for submarine, surface-ship and aircraft operations. According to the Ministry of Defence the Task Force's ROE were 'updated continually, reflecting changes in the Task Force's position and its composition; the allocation of new missions to the Task Force by the War Cabinet; and the nature of the Argentine response'.[41]

Substantial changes were translated into appropriate public warnings which announced what action could be expected from British forces in general terms. Such warnings consistently reserved the United Kingdom's right under Article 51 to take whatever additional measures were deemed necessary in self-defence. It was nonetheless the evolution of the Task Force's military needs rather than the development of political goals which prompted such detailed revisions of military policy.

Proposals for changes in the Rules of Engagement were usually initiated by the armed forces either through the Task Force Headquarters at Northwood or the Ministry of Defence. The standard procedure was for the Chief of the Defence Staff to submit requests to the War Cabinet after discussion by an *ad hoc* committee of officials, known as the 'Mandarins' Committee', which included all the Permanent Under-Secretaries of the Ministers in the War Cabinet chaired by the Cabinet Secretary. As a rule the group met each evening to consider changes which would be required for the following day or some days hence. In the process proposals were often modified before submission to Ministers.[42] Some changes were regarded as consistent with actions already agreed in principle and these were sanctioned only by the Secretary of State for Defence.[43]

According to Admiral Lewin, Ministers were often reluctant to approve a change and sometimes they resisted military advice, at least for a time.[44] Nevertheless, there appear to have been no rejections or delays which interfered with the progress of any of the stages of the campaign. Admiral Woodward reported that: 'Generally speaking, my rules of engagement were timely and apposite though they were more restrictive than I, as a military commander, would always have wished.'[45] In addition, the Ministry of Defence subsequently explained to the House of Commons Foreign Affairs Committee that there was only one important occasion when Ministers did not accept a proposed change in ROE. That occurred at the beginning of June but the MOD would not specify what the operation was or why the request was turned down.[46]

EXCLUSION ZONES AND THE CONTRADICTION IN MILITARY POLICY

If the divergent impulses behind military and diplomatic developments challenged the coherence of British policy and threatened the unity of the War Cabinet, military policy itself was also distinguished by a basic contradiction. Its public rationale relied upon the principle of the minimum use of force, but its strategic design demanded the maximum use of the forces available to optimise the prospect of achieving military victory. The one was still partially intent on pursuing the logic of politics, in the hiatus between Argentina's invasion and the arrival of the Carrier Group off the Falklands, while the other was dictated by the logic of conflict. As we have already observed, such a contradiction was tolerable only as long as the two dimensions of policy were kept separate, but the momentum of conflict ensured that they would ultimately clash. When they did so, over the weekend of 30 April–2 May, 'minimum force' became the maximum use of force consistent with the Carrier Group's operational plans, to the consequent political embarrassment of the War Cabinet and the near ruin of its diplomacy as well as much of its political rhetoric.

As the Secretary of Defence admitted to the House of Commons on 5 May, soon after the battle for the repossession of the Islands began:

> When we say that we wish to pursue minimum force that does not mean in any way that we are asking our forces to hold back on the pursuit of their objectives; nor in any way does it suggest that they are not totally free to defend themselves against attack and, when they are threatened, to attack the enemy first . . . [47]

Through its public warnings, and through carefully timed statements and debates in the House of Commons, the War Cabinet tried to prepare its international and domestic audiences for this eventuality. In large part it succeeded, but it suffered a damaging political defeat over the sinking of the *Belgrano*: partly because it mismanaged the final stage of the rite of passage to war, during which the contradiction between the rhetoric of military policy and the reality of conflict was brutally exposed, and partly because popular conceptions about the employment of force pay little attention to the power of military imperatives, or the bluntness of military capabilities as instruments of policy.

On 7 April the War Cabinet announced that a Maritime Exclusion Zone was to come into effect around the Falkland Islands on 12 April. The warning declared that

> any Argentine warships and Argentine naval auxiliaries found within the zone will be treated as hostile and are liable to be attacked by British forces. This measure is without prejudice to the right of the United Kingdom to take whatever additional measures may be needed in the exercise of its right of self-defence, under Article 51 of the United Nations Charter.[48]

12 April was chosen because it was the date on which the first of the Royal Navy's nuclear submarines (SSNs) was due to reach the Falklands.[49] Once on station the submarine commander required Rules of Engagement which would specify the action he could take. Michael Heseltine, Nott's successor as Secretary of Defence. explained to the House of Commons Foreign Affairs Committee later that as

we began to achieve a capability in the area of the Falkland Islands, it became necessary to establish what our military disciplines were to be, in terms of the Rules of Engagement and how we defined our military priorities.[50]

Although the military means open to the War Cabinet at that time were very restricted nuclear submarines were, of course, capable of inflicting considerable damage upon Argentine naval forces. Consequently a public warning was also issued because, according to Lewin, 'we did not want to prejudice negotiations by some unexpected actions'.[51] In addition, Argentina was engaged in large-scale reinforcement of its Falklands garrison and the British military command 'wanted to do something . . . to stop this reinforcement'.[52] Finally, Haig's mediation had just begun and the War Cabinet wanted to impress the United States as much as Argentina with its determination.

Imposition of the Exclusion Zone, therefore, was prompted by a variety of considerations: to deter Argentine intrusions; to warn-off third parties; to strengthen Britain's negotiating position by attempting to give some substance to its military policy; and ultimately to contribute to 'the process of our gaining control of the Falkland Islands'.[53]

The term itself appears to have been a new one in international law, although a zonal approach to questions of international jurisdictions has become common in recent years particularly through the work of the United Nations conferences on the law of the sea.[54] Like President Kennedy's Excom, which imposed a 'quarantine' on Cuba during the 1962 missile crisis, the War Cabinet chose an expression that avoided the use of the term 'blockade'.

None of the law of the sea conventions, however, address the jurisdictional context or breadth of security zones. Sea areas have been closed on international authority in the past but only in rare circumstances, such as the UN Security Council's authorisation of a blockade against Rhodesia during its Unilateral Declaration of Independence (UDI). More commonly security zones have been imposed as war zones, and blockades fall under this category, but the War Cabinet was determined to avoid all the collateral complications associated with declaring war on Argentina. Similarly, unrestricted submarine warfare against merchant shipping is outlawed in international law and would have been difficult to reconcile in any event with the War Cabinet's commitment to the limited use of force.

Consequently, only Argentine warships or naval auxiliaries were threatened in the MEZ announcement. Even then the War Cabinet seems to have been reluctant to become the first to inflict casualties. Although HMS *Spartan* (the SSN concerned) reportedly detected the Argentine naval auxiliary *Carlo San Antonio* laying mines off Stanley harbour, it did not attack the ship.[55]

Hence the MEZ seems to have been a hybrid term, novel in its form and coined from different traditions in the development of the law of the sea, which was adopted to suit the War Cabinet's complex politico-military requirements. Deep in the ambiguity of the invasion crisis, reference to an Exclusion Zone subscribed to the War Cabinet's many conflicting needs and gave it the appearance of having more control over events than it actually possessed. Effectively, the MEZ specified the 'operational zone' for the Falklands conflict, the outer limit of which was a radius of 200 nautical miles from latitude 51° 40' south longitude 59° 39' west. Quite a range of distances and forms of zone were considered including a 200-mile territorial limit around the Islands. That would have produced 'a very funny shape' which would have been difficult to police because of the problems of establishing whether a vessel is inside or outside a territorial limit. For this reason, therefore, a radius around a fixed geographical point was chosen instead. The criteria which governed the size of the zone were drawn partly from Royal Navy experience in fishery duties, the familiarity of the idea of a 200-mile zone which many nations claim as the extent of territorial waters, and operational considerations. These last included the requirement to have enough sea room to intercept ships before they could slip back to the safe haven of a port in the Falklands.[56]

Whatever political and psychological advantages were thought to be gained from the introduction of the zone, it was not a particularly effective obstacle to Argentine reinforcement because merchant ships and aircraft were at liberty to operate between the mainland and the Islands[57], although the presence of SSNs in the MEZ does appear to have been a powerful deterrent to the Argentine Navy.[58] Thus the announcement of the zone was intended, in addition, to bring into play the forces Britain had available in the area, to equip them with the political as well as the operational license which they would require if the need to use them arose, to intimidate Argentina and to convey the impression of a careful escalation of the conflict.

MILITARY IMPERATIVES AND THE MOMENTUM OF CONFLICT

The British carriers, HMS *Hermes* and HMS *Invincible*, arrived at Ascension Island on 16 April. The destroyers and frigates of the First Flotilla had preceded them there and immediately moved on into the South Atlantic. The amphibious assault ship, HMS *Fearless*, arrived the next day and other elements of the amphibious force which had been mobilised immediately Argentina had invaded the Falkland Islands followed in its wake. Over 16–17 April Woodward conferred with Admiral Fieldhouse (from Northwood), who had flown down for the conference, and with the commanders of the amphibious force to discuss and confirm the precise dates for the landing. 16 May was chosen, although later this was put back to 19–20 May to accommodate additional reinforcements which were being sent from the United Kingdom, and the progress of the Carrier Group's own operations. The carriers left Ascension on 18 April, after a stay of just two days, and rendezvoused with the advance party of destroyers and frigates on 24 April. Thereafter, the party sent to recapture South Georgia rejoined the main force, and the fully formed Battle Group proceeded directly to the Falklands where it arrived in the Exclusion Zone at the very end of April.[59] As it began the battle for the TEZ on 1 May, the leading elements of the Amphibious Task Group, the roll-on and roll-off landing ships (LSLs), left Ascension Island.[60] On 7 May the main amphibious force also left Ascension and received orders on 12 May from Northwood to conduct an amphibious assault, two weeks after the start of the Carrier Group's operations. On 13 May Brigadier Thompson briefed his land force commanders and gave his orders 'for the landing at San Carlos'.[61] The troops went ashore immediately after the Amphibious Force had regrouped and rendezvoused with the Carrier Force for the final run-in to the Islands.

Militarily, recapture of the Falkland Islands required reconnaissance, interdiction of Argentine reinforcements and the establishment of a measure of military supremacy before the amphibious operation could begin. Woodward summarised his contribution to these tasks as follows. He was

> to impose my will on the Exclusion Zone, to create conditions favourable for the landing, to get the essential recce done making the best use of the forces at my disposal while making life as difficult as possible for the Argentines ashore on the Falklands.[62]

All this had to be accomplished by the Carrier Group before bad weather and operational attrition exhausted the endurance of its ships and aircraft. To carry out its mission, therefore, the leading element of the Task Force had to go on to the offensive and gain a measure of control over the Exclusion Zone. Fourteen days were initially allocated for this stage of the campaign.[63] In the event the decision to reinforce the British amphibious force allowed Woodward an extra week. Although this allowed him longer to complete his job it was a mixed blessing because it also took its toll of the operational availability of his ships. That in turn began to cause concern about their ability to sustain adequate support for the ground forces throughout the land campaign.

It is now evident that Admiral Woodward's counter-attack upon the Islands was a deliberate attempt to seize the military initiative and that it was no mere device for bringing political pressure to bear upon Argentina.[64] Instead the Task Force Commander was engaged in a variety of carefully planned and dangerous military operations whose success was critical to the outcome of the entire war. Special Air Service (SAS) and Special Boat Service (SBS) forces had to be landed to discover Argentine strength and positions. The airport at Port Stanley had to be attacked and closed if possible, and the Argentine garrison had to be intimidated. Each was to be subjected to a combination of air attack and ship bombardment. Landing sites had to be surveyed and the sea approaches to them checked for mines and navigational hazards. Similarly the Argentine airforce had to be provoked into retaliation so that the combat range and performance of its various types of aircraft could be determined. In the process Woodward was also seeking to inflict an early and damaging blow that would give him a decisive military advantage. While such an attack might show Argentina that the British were 'in earnest', if such a demonstration was either required or thought likely to have some political effect at that stage, it would also be instrumental in securing an important measure of control over the Exclusion Zone prior to the landings.[65]

The one critical factor in all of this was air power. According to Hastings and Jenkins, 'London privately envisaged Woodward's little group destroying 30 per cent of the enemy's air capability before 3 Commando Brigade was sent in', but the carriers did not deploy a sufficient number of Harriers to be able to guarantee that sort of damage.[66] Their aircraft were few in number and had to be conserved. Ultimately, of course, Woodward could have lost the war in one attack if either of his capital ships had been severely damaged or sunk. They could not, therefore, be committed to an air and sea battle in the TEZ to the exclusion of other considerations, the most immediate of which was their continuing survival for the support of the land campaign. Consequently a trade-off had to be made between risking the fleet to provoke combat and preserving its strength.[67]

As it sailed south Woodward's Group faced several threats to its safety and the success of its operation.[68] These included: submarine attack; carrier-borne air attack from the Argentine carrier the *25 De Mayo*; land-based air attack from mainland bases in Argentina; Exocet attack from ships or from Super-Etendard aircraft which, it was thought at the time, might be launched from the *25 De Mayo*; and finally, attack by surface ships. To compound the Carrier Group's problems, airborne early warning from RAF Nimrods flying from Wideawake airfield on Ascension Island only provided aircover 1000 miles out from the American base. That left approximately 2000 miles to go without AEW support.[69] As the Carrier Group sailed beyond AEW cover, the air threat from the *25 De Mayo* became the dominant consideration, a 'unique threat' to the safety of the British force.[70] This did not diminish the danger from submarines but the British Fleet was at least expert in anti-submarine warfare. Military intelligence also warned that Argentine forces were planning to attack the British ships and this was later confirmed by the events of the weekend 30 April-2 May, as well as by accounts of the war subsequently published by Argentine sources.[71]

During its final approach to the Islands the Carrier Group adopted a 'deliberately provocative strategy'.[72] Woodward has since explained that his

> initial plan was to lay on a major demonstration of force well inside the Exclusion Zone to make the Argentine believe that landings were about to take place and thus provoke a reaction that would allow me to conduct a major attrition exercise before my amphibious forces arrived to complicate my problem. And at the very least I might discover whether they had a coherent defensive plan.[73]

The ruse appears to have been successful. Despite the fact that the British Fleet was overflown by Argentine reconnaissance aircraft the Argentine command did initially believe on 1 May that the Carrier Group was attempting a large-scale landing. Buenos Aires in fact claimed that the attack was heavily repulsed.

While Woodward wanted to provoke some military response from his opponents, he did not want to be subject to any devastating retaliation. Fearing Argentina's combined air and naval strength, the British by this stage in the campaign seem to have had few illusions about the danger to their ships, despite the hype which characterised the press conferences and private briefings held after the recapture of South Georgia.[74] Given its size there were doubts about the Carrier Group's ability to survive a determined and co-ordinated air and surface attack without major casualties, 'particularly if that threat had no obvious axis'.[75] The object therefore was to engage 'the opposition piecemeal' and establish some significant military advantage along with preparing the way for the landings.[76] As the British ships closed with the Islands neutralising the Argentine aircraft carrier became the top priority but, in addition, it seems as if the destruction of the *25 De Mayo* also became the object of that intimidatory blow which the Task Force Command wished to inflict upon the Argentine Navy.

South Georgia was recaptured on 26 April, although planning for its recovery had begun on 6 April quite independent of the operations being considered against the Falklands.[77] Specially devised Rules of Engagement for the attack were issued on 15–16 April.[78] A small Task Group of one Royal Fleet Auxiliary and three escorting warships screened by nuclear submarines, one of which was HMS *Conqueror*, arrived in the vicinity of the island on 21 April. After a very narrow brush with disaster the combined force of commandos, Special Boat and Special Air Squadron units, together with support elements, captured Grytviken on 25 April and received the surrender of the remaining Argentine garrison at Leith the following day.[79]

The South Georgia operation seems to have been a microcosm of the invasion crisis and, typically, conflicting accounts of the reasoning behind it have emerged since the War. Hastings and Jenkins have suggested that it was part of the process of escalation and indeed the separate planning does indicate that it might initially have been conceived as a way of bringing pressure to bear upon Argentina. But if that was the case, it had the opposite effect. According to one Argentine report, 'those who speculate that the sinking of the Argentine cruiser the *General Belgrano* on 2 May ruined any possibility of peace are wrong'.[80] This same account argues that the 1 May attacks were a probable cause of the failure of negotiations but it maintains, in addition, that Britain's attack on the Argentine submarine *Santa Fe* during the recapture of South Georgia could also have been the decisive factor.

Haig's account of the conflict lends some substance to this

argument. He recorded that Argentina's Foreign Minister, Costa Mendez, had previously warned him that 'the Argentinians would withdraw from negotiations should the British attack South Georgia' and on receiving news of the British assault Mendez cancelled a planned meeting with the Secretary of State.[81] Subsequently the Junta refused to accept a further visit from Haig and on 29 April it rejected his draft settlement requesting new proposals more suited to Argentina's demands. It is important to add, however, that talks did continue as the previous discussion of the Peruvian and UN initiatives indicates. Indeed, if Gavshon and Rice are to be believed, Argentina came close to accepting a settlement despite (or perhaps because of) the loss of South Georgia and the hostilities of 1 May.[82]

From the British perspective the decision to attack South Georgia before Haig had concluded his peace mission ran the risk of ruining whatever prospects those negotiations had of reaching a settlement. On a much reduced scale it was a dilemma which matched that of the entire invasion crisis. However, the island's remoteness ensured that there would be no major military confrontation between British and Argentine forces. It also offered an opportunity to take decisive military action, thereby improving political morale in Britain and retrieving the lost territory, while containing the escalatory impulses involved in the use of force, which an attack upon the Falklands themselves did not afford. That in large part is how it has been regarded since the War, but the motivations behind the operation seemed to have been even more complicated than this.

Because of the politics of advice through which the War Cabinet made its decisions, Ministers required the assurance that the Navy was capable of retaking the Falklands. Throughout the War Cabinet's discussions Lewin was not merely concerned to establish the Navy's capability; he was also engaged, according to his own account, in convincing Ministers that if the Task Force was to maximise its prospects of success it would require quick release from restricted ROE, and a license to undertake its mission at the earliest opportunity.[83] In this respect there is evidence to suggest that the Chief of Defence Staff and Naval Headquarters also regarded South Georgia as a chance to demonstrate the Navy's competence.

According to Woodward, 'The plan to retake South Georgia as soon as possible, and to push our surface and S/M forces as far south as possible, as fast as possible, were driven by political need'.[84] Hastings and Jenkins support this point, arguing that the operation was regarded by the Task Force commanders as a wasteful diversion of resources, claiming that 'virtually the entire Naval Staff, including Leach and Fieldhouse, argued against it'.[85] Woodward's article corroborates some of the journalists' argument. He complained that the operation divided his Carrier Group and caused unnecessary problems during its work-up to battle readiness as he sailed towards the Exclusion Zone:

> it committed me to splitting my assets and denying myself my prime military requirement, a work-up of the full battle group . . . Work-up as one approaches hostilities becomes an increasingly tricky not to say risky business, as fingers get itchy on the trigger and nerves tighten. I did not have as much time as I would have wished, but then few military commanders are blessed with that luxury.[86]

In complete contrast to these accounts Admiral Lewin is said to have succeeded in imposing his will 'on an uneasy and reluctant political hierarchy' in persuading the War Cabinet to sanction the attack.[87] Gavshon and Rice maintain that Lewin's objectives were as much 'political' as they were military. He is reported to have explained to them:

> We just about got the War Cabinet to agree that we should repossess South Georgia on the way down. There was quite a lot of opposition to that. They [the Ministers] thought that would take the eye from the main ball, that we could get bogged down or go wrong and absorb more forces . . . quite a strong body wanted to leave it on one side. But John Fieldhouse and I were quite keen to have a go because we thought we could do it and also felt we needed a success. We hadn't had many successes politically. We also needed a success militarily to get Ministers to believe in what we could do because a lot of my job was trying to give the Cabinet confidence that the services could deliver what they said they could deliver because we hadn't had a war for a long time . . .[88]

Given the plausibility of each of these accounts, as well as the conflict between them and the difficulty of substantiating either of them fully, it is reasonable to argue that the retaking of South Georgia was motivated by a complex of politico-military considerations. These no doubt reflected the politics of decision-making within the War Cabinet, the division of opinion amongst Britain's military and political leadership over how best to proceed with their military and diplomatic policies, as well as the processes by which they increasingly committed themselves to the full-scale implementation of their ultimatum.

All this was to come, however, only after a decisive week of intensive War Cabinet debate that coincided with the quickening tempo of the military campaign. The events of that week provide a further insight into the War Cabinet's decision-making, revealing a little more about the relations between its members, the politics of advice which governed its actions as well as the rest of the background to the sinking of the *Belgrano*. In particular, this final stage in the transition to armed conflict illustrates the confusion and uncertainty that was caused not only by the mounting intensity of the invasion crisis, and all the problems of communication and judgement that went with it, but also by the conflicting public warnings and announcements which were issued by the United Kingdom. These in turn demonstrated the War Cabinet's increasing inability to reconcile the deep divergences which existed between its military and diplomatic positions, and the closely related contradiction that obtained between the public and private dimensions of its military policy. Many detailed questions remain to be answered about the events of this week, but the major features can now be established with a measure of confidence on the basis of evidence produced since the extensive inquiries which have been conducted into the *Belgrano* affair, and these issues will be dealt with in the next chapter.[89] Although gaps in the record remain it seems reasonable to suggest that further information is more likely to confirm than deny the argument that the crucial decisions taken during the weekend of 30 April-2 May were determined more by the circumstances of crisis and conflict than by any other factors.

7 The Climax of the Conflict

We do not need a conspiratorial view of the military's role in decision-making to appreciate that if it comes to war the military suffer the immediate consequences and they, therefore, seek the freedom to wage it professionally, as they think fit. What evidence we have indicates clearly that, despite the War Cabinet's tacit ultimatum, Lewin was engaged in a sustained effort to free his forces for the coming conflict, to reduce the odds against them as best he could through timely decision taking and to maximise the War Cabinet's committment to a politically uncomplicated, if technically very difficult, military operation. Some of the evidence concerning the South Georgia operation supports these points, and what we now know about the decisions leading up to the sinking of the *Belgrano* confirms that the Chief of Defence Staff intensified his efforts to extend the Task Force's Rules of Engagement as the Carrier Battle Group sailed towards the zone of conflict. That evidence also reveals that the War Cabinet did not fully relax the ROE until the Carrier Group's operations against the Islands on 1 May had verified reports of Argentina's determination to counter attack. Only then, and with the additional receipt of ambiguous intelligence concerning the *Belgrano*'s role in a co-ordinated naval and naval-air attack against British ships, was the final decision made to free Woodward's Fleet to wage general war against Argentine forces in the South Atlantic, up to 12 miles from the Argentine mainland.[1] This Second World War cruiser was the first and immediate casualty of this extension of the conflict, and its accompanying escorts were fortunate not to have been destroyed with it.[2] Thereafter, within the confines of the South Atlantic, the war was fought will all the conventional means available, although the mainland remained a sanctuary from British attack.[3]

As the South Georgia expedition arrived off the island on 21 April the main force of the Carrier Group was also detected by an Argentine Air Force Boeing 707 reconnaissance aircraft which Woodward was not empowered to attack under his current ROE.[4] In response to the increasing momentum of the military campaign during the last week of April, British attention became concentrated upon the Carrier Group's two interdependent and dominating preoccupations—its

193

vulnerability to air and submarine attack and its ability to carry out its mission. From there on Lewin lobbied very strongly for Rules of Engagement appropriate to the military situation which was beginning to develop very rapidly. The details of military policy were, therefore, revised several times in swift succession as the War Cabinet, in response to Lewin's submission and the advance of British ships into combat radius of Argentine forces, finally accommodated itself to the imperatives of the campaign. These developments were also accompanied by two further public warnings–one in a message sent to Argentina on 23 April, and a second in the announcement of a Total Exclusion Zone on 28 April.[5]

Sometime between 21 and 23 April, after discussions about the general situation and the specific dangers which the Carrier Group faced, the Rules of Engagement were relaxed for the surface elements of the Carrier force. Lewin recalled:

> After putting all these points to Ministers over quite a considerable period (two or three days) we obtained approval for Rules of Engagement which allowed our ships to defend themselves against warships, aircraft and submarines who were intent on interfering with the mission of our force by approaching it.[6]

Such an important development also led to the issuing of a public warning on 23 April. Initially the note was sent direct to the Argentine Government via the Swiss Embassy in Buenos Aires, but it was also relayed by Parsons in New York to the UN Security Council.[7] The new warning declared:

> In announcing the establishment of a Maritime Exclusion Zone around the Falkland Islands, Her Majesty's Government made it clear that this measure was without prejudice to the right of the United Kingdom to take whatever additional measures may be needed in the exercise of its right of self-defence under Article 51 of the United Nations Charter. In this connection Her Majesty's Government now wishes to make clear that any approach on the part of Argentine warships, including submarines, naval auxiliaries or military aircraft which could amount to a threat to interfere with the *mission* of British Forces in the South Atlantic will encounter the appropriate response. All Argentine aircraft, including civil aircraft engaging in surveillance of these British forces will be regarded as hostile and are liable to be dealt with accordingly.[8] [Emphasis added]

A number of extremely important aspects of this statement are now evident and particular attention should be drawn to them. First, the announcement clearly gave the widest public warning to any Argentine forces in the South Atlantic which sought to interfere with the 'mission' of the British Fleet. Second, because of the wide scope of the warning certain members of the War Cabinet had grave reservations about whether it was specific enough to safeguard Britain's diplomatic and political position, as well as to satisfy the expectations which the War Cabinet had helped to raise about its limited and minimum use of force. The Foreign Secretary was to argue, on 1 May, when an attack outside the Exclusion Zone against Argentina's aircraft carrier was sanctioned, that a more precise statement was necessary, if not to satisfy Britain's legal responsibilities, which arguably had been punctiliously discharged, then at least to retain its high level of international support by keeping its political position absolutely clear.[9] Third, the warning went far beyond what British forces were actually empowered to do in terms of their current Rules of Engagement, despite the recent relaxation of ROE for the Carrier Group's ships and aircraft.

In this respect Clive Ponting seems to be mistaken in maintaining that during the week following the change in ROE on 2 May, which led to the sinking of the *Belgrano*, 'the UK Government had been in the position where the agreed rules by which its ships were operating in the South Atlantic went further than the public warnings indicated'.[10] For a period up to 2 May the position was in fact quite the reverse, but it was thoroughly confused by the War Cabinet's handling of the public announcements concerning the development of the conflict. Until then Britain's 23 April warning went beyond the Task Force's ROE, specifically where they applied to the operations of its nuclear submarines. It could plausibly be argued that the 2 May change merely gave military effect to that warning, and this is the position Lewin has maintained during the inquiries concerning the sinking of the *Belgrano*.[11] Many of the later difficulties, however, arose because of the confusion caused by the continued use of the 'zonal' language in statements about the operations of the British Task Force.

Fourth, and finally, therefore, the War Cabinet's continued reference to the Maritime Exclusion zone, and the prominence accorded to the MEZ/TEZ in official announcements, as well as public discussions, was thoroughly misleading. Ponting would have been nearer the mark had he argued, instead, that the War Cabinet's public statements were conflicting and unspecific, and that they consequently failed to deal effectively with the political and international problems raised by all the competing demands of the diplomatic, domestic and operational aspects of its policy. That its policy management was less than perfect in this regard is unsurprising. But its failure, combined with the arrogance and misjudgement which characterised the postwar handling of the *Belgrano* affair, provided fertile ground for conspiracy theories. There is every reason to believe that the War Cabinet was simply overwhelmed by the task of orchestrating its actions and concentrated on the problem which was its first priority. It was not until a statement was issued by the Ministry of Defence on 7 May, and submitted to the Security Council on 8 May, that the War Cabinet made clear that the Exclusion Zone was effectively superceded by the 23 April warning and the ROE changes of 2 May.[12] Even then, reference to the Zone continued to occupy a prominent and misleading place in the language of the conflict.

Towards the end of April it became evident that the United States was about to side with Britain and on 30 April a formal announcement was made to that effect. Consequently the War Cabinet was relieved of its greatest political fear just as the military aspect of the invasion crisis became dominant. As they made the final transition to war the majority of the War Cabinet seemed to have been much less concerned with the details of Britain's legal and international position, and increasingly preoccupied with the immediate military dangers and problems posed by the Carrier Group's approach to the Falklands. The diplomatic side seemed to have been taken care of in the announcement of an Exclusion Zone and the 23 April warning, and the associated political dividends had been secured. Ministers and officials were absorbed instead with the demands of the military contest which was now imminent.

These important developments were also directly reflected in the Parliamentary statements made by Ministers from 20 April onwards. The Prime Minister's announcements in particular showed a marked shift towards a preoccupation with the safety of the British forces. On 22 April, in preparation for the 23 April letter to the Security Council, she warned the House of Commons that force could not be ruled out and that negotiations could not go on endlessly.[13] On 26 April, announcing the recapture of South Georgia, she made a very lengthy statement which was quite clearly designed to prepare the House and the country for further military action. In reaffirming the 23 April warning the substance of her speech maintained that time was running out, that there were very few military options available and that the safety of British forces was now of paramount concern:

Time is getting extremely short as the Task Force approaches the Islands . . . One cannot have a wide range of choice and a wide range of military options with the Task Force in the wild and stormy weather of that area.[14]

She concluded: 'One must always consider the military options, and in doing so we must look after our soldiers and marines who have to undertake them'.[15] The following day (27 April) she repeated all these points and issued what amounted to a declaration that Britain's tacit ultimatum had finally expired:

> *It is Argentina that has flagrantly failed to comply (with Resolution 502), and it is because of that failure that we must now be free to exercise our right to self-defence under article 51.*[16] [Emphasis added]

On 28 April the Secretary of Defence announced the introduction of the Total Exclusion Zone (TEZ), and on 29 April the House of Commons held a fourth debate on the Falklands after the Government had accepted the Labour leader's earlier request for one.[17] No reference was made, of course, to the Carrier Group's forthcoming operations but the Prime Minister used the opportunity to review the Government's position, the problems in the negotiations and the intransigence of the Argentine regime. She also reminded her audience that 'it would be totally inconsistent to support the despatch of the Task Force and yet be opposed to its use. What is more it would be highly dangerous to bluff in that way'.[18]

As far as the War Cabinet was concerned implementation of its tacit ultimatum could not be delayed if the safety and success of the British Task Force was to be assured. The narrow margin between victory and defeat in the South Atlantic allowed little scope for delay and there seems to have been none. Nevertheless, although acceptance of the logic of conflict was quick it was also progressive because, despite the ease with which the United Kingdom finally went to war over the Falkland Islands, the outcome of the invasion crisis was uncertain and no one could assume at the time that Britain would secure the degree of national unity and international support which it actually achieved. Similarly, despite the jingoism of the popular press and some initial over-confidence at the official level, it quickly became clear that the Task Force would have to run considerable risks and take high casualties if it was to achieve its objective. Few senior decision-makers could have been cavalier about the price of military success, let alone failure, even though political ignominy threatened Britain's political leadership throughout the conflict. None could be certain, either, that the Task Force would not suffer some catastrophic losses. War Cabinet policies thus provided, as much by design as by effect, the indispensable rites of passage by means of which domestic and international support were mobilised and consolidated while the country was prepared militarily and politically for war. Moreover, wishing to avoid conflict while having no alternative but to threaten it caused internal strains and divisions within the Cabinet, particularly, as was suggested earlier, between the Prime Minister and the Foreign Secretary. By the end of April, therefore, all the various pressures to which the War Cabinet was subject had become intense and it faltered in its management of the processes of transition to war. This inflicted considerable damage upon its international position and created confusion which, together with its postwar handling of the *Belgrano* affair, helped to compromise the reputation that it had otherwise achieved in its handling of the conflict.

A second revision of military policy came on 30 April after the War Cabinet had debated the two most immediate military issues of the week: the threat from Argentina's aircraft carrier and the adequacy of the warnings which had been issued to cover Britain's military actions. There is every reason to believe that Cabinet discussion was not confined to specific threats to the British forces. The political and public background to a widening of the conflict had been prepared by the 23 April warning and subsequent Parliamentary statements on 26 and 27 April. What Lewin nevertheless still required was the operationalisation of these warnings in terms of a general extension of the Task Force's ROE, and there are several points which suggest that this was in fact the ultimate objective of his submissions to War Cabinet discussions towards the end of this critical week.

For example, Lewin is reported to have concluded by 26–27 April that 'the feeling in the War Cabinet and certainly in the military' was that 'a negotiated settlement was not on'.[19] Undoubtedly by 30 April, as he admitted later to the House of Commons Foreign Affairs Committee, 'My own view, and it was only a personal view, at that stage was that there was no hope of getting a negotiated settlement.'[20] Although others in the War Cabinet later claimed to be still uncertain at this point,[21] the Task Force Command was by now convinced that it would have to implement its military pland. Hence Lewin regarded Pym's visit to the United States on 1 May as instrumental to the development of the War Cabinet's military plans: 'My own feeling was that Mr Pym was going off to New York, to the United Nations, to try to explain more clearly the British position, before we got to another level of military action.'[22]

Furthermore, British strategy had by now been agreed and the objectives of the Task Force were quite clear. Consequently, the Carrier Group was quickly given orders to go ahead with that strategy by commencing operations on 1 May. As Lewin further explained to the Parliamentary Commttee on 29 April:

> Woodward's mission now he had arrived was twofold. He had to enforce the Total Exclusion Zone with all that that implied in stopping merchant ships, sinking warships, shooting down aircraft that are landing on the airfield, closing the airfield . . . The other part of his job was . . . because of the state of negotiations . . . to prepare for a landing with a view to repossession . . . He could not do either of these jobs if the Argentinian fleet were at sea.[23]

The speed with which the third and general extension of ROE was finally agreed on 2 May, so soon after the 30 April revision with apparently very little further debate by the War Cabinet and without going through the standard procedure that had been established for such changes, also indicates strongly that such an extension must have been contemplated for some time before 2 May. Presumably the arguments surrounding it had already been well rehearsed and resolved.

Lewin maintains, in addition, that on 30 April he asked only for a very specific change of ROE in order to allow the *25 de Mayo* to be attacked, whereas on 2 May he requested a general extension which *inter alia* sanctioned the attack on the *Belgrano*.[24] Although those of his political and military colleagues who have subsequently commented on the 2 May decision have accepted that it was a major one,[25] Lewin insists that it 'was not a change in principle . . . It was only a change in degree and it would not have needed a meeting of the mandarins'.[26]

Finally, therefore, the general extension of ROE on 2 May was not specifically required by the detection of the *Belgrano* or the immediacy of any threat which it may have posed. Such a change was demanded instead by the operations of 1 May, which demonstrated that the campaign to repossess the Islands had begun in earnest and that Argentine forces were going to resist the British attacks. Hence all Argentine ships thereby became a threat to the Task Force's mission.

It would be wrong to argue that the *Belgrano* was used simply as a pretext to overcome whatever final reservations the War Cabinet may have had about widening the conflict, because (as will be seen) she was playing an integral part in Argentine strategy; but the ship certainly seems to have been the last straw.

In order to support this argument we have to consider in greater detail the circumstances surrounding the 30 April revision, together with those that influenced the third and last change on 2 May. While doing so we can re-emphasise two additional points. First, Lewin had to press strongly for the general extension in ROE and the events of 1 May were instrumental in his case. Second, Ministers were divided over the adequacy of their public warnings and in granting the extension on 2 May, without clarifying their intentions along the lines which the Foreign Secretary recommended on 30 April, they mishandled the last stage in the transition to war. As things turned out that mistake was not to influence the outcome of the conflict, although it was, potentially, a serious diplomatic omission. Instead, it stored up political problems for the Government which were to damage its reputation subsequently.

According to Lewin, throughout the last week of April,

> I was briefing the War Cabinet on the actions of the Argentine Navy, our estimated position of them, the threat that they posed. Now, as we got even closer to the Falklands, the threat from the carrier with its aircraft with a range of 500 miles became more serious, and it would have been possible for the carrier to have come out of the River Plate—a distance of 150 miles or so—launch its aircraft and attack our ships without warning . . . so the carrier was a unique threat to our ships and, after considerable discussion over a number of days and as the threat got stronger as we got closer, Ministers agreed that this was a threat that they could no longer ignore and gave approval for the carrier to be attacked if it was detected by a nuclear submarine.[27]

At the beginning of that week the War Cabinet had authorised ROE for the ships and aircraft of the Carrier Group to take action against any Argentine forces which sought to interfere with their 'mission' (including any civil aircraft engaged on reconnaissance of the British Fleet). British SSNs operating in the South Atlantic, however, were still governed by ROE which limited their offensive actions to the Exclusion Zone; presumably these were the ROE granted on or about

12 April, when the MEZ first came into effect. As the Carrier Group sailed south from Ascension Island the SSNs were deployed out of the Exclusion Zone to act as a forward reconnaissance screen for the surface Force. It should be remembered that the British ships had no AEW and that 'the Task Force limit of reconnaissance was the radar horizon (about 20 miles) or the range which could be reached by helicopters or Harriers'.[28] However, as Lewin recorded,

> helicopters were needed for anti-submarine warfare; they were patrolling all the way down against the threat of attack by submarines. Again, as I have already said, the Task Group commander wanted to conserve his Harriers for much more important things later on.[29]

Redeployment of the SSNs did not immediately entail a revision of their ROE because reconnaissance did not require them to attack and their best form of defence, unlike the ships of the Carrier Group, was merely to avoid detection.[30] But an ROE change was required if one of them was to be used against the *25 de Mayo* outside the Exclusion Zone, from where the Argentine ship was capable of launching an air strike against the British Carrier Force operating within or on the periphery of the TEZ. According to Gavshon and Rice the Argentine aircraft carrier had been trailed by HMS *Splendid* until 23 April when, for reasons which remain obscure, this SSN had either been withdrawn from this task or simply lost contact with the vessel.[31] On 30 April Lewin persuaded the War Cabinet to authorise a further change in ROE and order HMS *Splendid*, which was patrolling north of the Exclusion Zone, to sink the *25 de Mayo* if the carrier entered its patrol area. The Chief of Defence Staff insisted that this was a very precise and very limited ROE revision: 'I only requested approval for the carrier to be attacked.'[32]; 'it was not an order to the submarine "Go and sink the *25 de Mayo*", it was an order to the submarine. If the *25 de Mayo* finds you in the patrol area which you are in, you have approval to attack'.[33]

As the *Belgrano* affair subsequently made clear, these extended Rules of Engagement were confined to HMS *Splendid*. HMS *Conqueror* was still operating under the original ROE which applied to the MEZ when she confirmed her detection of the Argentine cruiser group to the south of the TEZ on 1 May, and consequently her commander was not empowered to attack the *Belgrano*. Indeed he was specifically ordered not to do so unless the ship entered the TEZ.[34]

On 1 May the Carrier Group conducted its 'major demonstration of force, simulating an amphibious landing off Port Stanley, which successfully drew the Argentines and revealed some of their defensive positions'.[35] Up to this point the War Cabinet seems to have resisted the idea that the Carrier Force required a general extension of its ROE. As Lewin explained:

> Although our intelligence appreciation was that the Argentines intended to attack our ships as they got close to the Falklands *we had no confirmation of this* and Ministers were very reluctant to authorise too overt a military action on our part until the Argentine intention, which we were pretty sure of, had been made clear.[36] [Emphasis added]

It is difficult to imagine what other reaction Ministers expected from Argentina as the Carrier Group counter-attacked the Islands on 1 May. But it is evident, nevertheless, that Argentina's response served both military and, as far as War Cabinet decision-making was concerned, political purposes. As they drew Argentine forces into combat these attacks provided Lewin with the final confirmation he needed to persuade the War Cabinet that Argentina, like the United Kingdom, had a military strategy and was determined to act upon it. Amid reports of attack and counter-attack on 1–2 May, and Argentine claims of major British losses, the War Cabinet was asked not simply for an ROE change that would allow HMS *Conqueror* to attack the *Belgrano* but for a general extension of the Rules of Engagement in the South Atlantic. Even then it seems Ministers were only persuaded to grant such a license because they were advised, in addition, that the *Belgrano* was engaged in a co-ordinated offensive against British forces.

However, there was nothing in the detection of the *Belgrano* or the nature of the threat which it presented to the Task Force which made it any more dangerous to Woodward's force than Argentina's aircraft carrier. On the contrary it was a much less powerful naval unit and there was certainly nothing which distinguished it in such a way as to require a general extension of the Carrier Group's ROE. John Nott agreed that the carrier was in 'a quite different category to the *Belgrano*'[37]; and Lewin has insisted that 'it was a matter of the surrounding circumstances which affected the way in which the decision was taken on 2 May'.[38]

Indeed the postwar preoccupation with the *Belgrano* has served to divert attention away from a serious military failure, losing the *25 de Mayo*, which could have had disastrous consequences for the British Fleet. The cruiser had the misfortune to be discovered at precisely the moment when the War Cabinet's residual reservations about extending the conflict were about to be overcome, and as the Task Force Command, having failed to find and destroy the Argentine aircraft carrier, urgently required that intimidatory strike which it had been planning as part of its campaign strategy. 'Ministers and other people', Lewin was to argue in response to a question about why Ministers did not inquire about the course of the *Belgrano* once they had relaxed the ROE, 'were pretty busy fighting a war'.[39] In other words the engagements of 1 May helped to resolve the remaining ambiguity of the invasion crisis and encouraged the War Cabinet to cross its own final threshold to conflict by lifting the ROE restrictions on the British forces.

Subsequently it has become clear that for the Chief of Defence Staff, Task Force Headquarters and Admiral Woodward, it was the *Belgrano*'s potential threat 'and the constraints which that potential threat might impose on the British Fleet's future activities', rather than the immediacy of it, which was uppermost in their minds.[40] Certainly it was this consideration which resulted in a request for a general relaxation of the ROE:

> The *Belgrano* was a threat to Woodward carrying out his mission, because if Woodward kept himself safe and went off to the eastward at 20 knots he could not carry out his mission. His intention the next day was to bombard the airfield again, and his intention that night was to put in and re-supply more of the special forces. That was his job. *He could not do his job while Belgrano was where she was or even at sea.*[41] [Lewin: emphasis added]

Many aspects of the 2 May decision remain very uncertain despite the publicity it has received through the leaks and Parliamentary inquiry to which it has been subject. But one important question in particular has not received the consideration it deserves. Here, as in almost every other respect, the *Belgrano* affair has helped to obscure as much as it has revealed about the nature of British decision-making. Most discussion has focused upon whether it was militarily justifiable to sink the cruiser or not, but the real significance of Lewin's approach to the War Cabinet on 2 May was that it was designed to widen the undeclared war which had finally broken out the day before. Just as the *Belgrano* was part of the final act in the War Cabinet's accommodation to the imperatives of the South Atlantic campaign, so the Argentine vessel became the first and costliest victim of the War. Its fate, as Lewin himself persistently argued to the House of Commons Foreign Affairs Committee, cannot therefore be considered in isolation from those dynamics of conflict which propelled British policy once Argentina had seized the Falklands, and from the high degree of stress and danger to which they had been raised by the weekend of 1–2 May.

We have to ask *first*, why Lewin requested a general extension of the Rules of Engagement, just to deal with the *Belgrano*, instead of a specific extension such as that which had been granted two days previously in respect of the *25 de Mayo*? Only then can we appreciate the widernature of the considerations involved, the *Belgrano's* relationship to them and the complex of circumstances which led to the ship being attacked. The answer lies in the convergence of a variety of factors whose influence became decisive as Britain's ultimatum ran out. These included the fearful uncertainty which surrounded the rapidly developing military situation in the South Atlantic, the general strategy to which the British Task Force was committed, the intelligence information available to the Task Force Command through signals interception, together with its timing, and finally the tactics involved in giving military advice to the War Cabinet.

British forces had purposefully provoked Argentine counter-attacks on 1 May and so required freedom to respond as military circumstances dictated. Having detected the Argentine cruiser, HMS *Conqueror* had also presented the Task Force Command with what Lewin reportedly advised the War Cabinet was 'an opportunity to knock-off a major unit of the Argentinian fleet'.[42] Militarily the *Belgrano* was a much inferior target to the Argentine carrier but, as the *25 de Mayo* continued to elude its British pursuer, sinking the cruiser besides removing a potential problem offered a comparable symbolic substitute for the destruction of the more powerful ship. With the conflict widening according to its own logic, the War Cabinet was teetering on the brink of releasing the British forces from their restricted ROE. Nevertheless, it seemed to require one final indication of the 'immediacy' of the threat to Woodward's Group before doing so. There are good grounds for arguing, therefore, that against the background of all the actions which took place on 1 May, Lewin used the additional knowledge that the *Belgrano* was an integral part of Argentine naval strategy, the principal object of which was to launch an air strike against the British Carrier Group, to secure the military freedom which he had been seeking.

Woodward maintains that on 2 May 'I sought, for the first and only time throughout the campaign, a major change to the Rules of Engagement (ROE) to enable *Conqueror* to attack *Belgrano* outside the Exclusion Zone'.[43] This, incidentally, confirms that Lewin and Northwood, rather than the operational commander, set the pace with respect to changes in the ROE, directing the campaign as well as responding to military developments.[44] Lewin similarly records that

> the fact that *Conqueror* was in touch with the *Belgrano* was reported to me on the morning of the 2nd with a request from Admiral Fieldhouse, Commander of the Task Force . . . that the Rules of Engagement should be changed to allow the *Belgrano* to be attacked. He told me that not only was that his view but that Admiral Woodward had signalled during the night that he was concerned about the position of the *Belgrano* and wished the Rules of Engagement to be changed so that it could be attacked because it was threatening his ability to do what he had been told to do.[45]

It was the Chief of Defence Staff who translated Woodward's request into a recommendation that the War Cabinet grant a general relaxation of the ROE. From his unique vantage point at the interface between the military and political loci of decision-making he judged that the time had come to provide the Task Force with that operational license without which it could not proceed effectively with its purpose. While the military developments of 1–2 May gave him the confirmation which he needed to convince the War Cabinet of Argentine hostility, the sighting of the *Belgrano* provided him with the specific grounds upon which he was able to clinch his case. Taken together all the events of 1–2 May provided Britain's military leadership with *what it expected* by way of an Argentine response to the Carrier Group's attack, with *what it wanted* by way of an opportunity to inflict an intimidatory blow on the Argentine Fleet, and with *what it needed* to persuade the War Cabinet to allow it to engage in general warfare and prepare the way for the British landings. In such compelling circumstances the course which the *Belgrano* happened to be steering became, as Lewin himself observed, 'an insignificant detail'.[46]

1 May had not only witnessed the opening of the British campaign for the recovery of the Islands; by the same token it had exposed

Buenos Aires' counter-strategy. Argentina's military command had naturally planned to attack the British forces when they were at their most vulnerable, that is to say as they attempted to mount their amphibious assault. One Argentine account has since explained: 'With the Royal Navy's Task Force having reached the vicinity, the mission of the Argentine force was made manifest—to find and destroy the British if they attacked the Islands or Mainland'.[47]

On 27 April Argentina had deployed a Naval Task Force (Task Force 79), composed of the bulk of the Argentine Fleet, in preparation for a defence of the Falklands. The force was initially divided into three groups; two Northern Groups (79.1 and 79.2), one of which included the *25 de Mayo* and two British Type-42 destroyers (the *Santisima Trinidad* and the *Hercules*); and a third group (79.3) deployed to the south of the Exclusion Zone operating in the region of Isla de los Estados (States Island) at the foot of Tierra del Fuego. This was composed of the *Belgrano*, escorted by two Exocet-equipped destroyers, the *Piedra Buena* and the *Hipolito Bouchard*. On 1 May a fourth group (79.4), composed of three French-built Type-69 frigates, was formed and instructed to operate in conjunction with the two Northern Groups. Each group was also accompanied by an oil auxiliary.[48] According to some British reports, British signals intelligence disclosed sometime between 29 and 30 April that the *Belgrano* group's orders were 'to patrol in a straight line out from the Argentine coast, keeping south of the Falklands and the Exclusion Zone, until they reached a set point beyond the Islands. There, they were to turn round and patrol back again'.[49]

British operations on 1 May began with an unsuccessful attack on Port Stanley airfield by an RAF Vulcan bomber which had flown from Ascension Island. Its objective was to close the runway with heavy 1000 pound bombs, although some suggest that its purpose was a political one, an attempt by the RAF to reduce the Navy's monopoly of the campaign. Later that day Harriers from the British carriers attacked the Argentine garrisons and shore installations at Goose Green and Port Stanley. In addition, Woodward's destroyers moved close inshore to bombard other Argentine positions around the Islands' capital. Argentina's military command also committed its forces to battle, deceived into thinking that an amphibious assault was about to take place. Land-based Mirages attacked the ship bombardment groups from the British Fleet, and two Canberra bombers attacked the Battle Group's ASW frigates. An Argentine submarine was also detected amongst the ships of the Carrier Force and was hunted unsuccessfully for about 20 hours. Sometime between 1–2 May an Argentine Super-Etendard also flew an abortive mission to make an Exocet strike on the carriers. It failed to make its in-flight refuelling rendezvous and returned to base.[50]

At 15.55 local time (19.55 BST) on 1 May, Argentina's Fleet Commander ordered Task Force 79 to retaliate against the British Carrier Force.[51] These instructions seem to have been confined to the Northern Groups with the object of bringing 'the carrier's eight A-4 Skyhawk aircraft within range' of the British ships.[52] A well-informed Argentine source also explained that the job of the *Belgrano* was

> to provide an early warning for the southern mainland and to be in position to intercept any British reinforcements which might come from the Pacific. While on station the cruiser plied back and forth between Isla de los Estados and the Burdwood Bank.[53]

Again, according to British reports, British intelligence at the Government Communications Headquarters (GCHQ) also intercepted and decrypted the Argentine fleet order immediately after it was issued.[54]

The flight deck on the *25 de Mayo* was apparently too small for night recoveries and the ship had to await the approach of dawn, while closing with the British Fleet, before it could launch its aircraft. Accordingly on 2 May it was almost morning in the South Atlantic before the carrier attempted to launch its small complement of Skyhawks, expecting few if any to survive the mission. *25 de Mayo* could make 22 knots, but 35 knots of wind over the deck were required before aircraft could be launched. Conditions were unusually calm and the carrier failed in its efforts to get its Skyhawks airborne, although it reportedly came within 150 miles of its target.[55]

By this stage Argentina's military command had also concluded that the Carrier Group's assault was a feint and that the British were not in fact attempting a landing.[56] Consequently a withdrawal signal was sent out which, according to Argentine sources, instructed the Northern Groups of Task Force 79 'to return to safer waters in order to wait for more suitable weather'.[57] It also directed the *Belgrano* group to return to the vicinity of Isla de los Estados, specifically to a position 'in less deep water—no more than 120 metres—to avoid the presence of nuclear submarines'.[58] The signal was issued at 20.07 local time 1 May (00.07 BST, 2 May) and confirmed at 01.19 local time 2 May (05.19 BST, 2 May).[59] Both signals were intercepted and decoded by

GCHQ.[60] Gavshon and Rice seem to be alone in claiming that the instruction directed the Argentine ships 'the *Belgrano* group included, *"back to port"'* [emphasis added].[61] Neither of the most detailed Argentine accounts supports this point. Both maintain instead that Argentina was effectively engaged in a tactical military withdrawal beyond the strike range of the Carrier Group and away from the SSN threat.[62]

In the meantime HMS *Conqueror*, having detected the *Belgrano*, was shadowing the cruiser's movements. The British SSN had left the South Georgia region on 28 April under orders to detect the Southern Group of the Argentine Task Force.[63] Arriving in her patrol area sometime on 30 April the nuclear submarine quickly discovered the oil auxiliary accompanying the *Belgrano* and its escorts.[64] The following day, at 14.00 (BST), *Conqueror* established visual contact with the *Belgrano* itself which was refuelling from the auxiliary.[65] At 15.00, as *Conqueror* reported to Fleet Headquarters, the Argentine group moved off in a south-easterly direction along its patrol line.[66] According to Ponting:

> This information was signalled back to Fleet Headquarters at Northwood where it was immediately acknowledged. It would also have been available to Admiral Sandy Woodward in charge of the Task Force on board HMS *Hermes*.[67]

Thereafter, the SSN shadowed the group, making periodic status reports to Fleet Headquarters.[68]

As *Conqueror* trailed the *Belgrano* throughout 1 May and into 2 May, Woodward was also assailed by doubts about his position:

> Early on the morning of May 2 all the indications were that *25 De Mayo*, the Argentinian aircraft carrier, had slipped past my forward SSN (nuclear submarine) barrier to the north, while the cruiser *General Belgrano* and her escorts were attempting to complete the pincer movement from the south, still outside the Exclusion Zone.[69]

The idea of a 'pincer movement', implying an aggressive role for the *Belgrano*, is not supported by the evidence which is now available. But British intelligence may well have been quite uncertain about what precise contribution the southern group of TF 79 was making to the development of Argentine strategy. Nonetheless, there is some considerable dispute about this point; not so much with regard to the effectiveness of British signal interceptions, but about the intelligence assessments that were made on the basis of them, and whether these assessments were made available to Lewin and the War Cabinet before the lunch-time decision, on 2 May, to relax the ROE and attack the *Belgrano*. We will return to these issues shortly, but the 'pincer' explanation itself strongly suggests a rationalisation (no doubt related to the fears of the time and the need to provide a good justification for the attack later) which was designed to give a simplified account of what was likely to have been a much more confused and complicated situation.

Woodward might well have considered that he had enough problems to deal with and that, whatever its designated purpose, the *Belgrano* was at least one threat which he was in a position to eliminate altogether before its status changed. There was no guarantee, for example, that the *Belgrano* would not be ordered to attack units of the Carrier Group, engaged in bombardment and other sorties against the Islands or clandestine operations against the mainland, or that *Conqueror* would not lose the cruiser in the changing weather and maritime conditions of the area.[70] In either case Woodward could have become as ignorant of the threats developing on his southern flank as he was about those currently developing to the north.[71] It is not difficult to imagine, therefore, that from the perspective of the Carrier Group Commander it was better to sink the *Belgrano* than have it complicating his calculations and increasing his problems. Accordingly, in the early morning of 2 May, he requested a change in the Rules of Engagement to permit an attack on the ship.

Although *Conqueror* had sent a report of its sighting of the cruiser to Northwood at 15.00 (BST) on 1 May,[72] Fleet Headquarters did not warn Lewin or the War Cabinet that the *Belgrano* had been discovered.[73] The explanation of this, according to Lewin, was that the news was operational information,

> which went to the operational headquarters. Their first duty is to make sure that the man on the spot is aware of it. Once he is aware of it his safety is assured because he can make off to the eastward at 20 knots and this will extend the time that it takes for the *Belgrano* or anybody to catch up with him, to a very, very great number of hours.[74]

In short the priority was to let Woodward know about the contact. Any further action would have required change in the ROE and that, in turn, would have had to await the War Cabinet meeting planned for the afternoon of the following day. Fleet Headquarters knew

> very well, from my exchanges with Fieldhouse in keeping him aware of how things happened in Whitehall, that they were not going to change the Rules of Engagement without assembly the full War Cabinet. They knew the War Cabinet was due to assemble the next day and they decided that they could wait until that time.[75]

Despite these considerations, no effort was in fact made to follow the established procedure for putting the item before the War Cabinet by alerting the 'Mandarins' Committee', which had been established during the early days of the invasion crisis for precisely this purpose. Fleet Headquarters, Lewin and Woodward all knew from intelligence reports that the cruiser was operating somewhere to the south of the Carrier Group. Indeed *Conqueror* had been brought back from South Georgia to locate her and, according to a Ministry of Defence Memorandum, the SSN was instructed at 01.00 (BST) to intercept and attack the *Belgrano* group if it penetrated the TEZ.[76] Evidently the *Belgrano* was not considered to be a particularly significant threat at this stage because no alarms went off in Northwood on the afternoon of 1 May, when *Conqueror* signalled its first contact with the cruiser back to Fleet Headquarters. Attention was focused instead on the *25 De Mayo*. A careful scrutiny of the timing of events substantiates the argument that the cruiser could only have assumed the proportions of a major danger during the early hours and morning of 2 May, once Woodward had requested a change in the ROE and the matter had been discussed between Fieldhouse and Lewin. Clearly the only thing which had changed in the interim (saving some vital intelligence report which has not been leaked) did not relate especially to the *Belgrano*. This discussion was concerned instead with British reactions to the status of the conflict in the South Atlantic, following the engagements of the previous day, and the assumption that they would continue in one form or another from there on.[77]

Timing alone is not the only important consideration here. Both sides were now running very considerable risks around the Falklands and it is commonplace in the analysis of crises to observe how the speed and unpredictability of events influences the judgment of decision-makers. The pressures involved subject individuals to enormous stress and elicit familiar patterns of behaviour to which British decision-makers were no exception. Worst-case assumptions, stereotyping of the opponent, simplified models of the situation and resistance to changing established assumptions, all tend to prevail over the quite unrealistic ideal of the rational and infinitely responsive control over events which figure in decision-making models. Such rules of thumb are employed to select information, so helping decision-makers to decide on an appropriate course of action, despite the typical crisis problems of information-overload and uncertainty.

The Chief of Defence Staff maintains that the first he knew of the contact was when he arrived at Fleet Headquarters, about 09.15 (BST) on 2 May, to be briefed on the latest intelligence reports before attending the War Cabinet meeting scheduled for later that day.[78] Fleet Headquarters, it seems, also failed to inform Lewin that Argentina's Fleet Command had ordered the tactical withdrawal of TF 79 at 00.07 BST (2 May), confirming the order at 05.19 BST.[79] There seems to be little doubt that Argentine signals were being intercepted and decoded by GCHQ, although the Commons Foreign Affairs Committee has pointed out that it was by no means clear whether 'the signals referred to in the media [00.07 and 05.19] were the only orders issued to the various Argentine naval task groups between 30 April and 2 May 1982'.[80]

The report has also hinted darkly that perhaps 'other signals, with quite different purport' might have been intercepted and decoded by 'UK authorities'.[81] It backed these points by concluding that

such intelligence as we have seen actually strengthens the view taken by the British Government of the nature of the threat posed by the *Belgrano*, and we can only therefore commend the Government for its restraint in refusing to disclose it.[82]

Those on the Committee who drew up a minority report, however, were less impressed with what they had seen. As the additional evidence available to the Committee has not been made public, all we have to go on are the assurances of the majority report and the conflicting judgements and unallayed suspicions of the minority report. Even allowing for the political biases involved, many of the discrepancies and disparities cannot be evaluated with very much confidence. Consequently, there is not only an important unresolved dispute about whether the withdrawal signals were decoded and passed along the chain of command from GCHQ through Northwood and on to Lewin and the War Cabinet. In addition, there is a disagreement about whether the recall orders applied to the

Belgrano group, whether the units of TF 79 had been withdrawn to port or merely to a safe military distance from the Carrier Group's ships, and whether the British had other grounds than those which have so far been disclosed for believing that the cruiser now presented a more serious threat than it had 24 hours previously. Although Argentine confirmation of the withdrawal was issued at 05.19 (BST) the *Belgrano* continued on its easterly heading until about 09.00, at which point (virtually the same time as Lewin arrived at Fleet Headquarters for the morning briefing) she reversed course back towards the mainland.[83] Gavshon and Rice claim that the cruiser was included in the recall signals, but more recent reports in British newspapers and elsewhere argue that the orders did not apply to the *Belgrano* because the vessel had not been involved in the earlier instructions to attack the British Carrier Group.[84] On the basis of Argentine accounts, however, it seems evident that the *Belgrano* was a passive rather than an active component of TF 79, that it was recalled like other units of the Argentine Fleet and that the withdrawal was a tactical military manoeuvre rather than a political gesture.[85]

Whatever the status of the Southern Group of Task Force 79, official statements in Britain have repeatedly and consistently maintained that

> at the time of the decision to sink the *Belgrano* neither Ministers nor their senior military advisers were aware of any Argentine orders to withdraw their fleet, whether or not those orders applied to the *Belgrano* and her escorts.[86]

Nonetheless, news reports in the *Guardian* and the *Observer* have directly contradicted these assurances and claim that the contents of the intercepts of 1 and 2 May were decoded speedily 'and transmitted immediately by telex to Northwood and to the Prime Minister's office at Chequers'.[87] A question mark, therefore, still hangs over the transmission of intelligence information.

Woodward's request for a change in the Rules of Engagement was signalled to Northwood 'early in the morning of May 2nd . . . in time to be considered at the regular morning Chiefs of Staff meeting . . . .'.[88] It seems very likely that this request was related to a second signal which was received from *Conqueror* at 05.00 BST (2 May), reporting the *Belgrano*'s position, speed and course (due east at 090°).[89] Endorsed by Fieldhouse, Woodward's submission was presented to Lewin when he arrived at Fleet Headquarters. There the general situation seems to have been discussed in some detail, with attention focused on two particular dangers. First, as Lewin explained,

> we appreciated that there would be a co-ordinated attack by carrier aircraft, by the ships in the north, by shore-based aircraft, perhaps by submarines. As part of this co-ordinated attack, with some of our ships hit and damaged and maybe sunk, the *Belgrano* with her two escorts, armed with Exocet, was a very significant threat.[90]

Here again it was the general threat which the *Belgrano* posed, in conjunction with other attacks, that seemed to be the reason for making her a legitimate target for *Conqueror*. Second, Lewin reports that the possibility that the *Belgrano* might have been 'going across again to recapture South Georgia' was also discussed.[91] Given these considerations, 'coupled with all the circumstances' of the day before, he decided to seek a general extension of the Rules of Engagement from the War Cabinet.[92] According to a Ministry of Defence memorandum, Fleet Headquarters sent a signal to *Conqueror* at 10.15 BST (just as Lewin was about to leave Northwood for the War Cabinet meeting at Chequers) instructing her commander not to attack the *Belgrano* 'until allowed by ROEs'.[93] This strongly suggests that the SSN was being put on standby to receive new orders and Rules of Engagement later that day. If that was the case there can be little grounds for suggesting, as some of the War Cabinet's critics have done, that the submarine's commander may have queried the wisdom and 'legality' of the order to attack the *Belgrano* when it was first issued shortly after midday.[94]

Unlike almost all other ROE decisions this final revision was not considered by the 'Mandarins' Committee'. Neither was it considered by the full War Cabinet in formal session. According to the minority report of the Foreign Affairs Committee's inquiry into the *Belgrano* affair, it was considered at 'an informal gathering before lunch of some of those summoned to the War Cabinet meeting'.[95] By all accounts the discussion was short. Woodward believed that the decision 'was achieved in remarkably short order, reputedly in the entrance porch at Chequers'.[96] Ponting records that it probably took 'no more than twenty minutes' and that Sir Anthony Acland, Permanent Secretary at the Foreign Office, telephoned Washington to relay the news to Pym while Lewin telephoned Fleet Headquarters.[97] The order to sink the *Belgrano* was sent to Northwood before the War Cabinet was formally convened later that afternoon.[98]

If the speed of the decision suggests that there was a genuine sense of urgency about the need to attack the cruiser, it implies even more strongly that the War Cabinet was by now well prepared not just to eliminate individual threats to the Carrier Group but to widen the conflict. The considerations taken into account could not, therefore, have been confined to the Argentine ship. They must have included a general appreciation of the status of the confrontation and the prospects for a negotiated settlement. In short, by making this change to the ROE the War Cabinet effectively accepted that it was at war with Argentina.

In a statement issued by the Ministry of Defence on 7 May, designed to clarify Britain's position and dispel the confusion and recrimination caused by the sinking of the Argentine ship outside the Exclusion Zone, the War Cabinet made clear that it had granted Woodward the freedom to attack any Argentine units which did not remain within 12 miles of the Argentine coast line:

> Her Majesty's Government warns that any Argentine warship or military aircraft which are found more than 12 nautical miles from the Argentine coast will be regarded as hostile and are liable to be dealt with accordingly.[99]

Northwood signalled the change in ROE to *Conqueror* at 13.30 (BST), but according to official accounts the message was not understood aboard the SSN because of problems with its radio equipment.[100] At 15.00 (BST) *Conqueror* signalled Northwood with a report of the *Belgrano's* position at 09.00 (BST), together with a statement of its current westerly course and position.[101] The cruiser had been sailing westward since mid-morning and was taking no anti-submarine measures. According to Ponting, the submarine's message was received and decoded by Fleet Headquarters without delay at 15.40 (BST).[102]

News of the change of course was not reported to the War Cabinet. In another illustration of the military and organisational imperatives which were at work in the crisis, Lewin explained that 'Ministers had taken a decision that the *Belgrano* was a threat to our forces and she could therefore be attacked . . . what happen[ed] to the *Belgrano* after that [was] operational'.[103] Only some radical change of circumstances affecting the general situation could have granted the ship a last-minute reprieve. The cruiser's fate had been sealed by the conclusion that war had broken out in the South Atlantic and it seem evident that nothing dramatic enough to bring about a change in that appreciation had actually taken place. On 2 May the Peruvian initiative and the disengagement of the Argentine fleet were tentative developments that had come too late to arrest the momentum of conflict.

At 18.00 (BST) on 2 May Northwood repeated its order to HMS *Conqueror*. This time the submarine successfully received and decoded the signal.[104] Two hours later (20.00 BST) it pressed home its attack, hitting its target with two Mark 8 torpedoes.[105] An hour or so after that the *Belgrano* rolled over and sank with the loss of 368 lives. At that point the cruiser had been sailing away from the British Carrier Group for about 11 hours. She was approximately 260 miles from the nearest units of the British Fleet, or about 14 hours sailing time at a cruising speed of 18 knots, and was steaming approximately 30 miles south of the Total Exclusion Zone.[106]

It is conceivable, as the minority report from the Commons *Belgrano* Committee observed, that if British 'plans and actions' had been confined to the engagements of 1 May 'they could have been represented as military actions in support of diplomatic pressure'.[107] The report further implied that such military pressure, combined with the United States declaration of support for the UK, might have persuaded Argentina's military leaders to reassess their policy and become more responsive to a 'further diplomatic approach'. Aside from the whole question of Argentine decision-making, this argument surely discounts the power of the military dynamics at work in the South Atlantic, the profound mistrust of Argentina's intentions which must have possessed British decision-makers, and the impact of crisis upon their decision-making, particularly during the extremely compressed time-scale of the specific events under discussion. It also makes unrealistic assumptions about the capacity of decision-makers to retain control over conflict in circumstances that displayed many of the classic dangers associated with the advanced stages of a military crisis.

John Nott, for example, recalled the pressure under which the War Cabinet was operating when he issued the following challenge to members of the Commons committee of inquiry:

If you or any other member of any political party or government had been in the position that we were in on the Sunday morning; had known that the Argentinians had claimed that morning that they had sunk our ships; had known that there had been a major attack on the Fleet the previous day, and had then failed to allow the submarine to attack the *Belgrano* (which we believed at that time to be closing in on the fleet), what would the history books have said of you, if in fact *Hermes* or one of the British ships had been sunk?[108]

In one sense it was immaterial whether or not British Ministers knew on 2 May that Argentine claims of British losses were false. Those claims could only have emphasised the risks which the War Cabinet was taking and intensified the anxiety to which it must have been subject.

Worst-case assumptions also seem to have been in operation in at least two ways: one specific and one general. According to official sources, Lewin's briefing on the morning of 2 May did not include any reference to a possible withdrawal of Argentine forces. Lewin implies that it was based instead upon information received when *Conqueror* first notified Fleet Headquarters at 15.00 (BST) on 1 May that it had positively identified the Southern Group of TF 79.[109] In a newspaper article and in evidence to the Commons Foreign Affairs Committee he further implied that the 'furthest-on circle' technique was applied to estimate the *Belgrano*'s position on the morning of 2 May. This technique requires a naval commander to assume that an enemy unit will be somewhere within a circle whose radius is the maximum speed multiplied by the elapsed time from its last known position. For safety's sake he has to assume also that the vessel is at the most dangerous point on that circle, the 'furthest-on point'. On the basis of such a calculation, 'the *Belgrano* would have been within hours' steaming of our Task Force. We had to make the worst assumption—you have to in war, you are very foolish if you do not.'[110]

More generally, the briefing on the morning of 2 May seems to have been based on intelligence assessments which had concluded that Argentina was likely to renew its offensive actions on the Sunday. Here we enter the difficult area of whether Argentine withdrawal signals had been intercepted and decoded by GCHQ and what construction was put upon them.

As we recorded earlier, Edward Rowlands, Junior Minister formerly in charge of Falklands affairs under Callaghan, revealed in the Commons emergency debate of 3 April that 'As well as trying to read the mind of the enemy we have been reading its telegrams for many years'.[111] From this and other revelations there seems to be little dispute about Britain's interception of Argentine radio traffic. Lewin effectively confirmed that at least one of the signals at issue (the 05.19 BST confirmation of Argentine withdrawal) was decoded by GCHQ when he recalled later that 'it was part of the intelligence material which was available on the 3rd but I could be wrong—it could have been the 4th'.[112]

According to his own evidence Lewin's pre-Cabinet briefing at Fleet Headquarters was based upon information that was '15 hours out of date',[113] suggesting that it was largely derived from *Conqueror*'s first report of its sighting of the *Belgrano* and any other data which may have been available at that time, although the SSN sent a further status report in the early hours of 2 May at 05.00 BST.[114] Besides claiming that Argentine signals were intercepted, some reports also maintain that they were sent directly to Fleet Headquarters, to Lewin and to the War Cabinet. One even claims that the MOD's own *Belgrano* inquiry subsequently failed to find any trace of the 05.19 Argentine signal intercept, which Lewin had said was included in the intelligence summaries available to him on 3–4 May.[115] The majority report of the Commons *Belgrano* Committee, which was otherwise sympathetic to the War Cabinet and endorsed its actions, accepted that the information upon which the decision to relax the ROE and sink the *Belgrano* was taken was not only out of date but 'maybe of an incomplete nature'.[116]

All these points raise important questions about the operation of British intelligence, the way it evaluated incoming data and how quickly its assessments and information were made available to senior decision-makers. We have no direct or reliable knowledge about how these matters worked but indirectly, on the basis of other evidence which is available, much that is familiar to decision analysts seems to have taken place.

First there are the problems of time, timing and communication to consider. It may seem extraordinary, for example, that Lewin could have been satisfied with a briefing that was '15 hours out of date', but it has to be stressed that *Conqueror* was not communicating at will with Fleet Headquarters.[117] Moreover, in the last signal (05.00 BST) known to have been received at Northwood before the CDS meeting at 9.15 a.m. on 2 May the SSN reported that the *Belgrano* was still sailing eastwards. If we assume that the CDS had no knowledge of Argentina's subsequent recall orders, this point serves to confirm Lewin's 'furthest-on' circle explanation of why the cruiser's position was deemed to be so dangerous.

Second, there are the usual problems of evaluation to take into account. Had reports of an Argentine withdrawal been available the 'hard data' from the submarine concerning the cruiser's last known

218

The Falklands, Politics and War

position, together with the many other uncertainties which would have surrounded the signal intercepts, could easily have outweighed the news. It is now almost 30 years since Herbert Simon first observed that decision-makers do not operate on the basis of full information and that they 'satisfice' instead. Since that time it has become equally well established that 'hard data' tends to drive out 'soft data' in decision calculations, and that decision-makers seek to avoid the 'cognitive dissonance' which conflicting information arouses. The impact of stress, information overload and other features of crisis on decision-making is also well documented.

Assuming, therefore, that GCHQ did intercept and decode Argentine naval orders, specifically the ones relating to the *Belgrano* group's mission (issued sometime between 29 April and 1 May) and the recall signals sent by the Argentine Fleet Commander in the early hours of 2 May, two standard sets of considerations could account for their failure to have had much of an impact upon British decision-making.

First, crisis does not reduce information; it exponentially increases the quantity and variety of it, thus testing to the limit the organisational processes through which it is received and assessed. Institutional inefficiency consequent upon the demands of crisis could conceivably have delayed the processing of Argentine intercepts in some way. The history of the conflict now abounds with rumours and reports of documents lost and signal intercepts pigeon-holed.[118] Neither is it hard to imagine that the increase in signals traffic would have created large backlogs of work, and placed an enormous premium upon the weighting and selection of material. From Lewin's account of what happened to the 05.19 Argentine recall signal, it seems as if GCHQ was approximately 24 hours behind in the processing and dissemination of at least some important signals traffic. And then, if Lewin's memory is to be relied upon, it merely stated: 'We believe that the Argentine forces have now been withdrawn to their mainland',[119] suggesting that many points had been condensed into a brief summary thought to be consistent with the needs of the Task Force Command.

Second, information overload compounds the problem of deciding upon what is important, something which in any event can only be done on the basis of judgement. As we have argued, judgement itself is informed by existing standards and expectations, which usually become more difficult to change under pressure. Without them the decision-maker is in danger of being immobilised by indecision. Indeed, had British decision-makers not effectively ignored the critical assumption that Argentina would escalate the Falklands dispute in the absence of sovereignty negotiations, they might not have descended into political immobility and found themselves in the predicament which they faced on 2 May. There can be little doubt that the British military authorities not only believed from intelligence reports that their opponent was determined to fight but also that this expectation had been forcefully confirmed on 1 May.

Despite the claims of some authors there is little evidence to sustain the argument that the recall of the Argentine fleet was a politically inspired move directly related to the imminence of a ceasefire proposal or a negotiated settlement. If Argentina's military leaders were beginning to have second thoughts by 2 May nothing had been resolved by the Junta even as the *Belgrano* was being sunk. British analysts would necessarily have treated conflicting reports of a tactical military withdrawal by units of the Argentine fleet with suspicion and mistrust. What if they were a feint designed to decoy British ships into more exposed positions? How did they relate to the wider intelligence picture? How dangerous would Woodward's position become if they were reversed as quickly as they had been issued? To what extent would the Carrier Group Commander be inhibited by the knowledge that Argentine naval units were in holding positions within a relatively short sailing time of the Exclusion Zone? What impact would that have upon the tight schedule of the whole campaign? Raising such questions (and doubtless others) it would have been safer to have assumed the worst and relied on existing assumptions until additional evidence justified a revision of what must have been the most sensitive aspects of military planning. Even though it was a critical item of information it would not have been surprising if news of an Argentine withdrawal had failed to have an immediate and radical impact on the military appreciations which were current at the time.

Opposition members on the Commons' *Belgrano* Committee have insisted that it is important to establish whether the War Cabinet's claim that the Argentine fleet was engaged in a 'pincer movement' 'was based on hard information or soft assumptions'.[120] They also criticised Fleet Headquarters for failing to make 'a clear distinction between information and assumption in intelligence appreciations'.[121] Inevitably the answer to their query has to be that the fear of a co-ordinated attack would have been based upon both considerations. Lewin is reported to have stated that, in addition to the information which was currently available, the estimation of the threat presented by the *Belgrano* was also based upon 'an assessment of what you would do if you were Argentina'.[122] To help the War Cabinet anticipate military and political developments a special intelligence unit was also reported to have been established at Northwood 'to forecast how Argentina would react in a variety of contingencies'.[123] None of this should cause much surprise either. It is common in crisis decision-making. What is more disturbing is that analysts and decision-makers should think that reactions to crises are not profoundly influenced by all these factors.

Nonetheless, despite these considerations, a military pause might have been established on 2–3 May through Argentina's fleet withdrawal if Woodward's Carrier Group had similarly retired to the east of the TEZ, out of range of Argentine ships and aircraft. This would also have coincided with some revival of the diplomatic process through Peruvian mediation. There is no knowing what might then have transpired. So much depends, for example, upon judgements about the Argentine Junta, its capacity to arrive at decisions and its willingness to settle for some compromise formula. These issues have not been addressed here but Argentine accounts raise serious questions about these matters as well. On the British side the outcome would also have depended upon whether Lewin was correct in judging that the War Cabinet would ultimately have found a Haig-type formula politically unacceptable. In the event the Junta was never shrewd, or capable, enough to put the matter to the test.

However, if it is reasonable to accept that the War Cabinet genuinely believed that the *Belgrano* was a direct threat to the Carrier Group, it is equally reasonable to ask why it did not order Woodward to withdraw. His retreat would have been covered not only by his own defences but also by HMS *Conqueror*, which remained in contact with the cruiser and was under orders to sink her if she penetrated the TEZ. Moreover, Lewin has confirmed that 'one thing we could be fairly sure of was that the *Conqueror* was still in contact because if she lost her she would have come up and reported'.[124] The answer must be that by then the War Cabinet was almost entirely in the grip of military logic.

CONCLUSION

Just as there is no knowing whether a settlement might have been negotiated along Peruvian lines had a military pause ensued on 2–3 May, so it is difficult to determine what Woodward would have lost in making a tactical retreat had he subsequently been ordered to return to the TEZ to complete his mission. What these points confirm, nonetheless, is that the sinking of the *Belgrano* was really a question of whether the War Cabinet was willing to lose the momentum of the British campaign, and trade the military initiative upon which its success was critically dependent, to gain some problematical improvement in the prospects for peace. The decision to extend the Rules of Engagement on 2 May, therefore, was a tribute to the momentum of conflict and to the Naval Staff's determination to seize the military initiative at the earliest opportunity, rather than an indication of the scale or the immediacy of the threat which the *Belgrano* posed.

To some extent that the Government's accusers have based their criticism upon unrealistic assumptions about the capacity for crisis management; and the Government itself aroused their suspicions by defending the War Cabinet's decision-making in terms of an ideal of 'rational' conduct which simply did not correspond to the evidence. Indeed, the term 'rational' has no meaning beyond those contained in its use; and its use in policy-making is almost always rhetorical. During the profound uncertainty of the invasion crisis, the claim to be making precisely rational responses formed part of the War Cabinet's rhetorical armoury. Through such means it legitimised its actions, mobilised support for them, and restored the Government's political authority. Using the cognates of 'rationality' prominent in the contemporary language of international security (particularly those related to the limited use of force, escalation management and coercive bargaining), together of course with extensive appeals to nationalism and other values which comprised Britain's political culture, the War Cabinet combined its diplomatic and military policies into an effective device for guiding the country successfully through the transition to armed conflict. In this way it maximised the chances of winning the war should diplomacy fail to find an acceptable formula for Argentine withdrawal. In part the Government took the same line in its initial defence of the attack on the *Belgrano*.

In each instance, however, the implausibility of its claim was manifest. Under a barrage of leaks and questioning this account of its actions was entirely discredited. In the process, a vast amount of evidence emerged which shed light not only upon the events of 1–2 May, but also upon many other features of War Cabinet decision-making. Many of those who took part were thus forced into giving a less superficial and inaccurate account of how they actually operated.

The resulting picture was far removed from the simplicities of rational management. Inevitably it was also more complicated and confusing, but by virtue of these factors it became more familiar and credible. Responding to the dynamics released by the invasion, the War Cabinet rode the tiger of conflict and kept its nerve as it quickly adapted to the dynamics involved. At the same time its luck also held. As Britain's tacit ultimatum expired, however, the War Cabinet's actions revealed that military expediency rather than political restraint determined its decisions.

This argument is best illustrated by a final reference to the evolution of the language of Exclusion Zones. On 7 April the War Cabinet had announced the introduction of a Maritime Exclusion Zone which was to come into effect on 12 April, and on 29 April the MEZ was extended to a Total Exclusion Zone. In each case the designation of the Zone was prompted by the arrival of British forces which were capable of giving some effect to the declaration. On 12 April it was the arrival of a nuclear submarine in Falkland's waters, and on 29 April it was the deployment of Woodward's Carrier Battle Group on the perimeter of the MEZ.[125] On both occasions the announcement of the Zone also deliberately exaggerated the degree of military control which those forces could expect to exercise over it. Enforcement of the MEZ largely relied upon the deterrent effect of the British SSNs, whose not inconsiderable impact was limited nevertheless to the surface units of the Argentine Navy. As Nott's successor at the Ministry of Defence has since explained, 'we could not enforce a more ambitious zone until we had an air capability.'[126]

When Woodward's force arrived the British were then able 'to do better with the interdiction of reinforcements', and the Total Exclusion Zone, as its new title implied, was extended 'to all ships and all aircraft, military or civil of any nation'. But, as Lewin repeatedly emphasised, the Carrier Group's limited air capability was a significant handicap and something much less than a total blockade was actually imposed when the TEZ was introduced:

> We had only 22 Harriers. They could not maintain a continuous air patrol over Stanley airfield. They were needed for the air defence of the Task Force at a later stage (if, indeed, it reached that stage), and they might later be needed for the ground support of forces who landed.[127]

We considered earlier how the introduction of the MEZ was

designed to serve a complex of military and political objectives. The TEZ simply followed suit at a later stage. However, although the introduction of each Zone was initiated by specific military developments and actually served particular military needs (such as designating a zone of operations and equipping the forces concerned with a political license to act), neither was especially suited to military purposes. Woodward complained, for example:

> Exclusion Zones may appear politically attractive to those who draw them as nice clean lines on maps and charts. They would seem to be the ideal tool in applying minimum military force to achieve a political aim. You can shoot inside, but not outside—it is all crystal clear. The problem is that it is not actually like that. In practical terms the boundary is not clear cut—it is very fuzzy and operating a 50-mile-across task group within a similar distance of that edge is a military nightmare.[128]

Consequently, the Zones were essentially a political and psychological device addressed to several different audiences simultaneously. Lewin made clear that they did not reflect any military preferences: 'I did not call it a Total Exclusion Zone, the War Cabinet did.'[129] Instead they formed part of the War Cabinet's dangerous and improvised rite of passage to war, by intimidating Argentina, reassuring the United Nations that the United Kingdom was respecting its international obligations, and satisfying the War Cabinet's various domestic audiences that the Government was reacting in a forceful but controlled manner. This latter point summarised the overall objective and the general impression which the announcement of the Zones was intended to convey. Force was being reconciled with restraint in a rational response to the invasion crisis. Ineluctably, however, just as the logic of conflict was to subordinate the War Cabinet's diplomacy to the requirements of its military response, so the language of Exclusion Zones was superseded by that of military necessity.

On 23 April the War Cabinet issued a public warning to Argentina that went far beyond the MEZ announcement and the existing Rules of Engagement for the British Task Force. It was not reconciled in any way with the MEZ and from then on, as the majority report from the *Belgrano* inquiry accepted, the purpose of the Exclusion Zones became 'unclear and ultimately misleading'.[130] Lewin explained, 'We applied the word "Total" because we wanted to put psychological significance to it. We meant that nothing must come inside this circle'.[131]

A natural corollary, despite Lewin's protestations to the contrary, was that although any Argentine unit which was inside the Zone was vulnerable, any which was outside was not. If Woodward believed that reference to Zones implied that 'you can shoot inside, but not outside' the *Belgrano*'s commanding officer can be forgiven for complaining:

> I thought that a Total Exclusion Zone must mean that if you were in it, then you get shot at. If you were not in it, you did not get shot at. But if you are going to be shot at in any case, then tell me, why have a Total Exclusion Zone at all?'[132]

Given the 23 April warning he may have been imprudent but he was not alone in being confused by the tacit rules of conflict which the War Cabinet had unsuccessfully tried to establish.

This confusion was only compounded by the introduction of the TEZ on 29 April. Woodward's later description of the ROE issued to the Carrier Group on 23 April, as simply a device to enable him to implement a 'cordon sanitaire' around his force, has made matters even worse.[133] Whereas the Maritime and Total Exclusion Zones were fixed and specific Woodward's 'cordon sanitaire' was neither. It followed wherever the Carrier Group went, extended as far as the operational range of its ships and aircraft, and was limited only by the vague reference to the Task Force's 'mission' contained in the 23 April warning. 'Cordon sanitaire' is, therefore, a misnomer. Instead Woodward was given a partial license to get on with the business of retaking the Islands. This confusion and uncertainty extended to the War Cabinet itself. '[it] is now clear', the majority report of the *Belgrano* inquiry has conceded, '*that there was, at the very least, considerable doubt amongst Ministers as to whether the 23 April warning was fully understood in those terms in Argentina or elsewhere in the world*'.[134] [Emphasis added]

On 30 April, during the War Cabinet discussions about whether to change the ROE to allow an attack on the *25 De Mayo* outside the TEZ, the Foreign Secretary argued strongly for a further and much more specific public warning to Argentina. Without dissenting from the decision to sanction the attack, and after discussions with the Attorney-General about 'the way in which our action would have to be publicly justified and its legality defended', he drafted a minute to the War Cabinet as he left for Washington on 1 May.[135] The covering letter apparently stated:

I attach a draft of a possible warning message which we could ask the Swiss to convey urgently to the Argentine Government. This in no way alters the substance of the decision we took yesterday. But I believe it would greatly strengthen our hand in dealing with criticism at home and abroad once an attack on the carrier had been carried out.[136]

The issue was whether the carrier should be warned to stay within a narrow zone that would confine it to 'territorial waters south of about 41 degrees south'. The minute itself was supposed to have recommended that Argentina should be warned that

The *Veinticinco de Mayo* was not to move east of forty-five degrees longitude or south of thirty-eight degrees latitude or outside a limit of twelve miles from the coast of the mainland or north of forty-one degrees latitude.[137]

If it did, the carrier was to be sunk. The minute is also reported to have suggested a further extension of the warning:

if any attack anywhere in the South Atlantic is made upon British naval or air forces by an Argentine unit, all other Argentine naval units operating on the high seas, including the carrier *The 25th Of May*, will be considered, regardless of their location, hostile and are liable to be dealt with accordingly.[138]

The Secretary of Defence, the Chief of Defence Staff and presumably the Prime Minister herself all regarded the existing announcements as sufficient. Nott has since stated that the Law Officers 'in the Foreign Office and the Attorney-General' also advised that the 23 April warning covered the proposed change in the ROE.[139] He believed also that additional warnings, including that actually issued on 7 May, were totally unnecessary. Nevertheless, and not for the first time in the conduct of Falklands policy, the political advice of the Foreign Office was overruled by the Prime Minister and her Ministerial colleagues to their subsequent discomfort and discredit.

8 Conclusion

In practice war is either the rejection of politics or a sign of political failure, rather than the pursuit of politics by other means. Twentieth-century experience suggests also that peace and war should be regarded as two different worlds, each with its own dynamic: one governed by the logic of politics, accepting the diversity and problematical nature of human conduct; the other determined by the logic of conflict, demanding uniformity and conformity in the pursuit of interests that are given rather than questioned. Paradoxically, these worlds are not so much divorced from one another as correlated.[1] In peace we prepare for war, running the risk that the logic of conflict entailed in these preparations will become obsessional and displace the values of politics. In war we seek some form of peace, but run opposite risks. Peace-seeking, for example, always threatens to undermine a war effort. Or, we might seek a peace that is unattainable so turning conflict into a more or less permanent way of life. Alternatively, a peace achieved through war may prove unsatisfactory and impermanent, merely postponing further conflict. And so we cannot discount the renewal of hostilities in the South Atlantic following Britain's victory there in 1982.

It also takes at least two parties to fight a war and each of them may add its own distinctive contribution to the outbreak of the conflict. The Falklands War, in particular, resulted not only from a rejection of politics by Galtieri's Junta but also from a gross failure of political judgement and leadership by the Thatcher administration. A full account of the origins of the struggle in the South Atlantic, therefore, would have to take both sides into consideration. But only the British side has been examined here because interpretation of Argentine policy-making is beyond the author's expertise, and access to Argentine sources beyond the author's reach.

British officials and their Ministers, however, were fully aware of the dangers inherent in the Falklands dispute. They were regularly and carefully briefed about it, and were charged with maintaining peaceful relations with Argentina while some satisfactory solution was found. Avoidance of a military confrontation was their basic goal and it was also an attainable one. All the evidence suggests that the invasion of the Islands was the product of political mismanagement on both sides, and consequently the Junta's share of responsibility for the outbreak of the conflict does not exonerate British decision-makers. Neither does it provide any reason to disregard the confusion and political immobility which characterised British policy-making.

The advice which British Ministers received was by no means perfect. It was not able to specify precisely when the point of conflict would be reached, for example, although it accurately forecast when it was most likely to occur. Unfortunately it did not warn, either, that confrontation was likely sooner rather than later (or indeed that it was imminent by 1982), because it failed to appreciate the degree to which the dispute had become militarised in the 1970s. But advice is never perfect. In any event sufficient official concern was expressed, particularly between January and March 1982, to have merited, in the normal course of policy-making, a Cabinet-level review of the dispute. There was none and this final political omission sealed the fate of Britain's Falklands policy.

Official advice, in short, was as sound in basic conception as most policy advice is likely to be. It was consistent with foreign and defence policy goals and it sought to reconcile the conflicting interests concerned. In particular it sought to make provision for the Islanders' welfare in so far as this could be reconciled with British interest in a withdrawal from the South Atlantic. It offered specific proposals and identified the difficulties of defending the Islands, as well as specifying what forces would be required if they should have to be recaptured. Finally, it apprised Ministers of their options and warned them that failure to make diplomatic progress would end in conflict. And all this was done under appropriate Ministerial direction.

In Britain Ministers supervise their departments while the Prime Minister supervises the Government. Two sets of relationships play a decisive role here: those between Ministers and their professional advisers within the Departments of State, and those between Ministers and their political colleagues in the Cabinet. These in turn are subject to the powerful direction of the Prime Minister.

Just as Ministers have to range widely within their Departments to provide political impetus, direction, arbitration and co-ordination through the exercise of their political judgement and authority, so it is the Prime Minister who has to do the same for the Government as a whole. The Cabinet and the Departments are separate but intimately related centres of debate in which the discourse of policy-making concentrates upon recurring issues as well as new problems and emergencies. Here, power and persuasion are the weft and warp of the policy community's relationships. The pressure of routine business and the sheer variety of issues are important disincentives to fundamental policy reviews, but incremental change is nonetheless constant.[2]

Neither individual Ministers nor the Prime Minister can be expected to acquire an intimate technical knowledge of all aspects of Departmental business. Each is concerned instead with the arts of supervision, intervention and direction. Such leadership requires timing, political judgement, style and resolution. By and large these qualities are exercised in and through Government committees, where the political superintendents of the policy process can change the idiom of policy-making (as the 1980s has clearly demonstrated) as well as the course of specific issues.

There is, of course, no formula for success in Government, although committeeship is a valuable skill. Instead Ministers have access to the many 'texts' through which professional advice is made available, but they also have to draw upon their own individual talents and experience in dealing with these analyses.[3] It is the interplay and not the dichotomy between Minister and civil servant, therefore, which is critical in understanding the conduct of Departmental policy-making in Britain. And that interplay is shaped by the general style of a Government, as well as the talents of individual Ministers, as much as it is governed by constitutional convention or the bureaucratic culture of Whitehall Ministries. Similarly, it is the tenor of national politics as well as the interplay between Ministers, and in particular between Ministers and the Prime Minister, which is crucial in understanding the style of a Government. And, finally, it is the Prime Minister, 'the keystone of the Cabinet arch',[4] who is the central figure in national politics and policy-making providing for the Government as a whole what a Minister provides for a Department.

At the centre of British Government power and persuasion are, therefore, intimately related. Once again it is the interplay between the two which reflects the character of politics in the policy-making community. And persuasion, as a student of the United States Presidency once argued, 'deals in the coin of self-interest with men who have some freedom to reject what they find counterfeit'.[5] Political skills and political assets are thus vital aspects of the policy process. And what the Falklands episode illustrates in particular is that political reputation (the power to persuade as well as the persuasiveness of power) counts heavily in this interplay, because it is a staple currency in all the language games of policy-making.

All Ministers and Governments begin life with a stock of political capital, but they cannot simply hoard it. Their reputations are constantly earned and spent in the investments required to make decisions, set priorities, pursue policies, reconcile interests and manage prejudices; that is, in the conduct of politics itself. Carrington's actions especially, for example, showed that Ministers and Governments have to speculate with reputation not only to get their way, but also to accumulate that political capital they need in order to advance their political goals and ambitions. Like any currency, however, reputation is a scarce resource which requires careful husbandry. But in the final analysis reputation and its use is the product of other people's judgements, and such judgements are always made by reference to collective standards. Consequently, an individual's reputation reveals as much about the community in which he or she operates as it does about the individual themselves. That is why the politics of reputation, or 'the artifice of renown', as George Steiner would call it, are central to the politics of any community and why individual events which rely particularly upon individual judgement tell us so much about the politics of that community.[6] All these factors, then, were not merely conspicuous in the political management of Britain's Falklands policy; they were decisive.

Thus it was that the Ministerial and Cabinet politics of the first Thatcher administration, directly involving the Prime Minister and her Foreign Secretary, were ultimately to determine the fate of the Falklands between 1981 and 1982. Similarly the war itself was to reveal much about the character of Britain's domestic political culture and its international self-image in the 1980s. Indeed the entire Falklands affair was formative of the politics of the Thatcher Government and of the political leadership which was to become its central motif. But, just as this study maintains that individual judgement and its cognates (style, leadership and reputation) are integral to policy-making, so it also prompts serious reservations about the political judgement of the Conservative leader, and the reputation which she and her Government acquired as a consequence of military victory over Argentina.

Under Mrs Thatcher Falklands policy imploded into a political vacuum created by an absence of political leadership and Cabinet responsibility which was without precedent in the handling of the dispute. Thereafter, the reputation for political leadership which the Prime Minister won through her conduct of the Falklands War obscured the political indecision which contributed directly to its outbreak. Throughout the military campaign which followed the War

Cabinet was also driven by the logic of conflict as much as it was guided by any political direction.

The conduct of British policy during the three years leading up to the invasion of the Falklands raises more questions about the political judgement of the senior politicians responsible for policy, therefore, than it does about the adequacy of the routine processes of policy-making. It also arouses deep concern about the style of Cabinet politics under Mrs Thatcher; a concern that is by no means restricted to the mishandling of Falklands policy.[7] Between 1981 and 1982 there was quite clearly a basic failure of political control at the centre of British Government on an issue which was known to be dangerous and volatile. And that lack of political control contributed directly towards the outbreak of war.

As Britain's machinery of government was put to the test in the handling of the Falklands dispute, the role of political leadership and the consequences of political immobility, in addition to the routines of Whitehall decision-making, were clearly revealed. The seizure of the Islands then challenged the seriousness, and revealed some of the selectiveness, with which British decision-makers regarded the symbols and ideals of national and international politics (sovereignty, self-determination, the peaceful resolution of international disputes, and, above all, national potency, unity and credibility).

It was evident throughout that no material interests were at stake in the South Atlantic. Nor was the conflict part of a wider global or ideological struggle. Initially, at least, the issue was no great test of the resolve of any Alliance or of the position of any Alliance leader. Neither of the states directly involved was caught unaware by their disagreement, although one (the United Kingdom) was badly surprised by the speed with which the dispute became critical. It was a long-standing one in which the positions of both sides were well known and no struggle for national survival was entailed in it. There were, in addition, no other parties to the quarrel whose interference might have compounded the difficulties of resolving it. Conflicting historical claims to territorial sovereignty over islands of little if any intrinsic value to Britain or Argentina, and of no interest to any but these two states, remained isolated from superpower rivalries and unconnected with any important regional strategic balance, or with global strategic relationships.

The dispute was an apparently uncomplicated international disagreement between two otherwise friendly states, which historically have shared some mutual regard, transformed by military gamble and political misjudgement into crisis and war. It ought to have been resolvable, and yet it proved intractable. One might reasonably have thought also that even if no solution was immediately negotiable or foreseeable, a sense of proportion ought to have been sufficient to contain the disagreement below the threshold of violence. The causes of the Falklands conflict, therefore, are not to be found in any simple axioms of international behaviour but in the respective policy processes of the states involved, the political cultures in which they operated and the conduct of the political leaders who held office at the time.

For Britain, the Falklands dispute was never simply a legal or a military problem, although it was often analysed in terms of the language of sovereignty or of strategy. It was and remains a political problem concerned with the evolution of British interests and the management of those interests by Britain's foreign and defence policy-making community. In particular, after 1965, it became a problem of post-imperial politics. And the nature of the problem was exactly the same as that which faced British decision-makers throughout the country's imperial retreat: to reduce Britain's overseas commitments and accommodate its political perceptions to the changing pattern of British politics, and to the new realities of international power, in the interests of the general prosperity and security of the United Kingdom. If the Falklands dispute demonstrates how incomplete in certain respects that accommodation still is, it nonetheless also illustrates how much progress has been made since 1945, and how much more difficult that progress might have been.

In January 1981 the Thatcher government decided to abandon sovereignty negotiations with Argentina altogether. Although specifically warned, as other Prime Ministers and Cabinets had been, that the consequences would be military confrontation (including the danger of an invasion), neither Mrs Thatcher, nor the Foreign Secretary, nor the Secretary of State for Defence, authorised any measures to provide increased protection for the Islands. On the contrary, the Government indicated its continuing lack of concern in several ways and confirmed the run-down of Britain's commitment to the South Atlantic. This was not a matter of misperception, or of inadvertently sending the wrong signals, of the sort that has been well documented in the literature of international conflict. It was, instead, a clear instance of the failure of political leadership in the management of policy. As we have seen, there was little misunderstanding in Whitehall about the construction which Argentina was to place upon

British actions. But the political style of the Government and the nature of its Cabinet politics had induced a dangerous indifference to the consequences of the signals which were being sent.

A further diplomatic crisis in Anglo-Argentine relations was thus precipitated between January and March 1982, and this was also effectively ignored at Cabinet level. There was no crisis management, despite intelligence warnings and the mounting concern of officials, and the situation rapidly moved towards the predicted military confrontation. There can be little doubt that Britain's failure to respond directly to this final diplomatic crisis contributed to the descent into invasion and war. Equally, there is no doubt that the political immobility of the Prime Minister and the Foreign Secretary was primarily responsible for the failure to do so, despite certain deficiencies in the intelligence appreciations which were available to them.

With Argentina's seizure of the Islands, on 2 April 1982, Anglo-Argentine relations entered an entirely new phase. A British naval force was assembled and despatched to the South Atlantic and the passage of that Task Force then became an unacknowledged rite of passage to war. Like all rites of passage the *invasion crisis* which succeeded the diplomatic tension at the beginning of 1982 was a period full of ambiguity and contradiction. Efforts to preserve peace, therefore, were also designed to prepare the country for armed conflict.

Many have subsequently found this paradox hard to understand. Some have concluded instead that Britain's political leadership had conspired to cause the war, in an effort to redeem its domestic political fortunes. Others have argued that the British Government had no interest in a negotiated settlement once the Islands had been seized. The widespread confusion which characterised British decision making in the months prior to the invasion, however, disproves the first proposition. The second suggestion, though more plausible, takes little account, conversely, of the confusion of the invasion crisis itself. This is much more accurately represented by the idea of an ambiguous transitional stage between peace and war. Indeed, Victor Turner's conception of a social drama fits the Falklands conflict far better than any conspiracy theory or, indeed, many models of international relations.[8] For drama captures the essence of the interplay between structure and agency which seems to distinguish all decision making. Nor does the second charge account for the seriousness with which negotiations were pursued or the genuine difficulties which they faced.

In short, during the invasion crisis of April 1982, Britain's War Cabinet was not engaged in an exercise in crisis management, for its opportunity to do so had been squandered through the political immobility which had preceded the invasion. Argentina's attack had crossed the threshold of conflict and breached the peace. By despatching the Task Force, the War Cabinet had issued a tacit ultimatum designed to restore relations to something approaching their pre-invasion status. The duration of that ultimatum was determined by the progress of the Task Force, because Admiral Woodward's ships lacked the power and the time to operate as the flexible instrument of coercive bargaining conceived by crisis analysts. Dangerously under-strength, especially in terms of air defence, it was launched upon a 'one-shot operation' at the limits of logistical and operational endurance. Engaged in a military adventure rather than a carefully rehearsed military campaign, the margin between its victory or defeat was almost irresponsibly thin.[9]

British diplomacy was employed to specify the terms and conditions of the ultimatum, seeking an escape from war while simultaneously mobilising international support behind the War Cabinet. In confirmation of Britain's post-1945 strategic dependence upon the United States, these efforts focused upon Washington, because Washington's positive diplomatic and military assistance was indispensable. Whereas only United States' support could underwrite the risks entailed in the despatch of the Task Force, Washington's opposition would have ensured a Suez-like retreat or conceivably even the military defeat of the British forces.

At the same time, Britain's domestic political response to the invasion transformed the issue from a failure of post-imperial politics into an intense national drama. All the mythology and symbolism of Britain's defence culture, derived largely from the legend of inter-war appeasement and the Churchillian epic of the Second World War, was allied to the language and values of international order. In the process, the deep frustrations which accompanied Britain's long decline were excited into a remarkably unified and nationalistic determination to demonstrate Britain's continuing potency, and restore its sense of national credibility. Leading as well as profiting from this response, the War Cabinet rescued the Thatcher administration from its prewar failures. The final irony for Britain was that a war precipitated by political incompetence, driven also by military exigency and fought for political symbols in circumstances of no material interest to the country's circumstances, should now stand as a model for political leadership. For despite the inadequacies exposed during the run-up to the invasion, the political skills displayed during the conflict, combined with simple good fortune, enabled the War Cabinet to redeem the political reputation of the Government and its political leadership. Domestic politics, therefore, complemented the other processes by which the country was rallied for a war that was Thatcher's War in more senses than one.

Whatever Argentina makes of its failures in the South Atlantic the one thing that can prove more distorting than failure is success. This is the danger to which Britain's unconditional and decisive military victory in the Falklands War has been subject. Such distortion has taken a variety of forms, in addition to the inflated reputation which it earned for those whose political future depended upon the outcome of the conflict. Victory also obscured the origins of the War, idealised its conduct and exaggerated the relevance of the whole expedition to the United Kingdom's defence interests.[10] Moreover, by reducing the Falklands issue to a military question, albeit an extraordinarily expensive one, victory has disguised the fact that the Islands remain a major political problem for the United Kingdom. The single most important safeguard against the influence of such distortions, nonetheless, is the manifest irrelevance of the Falkland Islands to the security of the British Isles and the problems this poses for Britain's defence decision-makers. And at some point these issues will have to be addressed directly once again.

A product of the Prime Minister's political failure, the Falklands War became one of the foundations of her political success. Yet the cost was astonishingly high and the dispute with Argentina remains. In the final analysis the major political achievements of the conflict were to restore the political fortunes of the first Thatcher administration and reinforce those reactionary sentiments which have persistently obstructed Britain's post-imperial transformation.

The Falklands problem is not going to disappear and Britain's military victory has left the fundamental issues unresolved. None of the political rituals of peace-making have yet been used to heal the breach with Argentina, and there has been no formal cessation of hostilities. A permanent discord backed by military confrontation remains, and in these circumstances the threat of further conflict, though small, cannot be entirely discounted. The costs of the dispute cannot be justified, either, and the United Kingdom has still to find a way of disengaging militarily from the South Atlantic, because it has no defensible reason for staying there.

Those costs have now to be measured in terms also of the human, financial and political consequences of the Falklands campaign. The human cost can be calculated by reference to the number of dead and injured. Arithmetically the casualties were not high compared with other conflicts, but that hardly seems an adequate measure for such an avoidable war, not least in regard to those directly affected. Financially, including the losses incurred during the fighting and the price of Fortress Falklands, the expenditure was in excess of 5 billion (see Appendix, The Price of Victory). But even this figure is an underestimate and excludes many additional costs including, for example, the loss of trade with Argentina. Politically, the price has to be assessed in terms of all the additional difficulties of restarting the process of British disengagement.

What the Falklands conflict demonstrates above all is that foreign and defence policy-making cannot be understood as the pursuit of national interests as if these were given or axiomatic. Instead, the War shows that the managment of a state's external affairs takes place at the interface between its domestic and international environments. As a consequence, foreign and defence policy-making acts as an identity-defining activity imbued with political invention and ideology which determines, as well as reflects, the character of domestic politics. In other words, the Falklands conflict reaffirmed that political communities define and sustain themselves through their external as much as their internal relationships, and that they regularly do so by shaping the discussion of international issues through the operation of domestic politics. Questions of international relations and international security can never be divorced, therefore, from their domestic contexts because their outcome is critically dependent upon the nature of domestic political discourse. And that discourse is, of course, shaped by the subtle interplay between individual policy-makers, the economic, social and political structures within which they act, and the political vocabulary made available to them through their respective political cultures.

The Falklands dispute, for example, never lacked suitable peace formulas. The real difficulties were domestic and political rather than technical. In the first instance they concerned the reluctance of the Islanders and their sympathisers to accept that Britain's sovereignty over the Falklands was anachronistic and a quite absurd inversion of national priorities for a declining regional power. More generally the problems were rooted in a deep and widespread aversion to the decline of British power and a reluctance to accept its political consequences. Fortress Falklands has been the result but it makes neither political, strategic nor economic sense.

What is needed now is the statesmanship to translate military victory (and, for Buenos Aires, defeat) into a politically secure peace. For the moment Britain has the valuable advantage of a politically committed negotiating partner in the Alfonsin government. Thus a Falklands treaty that solves the sovereignty dispute, and by doing so helps to secure democratic politics in Argentina, would do more in the long term to stabilise relations in the South Atlantic and so secure a peaceful future for the Falkland Islanders, than a continuing military stand-off between the two countries. The War, therefore, changed everything, and yet it changed nothing.

Appendix: The Price of Victory

According to official estimates and public statements, the War itself cost £800 million, replacement of equipment lost during the campaign cost £1172 million and the total capital costs incurred since 1982 have amounted to £2005 million (Figure A.2). The additional postwar defence costs will amount to almost £3.6 billion over ten years (Figure A.1). A large amount of this expenditure has already been spent or committed, not only on the replacement of equipment but also on the building of a new strategic airfield at Mount Pleasant, 20 miles from Port Stanley, on the development of a military base, also at Mount Pleasant, to house the Islands' garrison, and on the related infrastructure facilities such as roads (almost non-existent outside the Islands' capital) and docks required for these developments (Figure A.1). But large capital expenditures remain outstanding together with the large running costs of the garrison. The postwar economic aid programme, including immediate rehabilitation and compensation of civilian losses and a six-year development plan, but excluding longer-term claims for compensation from the Islanders, totalled £51 million (Figure A.3).

By 1992, therefore, the total expenditure on the War, on Fortress Falklands and on the economic aid extended to the Islands since 1982 will amount to at least £4.5 billion (Figure A.4, 1983–84 average prices). But this figure is almost certainly a large underestimate of the final cost which for various reasons is likely to be well in excess of £5 billion.

The £4.5 billion figure, for example, excludes a number of additional items of expenditure for which figures are not currently available or are difficult to estimate. These include the increased rates of depreciation and the opportunity costs of aircraft, ships and other equipment deployed in the South Atlantic and in the maintenance of the air bridge to the Falklands. Reduction of running costs afforded by the new airport are estimated to be in the region of £25–£30 million per annum but these have to be set against the very high capital cost of its construction and the high level of running costs which are nevertheless projected for the future.

Royal Navy submarines, Frigates, Destroyers, Patrol Vessels, Royal Fleet Auxiliaries and ships taken up from trade (STUFT) are all engaged in the South Atlantic. Although the MOD claims that the meantime at sea and the usage of the ships operating off the Falklands will be of the same order as if the Falklands commitment did not exist, it has been reported that four Frigates/Destroyers are normally on station there. Despite the opening of the new airport on 12 May 1985, it has been estimated that in all a total of 15 naval vessels are involved in patrolling and keeping the Islands supplied. That means that the Frigate/Destroyer commitment alone represents about 10 per cent of Britain's operationally available Frigate/Destroyer strength.

Between 1982 and 1985 the RAF Hercules aircraft and air tankers operating the air bridge between Ascension and the Islands were flying at about 30 per

	1983-84	1984-85	1985-86	1986-87	1987-88	1988-89	1989-90	1990-91	1991-92	1992-93	TOTAL TEN YEAR DEFENCE COST
1. GARRISON COSTS	(b) 233.2	(b) 183.7	(b) 127.6	150	150	150	150	150	150	150	
2. INFRASTRUCTURE AND OTHER CAPITAL COSTS	(b) 190.8	(b) 150.3	(b) 104.4	(c) { 300 }	(c) { 150 }	(d) { 119.75 }	(d) { 119.75 }				
3. EQUIPMENT REPLACEMENT etc.	200	350	320								
TOTALS	624	684	552	450	300	269.75	269.75	150	150	150	3599.5

SOURCES:

(a) *Statement on the Defence Estimates 1983*, Cmnd 8951–1; *Statement on the Defence Estimates 1984*, Cmnd 9227–1; House of Commons Third Report from the Defence Committee. Session 1982–83, *The Future Defence of the Falkland Islands*, HC154, 1983; House of Commons Third Report from the Defence Committee. Session 1984–88, *Defence Commitments and Resources and The Defence Estimates 1985–6*, HC37-I–II–III. Annual running costs for the garrison were first given as between £175 million and £200 million, but the official figure is now £150 million (all figures average 1983–84 prices).

(b) The figures for cost categories 1 and 2 were calculated in the following way. The MOD explained to the Commons Defence Committee (*HC154*) that the combined figure for these categories in each of the years specified (1983–84, 1984–85, 1985–86) was £424 million, £334 million, and £232 million respectively. The capital cost was said to be about 45 per cent of these sums. That percentage has been applied here to give the figures in the able. [in *HC37-I*, p. xxxi, para. 81(f).]

(c) Estimate based upon subtraction of annual running costs from total figure given by the MOD in *HC37-I*, p. xxix.

(d) Estimate based upon dividing the sum outstanding from a total capital cost of £1980 million (*HC37-I*, p. xxix) equally between the following two years.

TABLE A.1 ... Additional Defence Costs 1983–84 to 1992–93[a]

REPLACEMENT OF EQUIPMENT		COST £ (m)
4 Type 22 Frigates (including costs of running on ships to maintain numbers during construction period)		705
Equipping and fitting of 4 Type 22 Frigates		132
Logistic landing ships		46
Aircraft (including: 12 PHANTOM F4Js; 5 CHINOOK Helicopters; 6 SEA KING ASW helicopters; and 7 SEA HARRIERS)		108
Weapons and ammunition stores (including 24 additional RAPIER fire units)		53
Other items (spares, support etc.)		128
	SUB-TOTAL	1172
NEW FALKLANDS AIRFIELD		240[b]
OTHER WORKS (including Ascension Island)		200[c]
NEW EQUIPMENT (including 6 wide-bodied TRI-STAR jets for tanker and transport roles)		265
OTHER ITEMS (spares, support etc.)		128
	TOTAL	2005

SOURCES:
(a) Average 1983–84 prices unless specified otherwise. Cost details taken from *HC37–I*, unless a different source is quoted. Details of weapon purchases are taken from *The Falklands Campaign: The Lessons*, Cmnd.8758, 1982.
(b) This figure is the revised July 1984 cost estimate given by the Property Services Agency which is the Department responsible for meeting the MOD's requirements for major works in the Falklands. It was reported and discussed in the National Audit Report by the Comptroller and Auditor General, *Property Services Agency: Defence Works in the Falkland Islands*, HC 31 (13 November 1984), p. 1, para. 2.
(c) This figure is taken from *HC37–I*, p. xxix. However, in an announcement on 21 September 1984 the Government revealed that an additional £119 million was to be spent to enable the Falklands Garrison to be concentrated at the airport site. It is not clear whether this £200 million figure refers to these new works or whether an extra £119 million should be added to the capital cost bill.

FIGURE A.2   *Falklands Expenditure: Capital Cost Breakdown*

ITEM	COSTS £ (m)
IMMEDIATE REHABILITATION AND COMPENSATION OF CIVILIAN LOSSES	15
POSTWAR SIX-YEAR DEVELOPMENT EXPENDITURE PLAN	31
ROAD CONSTRUCTION STANLEY-DARWIN	5
TOTAL	51

FIGURE A.3   *Falklands Expenditure: Economic Reconstruction Costs*

ITEM	COST £ (m)
WAR COSTS 1982-83	800
ECONOMIC RECONSTRUCTION	51
TEN-YEAR DEFENCE COST	
(a) CAPITAL COSTS	2005
(b) GARRISON RUNNING COSTS	1594.5
TOTAL	4450.5

(a) Average 1983–84 prices

Figure A.4   *Falklands Expenditure: Total Ten-Year Costing, 1982–1993*[a]

cent higher than normal rates, as were the RAF Sea King helicopters in operation in the South Atlantic. The composition of the Falklands garrison is officially described as one Infantry Battalion Group, together with supporting arms and services including Phantoms, Harriers, Hercules, Chinook and Sea King helicopters, and an RAF Regiment Rapier squadron. Unofficially the size of the garrison has been put at between 3–4000 men.

In addition, there is the cost associated with the retention of HMS *Invincible* (at £30 million per annum), which was scheduled to be sold to Australia before the War broke out, and of HMS *Fearless* and *Intrepid* (at £16 million per annum) which were scheduled to be scrapped. Together these items more than compensate for the fact that replacement equipment will last longer and is presumably of a higher quality than that destroyed in the War.

Above all the costs of the strategic base in the Falklands have already exceeded initial estimates, and neither the running costs nor the final construction costs can be fully determined.

The MOD estimated that once the strategic airfield at Mount Pleasant was completed and the level of forces on the Islands stabilised, the additional annual cost of maintaining the garrison, the Royal Navy and supporting shipping would be between £175 million and £200 million. Subsequently it has revised this figure without explanation down to £150 million. This lower cost has been used in Figure A.1 but there must be some doubt about its accuracy, particularly as the garrison is not likely to be operating on a care and maintenance basis until the end of the 1980s.[1]

Estimates for the new Falklands airport, in particular, are considerably understated. At the end of July 1982 Ministers decided in principle that a new airfield should be provided to meet the MOD's requirements 'for air defence, troop roulement and rapid reinforcement'. At first it was envisaged that the Army's Royal Engineers would undertake the construction, but in September 1983 the Government's Property Services Agency (PSA) was asked to assume responsibility for planning the works. The Mount Pleasant site was selected by the Royal Engineers in July 1982 but in November, after a detailed survey by a joint MOD/PSA team had produced an initial costing, Ministers asked for an alternative assessment based on the improvement of the existing airfield at Stanley. Further consideration was also given to the Royal Engineers reassuming responsibility for the task.

In January 1983, however, the assessment strongly recommended that the new airfield be constructed at Mount Pleasant by civil contractors rather than the Royal Engineers. Tenders put out in February confirmed that construction at Mount Pleasant 'would be cheaper, quicker and involve fewer risks than at Stanley', and Ministers approved this alternative on 20 June 1983. Construction began on 31 December and the airport became partially operational in May 1984. Additional work designed to allow it to cope with wide-bodied civilian airliners were completed in 1986. The National Audit Office reviewed the project in November 1984 and concluded:

> the final out turn on . . . contracts cannot be predicted confidently even during construction. Moreover, the airfield contract contains substantial elements of work for which only provisional sums have been included; shipping costs are subject to currency fluctuations; transport and catering costs will rise if the work force is increased; and any delays attributable to PSA or MOD could give rise to claims by the contractors. *The final cost of the airfield contract is therefore vulnerable to considerable risks.*[2] [Emphasis added]

A written answer to a Parliamentary question on 30 January 1985 revealed that the June 1983 estimate of £215 million was revised on 21 September 1984 to £250 million. A further increase to £260 million was also reported, together with new contracts to enable the garrison to be concentrated at Mount Pleasant, at a cost of an additional £119 million.[3]

The new strategic airport, therefore, is the centrepiece of a powerful strategic base whose estimated cost was revised upwards once more when the airport was priced at £276 million on 30 April 1985. The current total estimated cost for the Mount Pleasant complex now stands at £395 million (September 1984 prices. See Figure A.5).

ITEM	COST £ (m)
NEW AIRFIELD	276
NEW GARRISON FACILITIES	
Phase I	25
Phase II	94
TOTAL	395

FIGURE A.5 *Falklands Expenditure: Mount Pleasant Strategic Base 1985 Cost Estimates*

Fortress Falklands, therefore, cannot be viewed as anything other than an expensive diversion of financial and military resources, and political pressure for a settlement of the Falklands dispute is bound to be increased by these financial considerations. Nonetheless, British defence statements still declare that the 'limited forms of involvement' which the UK maintains overseas 'can represent some of the most economical and cost effective ways of protecting and advancing the United Kingdom's interests outside the NATO area'.[4] If there are any lessons to be learnt from the Falklands conflict, this is certainly not one of them.

Notes

1 A Post-Imperial Problem

1. For an excellent account of the early history of the dispute see Peter J. Beck, 'The Anglo-Argentine Dispute Over Title to the Falkland Islands: Changing British Perceptions on Sovereignty Since 1910', *Millenium Journal of International Studies*, Vol. 12, No. 1 (Spring 1983). For a general history of Anglo-Argentine relations see H. S. Ferns, *Britain and Argentina in the Nineteenth Century* (New York: Arno, 1977); see also his *Argentina* (London: Ernest Brown, 1969).

2. The Falklands invasion led to the publication of many accounts of the history of the sovereignty dispute. The official British version can be found in *The Falkland Islands. The Facts* (London: HMSO, 1982); and *The Disputed Islands. The Falklands Crisis. A History and a Background* (London: HMSO, 1982). See also Peter Calvert, *The Falklands' Crisis: the Rights and the Wrongs* (London: Frances Pinter, 1982), and his article, 'Sovereignty and the Falklands crisis', *International Affairs*, Vol. 59, No. 3 (Summer 1983). Calvert's analysis ought to be read in conjunction with Peter Beck's article. See in addition two other papers in the journal *Millenium* (Spring 1983), Jeffrey D. Myhre, 'Title to the Falklands-Malvinas Under International Law', and Alfredo Bruno Bologna, 'Argentinian Claims to the Malvinas Under International Law'. The classic historical analysis by Julius Goebel is critical of the British claim. See his *The Struggle for the Falkland Islands* (New Haven: Yale University Press, 1982). See, in addition, International Commission of Jurists, 'The Argentinian Claim to the Falkland Islands', *The Review*, No. 28 (June 1982); James Fawcett, 'Legal Aspects' in *The Falkland Islands Dispute International Dimensions* (London: Royal Institute of International Affairs, April 1982); J. C. J. Metford, 'Falklands or Malvinas?: The Background to the Dispute', *International Affairs*, Vol. 44, No. 3 (1968); and Adrian F. J. Hope, '*Sovereignty and Decolonization of the Malvinas (Falkland) Islands*', *Boston College International and Comparative Law Review*, Vol. 6, No. 2 (Boston: 1983). More recent but no less conflicting accounts can be found in the reports and evidence of the House of Commons Foreign Affairs Committee, which has reviewed Falklands policy since the War. Contrast, for example, the conclusions in 'Chairman's Draft Report on a Policy for the Falkland Islands', *HC 380* (May 1983) pp. XIX–XXVII, with *Fifth Report from the Foreign Affairs Committee Volume I Report*, HC 268–I, pp. XIV–XVII (October 1984). For further argument and evidence see Appendices 12 and 19 in *House of Commons Foreign Affairs Committee Session 1982–3 Falkland Islands*, HC 31–XV. Note: The Foreign Affairs Committee decided on 12 July 1982 to inquire into Falklands policy. It published its minutes of evidence as *House of Commons Papers 31–i to 31–XIV*, and its appendices in *HC 31–XV*. Because of the General Election of June 1983 the Committee was

unable to complete its consideration of the Chairman's draft report (see *HC 380*, May 1983). In the next Parliament the new committee took up the suggestion of its predecessor (given in a Special Report, *HC 378*, May 1983) that the investigation should be completed and a report produced. This led to the submission of *HC 268, Vols. I and II* (October 1984).

3. *Falkland Islands Review. A Report of A Committee of Privy Counsellors* (Chairman: the Rt Hon. The Lord Franks), (London: HMSO, January 1983) Cmnd. 8787, para. 22. Hereafter referred to as *Franks Report*.
4. Ibid.
5. Ibid., para. 23.
6. Mary Cawkell, *The Falkland Story 1592–1982* (London: Antony Nelson, 1983) pp. 61–2n. See also *Franks Report*, para. 25.
7. Ibid.
8. Ibid.
9. Ibid.
10. *Official Report*, House of Commons, 11 December 1968, cols 424–34.
11. *Franks Report*, para. 19.
12. Ibid., para. 26.
13. See Max Hastings and Simon Jenkins, *The Battle for the Falklands* (London: Pan, 1983) Chapter 2. Cawkell, *The Falkland Story*, Chapter 7. *Franks Report*, pp. 7–9.
14. Hastings and Jenkins, op. cit., especially pp. 39–40.
15. *Franks Report*, para. 30.
16. Ibid.
17. Ibid., para. 33.
18. Ibid., para. 34. See also, Lord Shackleton, *Economic Survey of the Falkland Islands* (London: Economist Intelligence Unit, 1976; hereafter referred to as *Shackleton I*). The second Shackleton report was *Falkland Islands. Economic Study 1982*, Cmnd 8653 (London: HMSO, September 1982; hereafter referred to as *Shackleton II*).
19. *Franks Report*, para. 58.
20. Ibid., para. 48.
21. Ibid., para. 49.
22. Ibid., para. 58.
23. Ibid., para. 60.
24. Ibid.
25. Ibid., para. 61.
26. Ibid.
27. Ibid., paras 67–9.
28. Ibid., para. 69.
29. Ibid., para. 32.
30. Such as 'Operation Condor'. See *Franks Report*, para. 21; Hastings and Jenkins, op. cit.; and Cawkell, *The Falkland Story*.
31. *Franks Report*, para. 31.
32. Ibid., paras 36–9.
33. Ibid., para. 42.
34. Ibid., and interviews.
35. *Franks Report*, para. 46.
36. Ibid., paras 44–5.

37. Ibid., para. 43.
38. Ibid., para. 47.
39. Ibid., para. 49.
40. Ibid., paras 52–7.
41. Ibid., para. 55.
42. Ibid.
43. Ibid.
44. Ibid., para. 59.
45. Ibid., para. 62.
46. Ibid., paras 63–6.
47. Ibid., para. 63.
48. Ibid., paras 64–6.
49. Ibid., para. 66.
50. Hastings and Jenkins, op. cit.; and interviews.
51. Hastings and Jenkins, op. cit., pp. 51–2.
52. *Franks Report*, para. 70.
53. On developments in British politics, and changes in the Conservative Party, which preceded Mrs Thatcher's election victory in 1979, see the following: R. Behrens, *The Conservative Party from Heath to Thatcher* (Aldershot: Saxon House, Gower, 1980); N. Bosanquet, *After the New Right* (London: Heinemann Educational Books, 1983); S. Hall (ed.), *The Politics of Thatcherism* (London: Lawrence and Wishart, 1983); P. Riddell, *The Thatcher Government* (Oxford: Martin Robertson, 1983); Robert Blake, *The Conservative Party From Peel to Thatcher* (London: Methuen, 1985); Philip Norton and Arthur Aughey, *Conservatives and Conservatism* (London: Temple Smith, 1981). Martin Holmes provides a survey of Thatcher's first administration in *The First Thatcher Government 1979–83. Contemporary Conservatism and Economic Change* (Brighton: Wheatsheaf Books, Harvester Press, 1985).

2 Ministerial and Cabinet Politics

1. *Franks Report*, para. 71.
2. Ibid., para. 72.
3. Ibid., para. 73.
4. Ibid.
5. Ibid., para. 74.
6. Ibid., paras 75–6.
7. Ibid.
8. Ibid., para. 74.
9. Ibid., para. 78.
10. Ibid. For the details of those terms of reference see para. 60.
11. Ibid., para. 79.
12. Ibid., para. 80.
13. Hastings and Jenkins, *Battle for the Falklands*, p. 54. See also Anthony Barnett, *Iron Brittania* (London: Allison and Busby, 1982) pp. 74–5.
14. *Official Report*, House of Commons, 2 December 1980, Cols 195–204.
15. The text of Ridley's statement and the subsequent exchanges is

reproduced in Anex F of *Franks Report*, pp. 101–5. See also Hastings and Jenkins, op. cit., p. 55, and Barnett, op. cit.

16. *Franks Report*, para. 82.
17. Ibid., paras 83–4.
18. Interviews. See also the discussion below in chapter 3, and the *Franks Report*, para. 90.
19. Peter Riddell, *The Thatcher Government*, Chapter Ten, 'Foreign Affairs and Defence'. See also *Financial Times* 6 April 1982.
20. Riddell, op. cit.
21. Debate still surrounds the issue of precisely when the Junta took its decision to invade. Franks deals with the immediate decision and concludes that 'the actual order to invade was probably not given until at least 31 March and possibly as late as 1 April' but overlooked evidence that planning began in December 1982, soon after Galtieri took over the Junta. For discussion of this issue see Lawrence Freedman, 'The Falklands War 1982', *Foreign Affairs* (autumn 1982), plus the review article by Freedman, 'British Falklands Literature' in *International Affairs*, Vol. 59, No. 3 (1982); and that by Walter Little in 'The Falklands Affair: A Review of the Literature', *Political Studies*, Vol. XXXII (1984). See also Juan Carlos Murguizur, 'The South Atlantic Conflict: an Argentinian Point of View', *International Defence Review* (2/1983) pp. 135–40.
22. *Franks Report*, paras 87, 90 and 91.
23. Ibid.
24. A standard feature of Islands politics which the Governor shared with many Islands councillors. See the discussion below in chapter 3. In addition, see the discussion of Islanders' views contained in *HC 380*, paras. 4.21–4.27; *HC 268–I*, pp. XLIV–LX; and the *Franks Report*, para. 92.
25. *Franks Report*, para. 93.
26. Ibid.
27. Ibid., para. 104.
28. Ibid. para. 100.
29. Ibid., paras 107, 133, 156, 187 and 225.
30. Ibid., paras 46, 48 and 61.
31. Ibid., Annex B 'Aspects of the Machinery of Government in Relation to the Falkland Islands', p. 93, para. 2.
32. Ibid., para. 292.
33. Ibid., para. 108.
34. Ibid., para. 109.
35. Ibid., paras 108, 110, 111 and 112.
36. Ibid., para. 106.
37. Ibid., para. 113.
38. Ibid., para. 291.
39. Ibid., para. 114.
40. Ibid., para. 115. A copy of the latter can be found in *House of Commons Foreign Affairs Committee Session 1982–83 Falkland Islands*, HC 31–XV, Appendix 10.
41. *Franks Report*, para. 116.
42. Ibid., para. 17.

43. See her answer to a question in the House of Commons on 9 February 1982, *Official Report*, Col. 856; and the discussion in the *Franks Report*, para. 117 and paras 285–8. See also the minority report in the *Third Report from the Foreign Affairs Committee Session 1984–85 Events Surrounding the Weekend of 1–2 May 1982*, 22 July 1985, HC 11, pp. LXXV–LXXVI. Callaghan persisted in challenging the decision to withdraw the ship, attacking Richard Luce in the House of Commons on the issue on 23 March 1982. See *The Times*, 24 March 1982.
44. *Franks Report*, para. 118.
45. Hastings and Jenkins, op. cit., p. 74.
46. Robert Jervis, *Perception and Misperception in International Relations* (Princeton: Princeton University Press, 1976) p. 194. See also Roberta Wohlstetter, *Pearl Harbor: Warning and Decision* (Stanford: Stanford University Press, 1962); and Robert Jervis, 'Hypotheses on Misperception', in J. Rosenau (ed.) *International Politics and Foreign Policy* (New York: The Free Press, 1969).
47. See below, Chapter 4.
48. *Franks Report*, para. 122.
49. Ibid., paras 123, 163 and 164. See also below, 'South Georgia'.
50. *Franks Report*, paras 124 and 125.
51. Ibid., para. 126.
52. Ibid., para. 128.
53. Chapter 1. See also Guillermo Makin, 'Argentine Approaches to the Falklands/Malvinas: was the resort to force foreseeable?', *International Affairs*, Vol. 59, No. 3 (1983).
54. Makin, op. cit., pp. 399–402. See also *Franks Report*, paras 129–32.
55. Ibid., para. 133.
56. Ibid., paras 326 and 328.
57. Ibid., para. 137.
58. Interview. The point is only intimated in the *Franks Report*, para. 298. See also Ned Lebow's discussion of the need for such indicators in his 'Miscalculation in the South Atlantic: The Origins of the Falkland War', *Journal of Strategic Studies*, Vol. 6, No. 1 (March 1983) p. 8.
59. *Franks Report*, para. 138.
60. Makin, op. cit., and *Franks Report*, para. 139.
61. Ibid., paras 142 and 144.
62. Ibid., para. 148.
63. Quoted in R. N. Lebow, 'Miscalculation in the South Atlantic: The Origins of the Falklands War', *Journal of Strategic Studies*, Vol. 6, No. 1. (March 1983) p. 14. See also the *Franks Report*, para. 329.
64. Ibid., para. 330.
65. Ibid., para. 152.
66. Ibid., para. 153.
67. Ibid., para. 155. Lord Carrington finally wrote to Mr Nott on 24 March, para. 189.
68. Ibid.: November 1975, para. 40; 8 and 22 January, para. 41; July 1976, para. 50; 31 January 1977, para. 55; February 1977, para. 59; 11 October and 1 November 1977, para. 63.
69. Ibid., paras 77, 94 and 230.

70. Ibid., para. 306.
71. Ibid., paras 94 and 95.
72. Ibid., para. 316.
73. Ibid.
74. Ibid., para. 313.
75. Lebow, op. cit., pp. 6–7. See also the *Franks Report*, paras 312 and 313.
76. Lebow, op. cit.
77. See below, chapter 4.
78. *Franks Report*, para. 150.
79. Ibid., para. 151.
80. Ibid., paras 317–19.
81. Ibid., paras 162, 165 and 169. For an Argentine account of the South Georgia affair, see Robert C. Scheina, 'The Malvinas Campaign', *United States Naval Institute Proceedings* (1983) reprinted in Appendix 6 to *HC 11*, 1984.
82. *Official Report*, House of Commons, 23 March 1982, col. 798: the occasion when Callaghan objected to existing plans to withdraw HMS *Endurance* from service. See also the *Franks Report*, paras 169, 177 and 322.
83. *Franks Report*, para. 184.
84. Ibid., paras 190 and 192.
85. Ibid., para. 187.
86. F. M. Cornford, *Microcosmographica Academica* (London: Bowes and Bowes, Ninth Impression, 1973) p. 16. See also William Wallace, 'The Franks Report', *International Affairs*, Vol. 59, No. 3 (1983).
87. *Franks Report*, paras 188 and 189.
88. Ibid., para. 193.
89. Makin, op. cit., p. 401.
90. Coral Bell, *The Conventions of Crisis* (London: Oxford University Press) p. 9.
91. *Franks Report*, paras 212, 213 and 235.
92. Julian Thompson, *No Picnic* (London: Secker and Warburg, 1985) p. 3.
93. *Franks Report*, paras 188, 204 and 225.
94. Hastings and Jenkins, op. cit., p. 373. See also the *Franks Report*, paras 234 and 240.

3 Falklands and Lobby Politics

1. In a sense this is one of the excused which the *Franks Report* advances: see especially paras 268–71 and para. 283. It similarly runs through much of the first-wave Falklands literature affecting in some degree even the excellent analysis provided by Hastings and Jenkins, *Battle for the Falklands*.
2. This is a refrain which is repeated in much of the Parliamentary evidence on Islands politics that has been assembled since the War. See, for example, *HC 380*, para. 4.21; and *HC 268–I*, pp. XLIV–LX.
3. *HC 268–I*, para. 52. See also the *Franks Report*, pp. 4–9.
4. That is not to say that political discourse would automatically have solved the Falklands dispute. Neither is it intended to imply that all political

problems are resolvable. It is merely intended to argue that as a political problem the dispute could not be handled in any other way and that the evidence supports the view that it was, in fact, capable of being resolved.

5. Interview. See also Cawkell, *The Falkland Story*.
6. See David Greenwood, 'Defence and National Priorities Since 1945', in J. Baylis (ed.), *British Defence Policy in a Changing World* (London: Croom Helm, 1977); and D. Greenwood and D. Hazel, *The Evolution of Britain's Defence Priorities, 1957–76* (Aberdeen Studies in Defence Economics (ASIDES), No. 9: University of Aberdeen Centre for Defence Studies, 1977–78).
7. Hastings and Jenkins, op. cit., p. 368.
8. Ibid., p. 368.
9. Ibid.
10. Ibid.
11. Cawkell, op. cit., is an especially good and typical example, but it was a theme of the Falklands lobby and other Falklands propagandists as well. Interviews, *Penguin News* (the Islands' newspaper), and *Falkland Islands Newsletter*, published by the Falkland Islands Association.
12. *Shackleton I*, 1976.
13. *HC 380*, para. 2.20.
14. *HC 268–I*, para. 22.
15. For the details of which see Cindy Cannizo (ed.), *The Gun Merchants: Politics and Policies of the Major Arms Suppliers* (New York: Pergammon Press, 1980); Andrew J. Pierre, *The Global Politics of Arms Sales* (Princeton: Princeton University Press, 1982); US Arms Control and Disarmament Agency, *World Military Expenditures and Arms Transfers, 1967–1976* (Washington DC: US Government Printing Office, 1978); and SIPRI, *The Arms Trade with the Third World* (Stockholm: Stockholm International Peace Research Institute, 1971).
16. Cawkell, op. cit.; Ian Strange, *Falkland Islands* (London: David and Charles, rev. ed., 1983); and especially evidence given to the House of Commons Foreign Affairs Committee, *HC 268–II*, Minutes of Evidence and Appendices.
17. *HC 380*, paras 4.21–4.27; *HC 268*, Vols. I and II, especially Vol. I, paras 121–3; Cawkell, op. cit. A very good illustration is provided in a copy of letter sent by an Islander to the House of Commons Foreign Affairs Committee, 11 January 1983. See *HC 31– XV*, Appendix 27, p. 491, especially the paragraph which discusses political representation and the economic interests of Coalite.
18. *HC 31–i*, Q. 31.
19. *HC 31–iv*, Q. 324.
20. *HC 31–XV*, Appendix 24, 'Memoranum by Mr L. Melchoinne, Department of Anthropology, Rutgers University, New Brunswick, NJ, USA', p. 485.
21. Ibid.
22. Ibid.
23. A summary of the observations of *Shackleton I* and *II*. See Also *HC 268–I*, paras 124–5.
24. *Shackleton II*, Section four, 'The Population, Social Aspects and

Immigration', para. 4.1. Shackleton's figures on the size of population differ marginally from those contained in *HC 268–I*, para. 117, for the same period because allowance was made for the 36 Royal Marines included in the previous census.

25. *Shackleton II*, para. 4.1.
26. *Shackleton II*, para. 4.2.3. Since this report the population trend has been reversed and there has been a small increase; see *HC 268–I*, para. 117.
27. *Shackleton II*, para. 4.1.
28. Ibid., para. 2.2.7.
29. Ibid., paras 3.3.1.– 3.3.3.
30. Ibid., para. 2.2.5. However, there has been some more progress towards diversifying land holdings since 1982. See, for example, *HC 268–I*, paras 140–2.
31. *Shackleton II*, para. 3.3.4. See also *Falklands/Malvinas: Whose Crisis?* (London: Latin American Bureau, 1982) Chapter 1.
32. *Falklands/Malvinas Crisis?*, p. 14.
33. Ibid., pp. 14–22. See also *Shackleton II*, paras 2.2.1.–2.2.8; and paras 3.3.1.– 3.3.4.
34. *Shackleton II*, para. 3.3.5.
35. Ibid.
36. Ibid., paras. 2.2.2.– 2.2.3.
37. *Falklands/Malvinas: Whose Crisis?*, pp. 17–18.
38. *Shackleton II*, para. 3.3.2.
39. *Falklands/Malvinas: Whose Crisis?*, pp. 14–22. Interviews.
40. *Shackleton II*, paras. 2.2.2.and 2.2.3.
41. *HC 268–I*, para. 51.
42. Ibid., para. 123.
43. Ibid.
44. Ibid.
45. *HC 31–VII*, Q. 696.
46. Ibid., Q. 717.
47. *The Sunday Times* Insight Team, *The Falklands War* (London: Sphere, 1982) pp. 42– 3.
48. Quoted in Barnett, *Iron Brittania*, p. 128.
49. *Shackleton I*, quoted in *Iron Brittania*, p. 128.
50. *Shackleton I*, quoted in *Iron Brittania*, pp. 128–9.
51. *Shackleton II*, paras 4.2.1.– 4.2.3.
52. Interviews.
53. Appendix 24, *HC 31–XV*.
54. Cawkell, *The Falkland Story*, p. 55.
55. Appendix 24, *HC 268–II*, p. 485.
56. *HC 380*, para. 4.21.
57. *HC 268–I*, para. 121.
58. *HC 31–XV*, p. 485.
59. Cawkell, op. cit., p. 82.
60. Hastings and Jenkins, op. cit., p. 65, and the evidence taken in the Falkland Islands by the House of Commons Foreign Affairs Committee during 1982–83, *HC 31–viii–xii*. See in particular the Governor's comments, Q. 778.

61. For details of the evolution of the Islands' Government see Strange, op. cit.; *HC 380*; *HC 268–I*; appendices 1, 5, 7 and 27 of *HC 31–XV*; and *Shackleton I*.
62. *HC 268–I*, paras 155– 62.
63. *HC 380*, paras 4.25 and 6.28.
64. *HC 268–I*, para. 158 and the Governor's reply to Q. 793 in *HC 31–VIII–XII*.
65. See Cawkell, op. cit. Interviews. The point about the Islanders' dissatisfaction with their own and the British Government is also made in *HC 268–I*, para. 159.
66. Cawkell, op. cit. Interviews.
67. *Shackleton I*, quoted in Barnett, *Iron Brittania*, p. 128.
68. Ibid., see also Appendix 27, *HC 31–XV*, p. 491.
69. Cawkell, op. cit., p. 86.
70. *HC 380*, paras 4.21–4.27.
71. See *Shackleton II*, which comments in particular on parallels with the Scottish islands, especially in para. 4.2.3.
72. *HC 31–VIII–XII*, paras 1540–2.
73. Ibid., para. 1542.
74. Hastings and Jenkins, op. cit., p. 55.
75. *HC 31–VIII–XII*, para. 1197.
76. Ibid., paras. 1543–5.
77. Ibid., para 912. More generally, see the evidence of the representatives of the Stanley Falkland Islands Committee, pp. 213–18.
78. Ibid., pp. 213–18.
79. Ibid., para. 1526.
80. Ibid., para. 1118.
81. See Hunt's comments, for example, in ibid., paras 772–4.
82. *Shackleton I* and *II* deals with these points in detail.
83. *Shackleton II*, pp. 95–7.
84. Antarctica is an increasingly important issue. For a discussion see *HC 380*, paras 6.30 and 6.31.
85. Self-determination is discussed in *HC 380*; *HC 268–I*; and in detail in *HC 31–VIII–XII*. And see, for example, the reply to the Foreign Affairs Committee from a leading Islander: 'We want to remain a colony or have something similar for the foreseeable future', *HC 31 VII–XII*, para. 980.
86. Interviews.
87. Interviews. See discussion below.
88. Interviews and evidence given in *HC 268–II*; see also Hastings and Jenkins, op. cit., p. 49 and *The Sunday Times* Insight Team, *The Falklands War*, pp. 45–6.
89. *HC 31–VII*, Q. 637.
90. Ibid., Q. 638.
91. *HC 31–VIII–XII*, especially pp. 213–18; Cawkell, op. cit., especially Hunter- Christie's introduction; and Interviews.
92. Hastings and Jenkins, op. cit., p. 49; *The Falklands War*, pp. 45–6; and *HC 31–XV* Appendix II, 'Further memorandum by the United Kingdom Falkland Islands Committee and the Falkland Islands Association'.
93. *HC 31–XV*, Appendix II, p. 436.

94. Ibid.
95. Ibid., p. 436; and *Falkland Islands Newsletter*, No. 12 (November 1982).
96. *Falkland Islands Newsletter*, No. 12 (November 1982).
97. Interviews.
98. Interviews and *HC 31–XV*, Appendix II, p. 436.
99. Interviews; and *Falkland Islands Newsletter*, No. 17 (November 1983).
100. Ibid.; and *HC 31–XV*, pp. 436–7.
101. Interviews.
102. Interviews.
103. *HC 31–VII*, Q. 621.
104. Interviews.
105. *Falklands Islands Newsletter*, No. 18 (February 1984) and No. 19 (May 1984).
106. *Falklands Islands Newsletter*, No. 17 (November 1983).
107. Interviews.
108. *HC 31–XV*, pp. 435–6.
109. Interviews; Hastings and Jenkins, op. cit., pp. 32–6; and Insight's *The Falklands War*.
110. Ibid., pp. 435–6.
111. Ibid., p. 437.
112. Ibid., p. 436.
113. Interviews; and Hastings and Jenkins, op. cit., p. 368.
114. Memorandum contained in *HC 31–XV*, Appendix II, p. 436.
115. Ibid.
116. Interviews.
117. Interviews.
118. See *HC 31–VII*, Q. 641–Q; especially Q. 646, where Sir John Barlow accepted precisely this definition.
119. Interviews. See also Hastings and Jenkins, op. cit.
120. Hastings and Jenkins, op. cit., pp. 32–6; and *HC 31–VII*.
121. *HC 31–VII*, Q. 625; and Hastings and Jenkins, op. cit., p. 45.
122. Interviews.
123. Hastings and Jenkins, op. cit., p. 49; and Joan Pearce, 'The Falkland Islands Negotiations 1965–82', in The Chatham House Special, *The Falkland Islands Dispute. International Dimensions* (London: Royal Institute of International Affairs, 1982) pp. 3–4.
124. Interviews; and see also *HC 31–VII*.
125. *HC 31–VII*, Q. 655.
126. Hunter-Christie in the introduction to Cawkell, op. cit.
127. *Official Report*, House of Commons, Col. 856 (9 February). See also the discussion in chapter 2.

4 The Structure of the Crisis

1. Thomas C. Schelling, *The Strategy of Conflict* (London: Oxford University Press, 1963); and *Arms and Influence* (New Haven: Yale University Press, 1966). O. Young, *The Politics of Force: bargaining during international crisis* (Princeton: Princeton University Press, 1968).

2. Charles Iklé, *How Nations Negotiate* (New York: Harper and Row, 1964); Roberta Wholstetter, *Pearl Harbor* (Stanford: Stanford University Press, 1962); Robert Jervis, *Perception and Misperception in International Relations* (Princeton: Princeton University Press, 1976).
3. See, for example, Herman Kahn, *On Escalation: Metaphors and Scenarios* (New York: Pall Mall 1965).
4. P. Williams, *Crisis Management* (London: Martin Robertson, 1976).
5. In a speech opening the debate in the House of Commons on 7 April; see *The Times*, 8 April 1982.
6. Mrs Thatcher in the debate on the eve of Britain's counter-invasion, *The Times*, 21 May 1982, p. 4.
7. *The Falklands Campaign: a Digest of Debates in the House of Commons, 2 April–15 June 1982* (London: HMSO, 1982) p. 146; hereafter cited as *Digest of Debates*.
8. Philip Williams, 'Miscalculation, Crisis Management and the Falklands', *World Today* (April 1983) pp. 144–9.
9. Ibid.
10. Ibid., p. 147.
11. For two studies of brinkmanship see R. N. Lebow, *Between Peace and War: The Nature of International Crisis* (London: Johns Hopkins University Press, 1981), especially pp. 61–82; and S. Maxwell, *Rationality in Deterrence* (London: International Institute for Strategic Studies, Adelphi Paper, No. 50, 1968).
12. Williams, *Crisis Management*, pp. 182–91.
13. Ibid., especially chapter 6.
14. Ibid.
15. Ibid.
16. Glenn Snyder, 'Crisis Bargaining' in C. F. Hermann (ed.), *International Crises: Insights from Behavioral Research* (New York: Free Press, 1972), p. 241.
17. Williams, *Crisis Management*.
18. R. N. Lebow, 'Miscalculation in the South Atlantic: The Origins of the Falkland War', p. 27.
19. Williams, op. cit.
20. *Digest of Debates*, p. 335.
21. Lebow, *Between Peace and War*, p. 57; and Lebow article.
22. Ibid.
23. Lebow, 'Miscalculation in the South Atlantic: The Origins of the Falklands War', p. 20.
24. Irving L. Janis and Leon Mann, *Decision Making: A Psychological Analysis of Conflict, Choice and Commitment* (New York: The Free Press, 1977). See also Lebow, *Between Peace and War*; and 'Miscalculation in the South Atlantic'.
25. See the discussion of these points and their application to British policy in Lebow, 'Miscalculation in the South Atlantic'.
26. Ibid., p. 17.
27. Ibid., pp. 13–14. For further details see Janice Stein, 'Intelligence and "Stupidity" Reconsidered: Estimation and Decision in Israel 1973', *Journal of Strategic Studies*, 3 (September 1980); and Avraham Shlaim,

'Failures in National Intelligence Estimates: The Case of the Yom Kippur War', *World Politics* (1976) pp. 348–80.

28. *The Times*, 6 April 1982; and Lebow, 'Miscalculation in the South Atlantic', p. 19.
29. *The Economist*, 19 June 1982, p. 44; and Lebow, 'Miscalculation in the South Atlantic', p. 19.
30. Lebow, 'Miscalculation in the South Atlantic', p. 19.
31. *HC II–iv*, para. 506.
32. See previous chapter, especially the discussion of the emergency meeting in the House of Commons on the evening of 31 March; see also the *Franks Report*, pp. 61–7.
33. See Hastings and Jenkins, op. cit., pp. 85–7.
34. *Franks Report*, para. 258.
35. Hastings and Jenkins, op. cit., p. 129. See also the general account of British mobilisation, pp. 102–19.
36. See below.
37. Williams, *Crisis Management*.
38. O. R. Cardosos, R. Kirschbaum and E. Van der Kooy, *Malvinas: La Trauma Secreta* (Buenos Aires: Sudamericana/Planeta, 11th edition, January 1984). Robert L. Scheira, 'The Malvinas Campaign', *United States Naval Institute Proceedings* (1983); and 'Where were those Argentine Subs?', *United States Naval Institute Proceedings* (1984).
39. Williams, *Crisis Management*, p. 153.
40. Holsti, op. cit., quoted in Williams, p. 13.
41. Quoted in *HC II*, para. 3.5, 'Minority Report'.
42. *HC II–v*, para. 582.
43. *HC 268–vi*, para. 377.
44. Sir Nicholas Henderson, 'America and the Falklands. Case Study in the Behaviour of an Ally', *The Economist* (12 November 1982), p. 53.
45. Ibid., p. 54.
46. Ibid.
47. The classical account is Arnold van Gennep, *The Rites of Passage* (Chicago: Chicago University Press, 1960).
48. *HC II*, para. 7.5, 'Majority Report'.
49. Lawrence Freedman in a review of the Gavshon and Rice book in the *Times Literary Supplement*, 9 March 1984, p. 244.
50. Ibid.
51. Freedman, letter, *Times Literary Supplement*, 6 April 1984. See also Freedman, 'The War of the Falkland Islands, 1982', pp. 208–10.
52. In a debate on 29 April, *Digest of Debates*, p. 147.
53. Williams, *Crisis Management*, provides an especially good analysis of the arguments and the literature.
54. See the evidence in *HC II–iv*, and especially Lewin's supplementary memorandum, 'Timing and the Falklands Crisis', p. 96.
55. Hasting and Jenkins, op. cit., p. 359.
56. Lewin, *HC II–iv*, p. 96.
57. Ibid.
58. Ibid.
59. Ibid.

60. Major-General Sir Jeremy Moore and Rear-Admiral Sir John Woodward, 'The Falklands Experience', *Royal United Services Institute Journal* (March 1983) p. 30.
61. Ibid., p. 27.
62. Ibid.
63. Ibid., p. 30.
64. Ibid., p. 29.
65. *HC II–iv*, p. 96.
66. Ibid.
67. Ibid.
68. The Prime Minister, 25 May, *Digest of Debates*, p. 315.
69. Hastings and Jenkins, op. cit., p. 129.
70. Schelling, *The Strategy of Conflict*, p. 22; Williams, *Crisis Decision Making*, p. 142.
71. In the fifth House of Commons debate on the Falklands, 13 May 1982, *Digest of Debates*, p. 268.
72. Ibid.; although on television he was claiming that the Task Force was capable of maintaining a long blockade, p. 140.
73. Woodward and Moore, op. cit., p. 28.
74. Apart from the crisis literature already cited see Colin Seymour-Ure, 'British "War Cabinets" in Limited Wars: Korea, Suez and the Falklands', unpublished paper presented to the European Consortium for Political Research Workshops (Freiburg, March 1983) which together with that of Hastings and Jenkins are the only two extended accounts of War Cabinet decision making during the War.
75. Hastings and Jenkins, op. cit., pp. 100–1, 128–9, and 372–3.
76. Seymour-Ure, op. cit.; and Hastings and Jenkins, op. cit.
77. Hastings and Jenkins, op. cit., p. 101.
78. Hastings and Jenkins, op. cit., pp. 128–9; and Seymour-Ure, op. cit.
79. Hastings and Jenkins, op. cit., p. 102.
80. Ibid., p. 128.
81. Ibid.
82. Ibid.; and Seymour-Ure, op. cit., pp. 19–21..
83. Woodward and Moore, op. cit.
84. *Digest of Debates*, p. 21.
85. See chapters 5 and 6.
86. See the fifth and sixth House of Commons debates on 29 April and 10 May, in particular *Digest of Debates*, pp. 143–81 and 274–305.
87. Ibid. See also chapter 6.
88. One of the principal arguments of the MP whose constant questioning helped to expose much of the *Belgrano* affair. See, for example, Tam Dalyell, *One Man's Falklands* (London: Cecil Woolf, 1982); and *Thatcher's Torpedo: The Sinking of the Belgrano* (London: Cecil Woolf, 1983).
89. Nevil Johnson, 'The British Political Tradition, A Review Article', *Political Studies*, Vol. XXXII (1984) pp. 471–73.
90. The MORI Polls were reported in *The Economist*, on 17 April, 25 April, 5 May and 29 May 1982. The Gallup Polls are taken from *The Gallup Political Index* (London: Gallup Organisation).

91. In particular the argument presented in Lucinda Broadbent *et al.*, *War and Peace News* (Milton Keynes: Open University Press, 1985, The Glasgow University Media Group).
92. On defence and public opinion in Britain see D. Capitanchik, 'Public Opinion and Popular Attitudes Towards Defence', in J. Baylis (ed.), *British Defence Policy in a Changing World*; and D. Capitanchik and R. C. Eichenberg, *Defence and Public Opinion* (London: Routledge for RIIA, Chatham House Paper No. 20, 1983).
93. Johnson, op. cit.
94. Ibid.
95. *House of Commons First Report from the Defence Committee Session 1982–83. The Handling of Press and Public Information During the Falklands Conflict*, HC 17, Volumes I and II; especially the evidence contained in Volume II. In addition see also Robert Fox, *Eyewitness Falklands* (London: Methuen, 1982); Robert Harris, *Gotcha! The Media, The Government and the Falklands Crisis* (London: Faber and Faber, 1983). Lucinda Broadbent, *et al.*, *War and Peace News*.
96. See in particular the hostile views expressed in *HC 17–II*.
97. *The Economist*, 17 April, 1982.
98. Ibid.
99. See below, Chapter 6.
100. *The Economist*, 24 April 1982.
101. *The Economist*, 5 May 1982.
102. Ibid.
103. *The Economist*, 29 May 1982.
104. See Harris, *Gotcha! The Media, the Government and the Falkland Crisis*.
105. *The Economist*, 17 April 1982.
106. Ibid., 29 May 1982.
107. Ibid.
108. *War and Peace News*, p. 141. See also the general discussion on public opinion, pp. 136–43.
109. Lebow, 'Miscalculation in the South Atlantic', p. 27.
110. See Figure 4.5.
111. For an analysis of the 1983 Election see D. Butler and D. Kavanagh, *The British General Election of 1983* (London: Macmillan, 1984).
112. See especially the reports of the Parliamentary debates in *Digest of Debates*.
113. See *Digest of Debates*; also 'Labour is not giving Tories blank cheque', *The Times*, 8 April 1982; and 'Foot ends bipartisan approach to Falklands', *Financial Times*, 28 April 1982.
114. *Financial Times*, 7 April 1982; *The Times*, 10 April 1982; Hastings and Jenkins, op. cit., p. 161; Barnett, *Iron Brittania*; Dalyell, *One Man's Falklands*.
115. Minimum use of force and reference to the United Nations were constant themes in the Labour leadership's response. See *Digest of Debates*.
116. *Digest of Debates*, see the extracts from 7 April, 14 April, 29 April and 20 May in particular.
117. See *Gotcha!*; and *HC 17–I* and *II* for details. See also W. Miller, *Testing the power of a media concensus: A Comparison of Scots and English*

Treatment of the Falklands Campaign (Glasgow: Strathclyde Papers on Government and Politics No. 17, University of Strathclyde, 1983).
118. Miller, op. cit.; and *HC 17–1*, para. 14.
119. *HC 17–1* and *HC 17–1*, para. 14.
120. *HC 17–I*, para. 41.
121. See the MOD's memorandum and its appendices which replied to these charges, *HC 17–II*, pp. 408–33.
122. *HC 17–I*, paras 88–101.
123. One of which has recently been published; see Valerie Adams, *The Media and the Falklands Campaign* (London: Macmillan, 1986).

5 War Cabinet Diplomacy

1. *Digest of Debates*, p. 5.
2. Ibid., p. 35.
3. *Digest of Debates*, p. 26.
4. Sir Anthony Parsons, 'The Falkland Crisis in the United Nations, 31 March–14 June 1982', *International Affairs*, Vol. 59, No. 2 (Spring 1983) p. 170. See also, Assembly of Western European Union Twenty-Eighth Ordinary Session (Second Part), *The Falkland Crisis* (Paris: Report submitted on behalf of the Committee on Defence Questions and Armaments, 8 November 1982) Document 935, Appendix 1(2), pp. 24–5; hereafter referred to as WEU, *The Falklands Crisis*.
5. Points noted in WEU, *The Falklands Crisis*, pp. 6–7.
6. Jozef Goldblat and Victor Millan, *The Falklands/Malvinas Conflict—A Spur to Arms Build-ups* (Stockholm: SIPRI, 1983). The OAS, however, did declare its support of Argentina's claim to the Falklands.
7. *HC 268–v*, para. 336.
8. Philip Windsor, 'Diplomatic Dimensions of the Falklands Crisis', *Millenium: Journal of International Studies*, Vol. 12, No. 1 (Spring 1983) p. 95.
9. *Digest of Debates*, pp. 10–11.
10. See, for example, the government's arguments in the first Falklands debate on 3 April 1982, *Digest of Debates*, 4–21.
11. See in particular Barnett, *Iron Brittania*; and Harris, *Gotcha! The Media, The Government and the Falklands Crisis*.
12. *Digest of Debates*, p. 70.
13. Windsor, op. cit. p. 96. The Foreign Office was a favourite target. Apart from the Commons debate on 3 April, see also the *Financial Times*, 8 April and Ronald Butt in *The Times*, also 8 April 1982.
14. Windsor, op. cit. See also Lebow, op. cit.
15. *The Economist*, 19 June 1982.
16. *Digest of Debates*, p. 63.
17. In a speech to the annual conference of the Scottish Conservatives a week before the San Carlos landings, quoted in Barnett, op. cit., p. 69.
18. The language of the War was permeated by Churchillian rhetoric. See, for example, the discussion in Barnett, *Iron Brittania*, as well as the *Digest of Debates*. And see also the leaders in *The Times*, whose editorial on 5 May, for example, read:

We defended Poland because we had given our word and because the spread of dictatorship had to be stopped . . . As in 1939, so today; the same principles apply to the Falklands. . . . But there is a more important dimension now. The Poles were Poles, the Falklanders are our people. . . . When British territory is invaded, it is not just an invasion of our land, but of our whole spirit. We are all Falklanders now.

19. The Prime Minister in the Commons 6 April 1982, *Digest of Debates*, p. 70. see also the Parliamentary debate on 3 April. In the vote taken in the House of Commons at the end of the debate on the eve of the British landings 33 MPs voted against the Government. *Official Report*, 20 May 1982, Cols 559–61.
20. 3 April 1982, *Digest of Debates*, p. 14.
21. See Dalyell, *One Man's Falklands*.
22. 3 April 1982, *Digest of Debates*, p. 17.
23. As Hastings and Jenkins argued, for example, in *Battle for the Falklands*.
24. 3 April 1982, *Digest of Debates*, p. 16.
25. 21 April 1982, *Digest of Debates*, p. 118.
26. See Denzil Dunnett, 'Self-Determination', *International Affairs*, Vol. 59, No. 3 (Summer 1983).
27. See in particular Hastings and Jenkins, op. cit.
28. Quoted in *HC II*, paras 3.21–3.22.
29. *HC 268–vi*, paras 390–1.
30. Pym, 21 April 1982, *Digest of Debates*, p. 116.
31. Duality of purpose is a theme well explored in the literature of international relations, particularly that section of it which deals with force and crisis. See, for example, Schelling, *Arms and Influence*, as well as *Strategy and Conflict*; Stanley Hoffman, *The State of War: Essays on the Theory and Practice of International Politics* (London: Pall Mall, 1965); and W. W. Kaufmann, 'Force and Foreign Policy', in W. W. Kaufmann (ed.) *Military Policy and National Security* (Princeton, New Jersey: Princeton University Press, 1956).
32. *Franks Report*, paras 142 and 157.
33. See Windsor's criticism of the US in 'Diplomatic Dimensions of the Falklands Crisis.'
34. Sir Nicholas Henderson, 'America and the Falklands. Case Study in the Behaviour of an Ally', *The Economist* (12 November 1983) p. 60. See also his evidence to the House of Commons Foreign Affairs Committee, *HC 268–iv*.
35. Anthony Nutting, *No End of a Lesson: The Story of Suez* (London: Constable, 1967); and David Carlton, *Anthony Eden: A Biography* London: Allen Lane, 1981) chapter XI.
36. *The Economist*, 'America and The Falklands. Case Study in the Behaviour of an Ally', p. 60.
37. Ibid., p. 53.
38. Alexander M. Haig Jr, *Caveat: Realism, Reagan and Foreign Policy* (London: Weidenfeld & Nicolson, 1984), chapter 13. See also *The Sunday Telegraph*, 1 April 1984; and Sir Nicholas Henderson, *HC 268–IV*, para. 257.

39. Henderson, *HC 268–iv*, para. 265. On the provision of US military aid to Britain both before and after the US 'tilt' of 30 April see 'America's Falklands War: A Relationship Sweet and Sour', *The Economist* (3 March 1984).
40. Henderson in *The Economist* (12 November 1983), p. 50.
41. Ibid., p. 53.
42. Henderson in *The Economist* (12 November 1983), and in *HC 268–iv*, para 266. See also Haig, op. cit.
43. Hastings and Jenkins, op. cit., p. 135.
44. Desmond Rice and Arthur Gavshon, *The Sinking of the BELGRANO* (London: Secker and Warburg, 1984) Appendix 3 (A): 'The Haig Memorandum of Agreement, 27 April 1983', pp. 189–92.
45. Ibid., para. 8.1.
46. Ibid.
47. Ibid., para. 7.
48. Ibid. See also Rice and Gavshon, op. cit., Appendix (B) 'Reply to the Haig Memorandum by the Argentine Foreign Minister, 29 April 1982', p. 193.
49. *HC II–iv*, para. 485.
50. 21 April 1982, *Digest of Debates*, p. 118.
51. Senate Resolution 382, 29 April 1982:

   Resolved: that the United States cannot stand neutral with regard to implementation of Security Council Resolution 502 and recognises the right of the United Kingdom and all other nations to the right of self-defence under the United Nations Charter, should therefore prepare, through consultations with Congress, to further all efforts pursuant to Security Council Resolution 502, to achieve full withdrawal of Argentine forces from the Falkland Islands.

   See *HC, 11*, p. xcii, para. 4.9.
52. Rice and Gavshon, op. cit., Appendix 4: 'The Haig 'tilt' Statement, 30 April 1982', pp. 195–7.
53. See *The Economist* (3 March 1984) for details.
54. Henderson's phrase; see his article in *The Economist* (12 November 1983) p. 60.
55. A theme which runs through the evidence given by Henderson and Sir Anthony Parsons, Britain's Permanent Representative to the United Nations, to the House of Commons Foreign Affairs Committee, *HC 268–iv* and *HC 268–v*, as well as their respective articles.
56. Interviews and *HC 268–iv*.
57. *HC 268–iv*, para. 268.
58. See John Baylis, *Anglo-American Defence Relations 1939–1980: The Special Relationship* (London: Macmillan, 1981); and G. M. Dillon, *Dependence and Deterrence* (Aldershot: Gower, 1983).
59. Hastings and Jenkins, op. cit., p. 136.
60. *The Economist*, 3 March 1984.
61. In newspaper reports and leaks too numerous to cite. For some of the main publications involved in the *Belgrano* affair see Rice and Gavshon, op. cit.; Tam Dalyell, *Thatcher's Torpedo*; and Clive Ponting, *The Right to Know* (London: Sphere, 1985).

62. Arthur Gavshon in evidence to the Commons Foreign Affairs Committee, *HC II–ii*, para. 216.

63. See Hastings and Jenkins, op. cit.: Sir Anthony Parsons, 'The Falklands Crisis in the United Nations'; and Parsons' evidence to the Foreign Affairs Committee, *HC 268–V*, April 1984.

64. Pym's evidence to the Foreign Affairs Committee, *HC 268–vi*, June 1984.

65. See below, chapter 6.

66. Although they did not escape much of the blame for ending negotiations with the sinking of the *Belgrano*. It is important to note, however, that just as discussions about a settlement continued after the recapture of South Georgia so they continued after the sinking of the *Belgrano*. Haig records that Costa Mendez had told him that Argentina would withdraw from negotiations should the British attack South Georgia and cancelled a planned meeting on receipt of the news of its recapture by the British. Shortly thereafter Argentina rejected Haig's proposals for an agreement. *HC II*, para. 7.15, 'Majority Report'. These issues are taken up again in chapter 6.

67. Pym, *HC 268–vi*, para. 384. Pym had been at the War Cabinet meeting on 30 April which extended the Rules of Engagement to allow a submarine attack on the Argentine aircraft carrier. See chapter 6.

68. The ROE change of 30 April only applied to the Argentine aircraft carrier. Those of 23 April, however, were concerned with allowing the Carrier Battle Group to take defensive measures, for example by intercepting Argentine reconnaissance aircraft monitoring its advance towards the Falklands. See Admiral Lewin's evidence, *HC II–iv*, para. 455, and chapter 6.

69. A copy of the warning was sent to the UN Secretary General on 24 April. The text of the statement can be found in, *HC II*, Appendix 5, p. 142 and a discussion about whether it was adequate or not can be found in the 'Majority Report', paras 6.12–6.15.

70. See Rich and Gavshon, op. cit., chapter 5; also Haig, *Caveat*, chapter 13, p. 293.

71. See Henderson, *HC 268–iv*; Parsons, *HC 268–v*; Pym, *HC 268–vi*; and Wallace, *HC II–iii*.

72. *HC II*, 'Majority Report', para. 2.9.

73. *HC 268–vi*, paras 380–3.

74. Ibid., para. 385.

75. Memorandum by the Foreign and Commonwealth Office to the Foreign Affairs Committee, *HC 268–viii*, pp. 119–20, para. 17. The time was given here as 22.15 GMT (Greenwich Mean Time). But as far as possible all times in this and the following chapter have been standardised on BST, which is GMT plus 1 hour.

76. Wallace's evidence can be found in *HC II–iii*. This quotation is from para. 306, but see in addition Baroness Young's answers explaining that Pym had given a routine instruction to diplomatic posts to brief their host Governments on what was going on at that stage, *HC 268–viii*, paras 636–8.

77. *HC II–iii*, paras 305 and 307.

78. *HC 268–viii*, paras 640–1.

79. *HC II–iii*, para. 309. See also the account of the timing given by Wallace, ibid., para. 309 and paras 325–7.

80. Ibid., para. 309. Again I have standardised the time to BST. Wallace gives it as 01.00 GMT.

81. These are considerations which the 'Minority Report' in *HC II* raises.

82. HC II, 'Majority Report', para. 5.14.

83. Dalyell, *Thatcher's Torpedo*.

84. Pym, *HC 268–vi*; and Henderson, *HC 268–iv*.

85. Quoted in O. R. Cardoso, R. Kirschbaum and E. Van der Kooy, *Malvinas: La Trama Secreta*, p. 224. See also *HC II*, Appendix II and p. XIII, n. 19.

86. Rice and Gavshon, op. cit., pp. 89–93 and p. 115. The last telephone conversation between Peru and Argentina took place 'on 2 May at midday'. The last one which the authors mention was at 10.00 a.m. Argentine time (13.00 GMT or 14.00 BST because Argentina was three hours behind GMT). See p. 89.

87. For Argentine accounts of the Junta's decision making see *Malvinas: La Trama Secreta*.

88. Rice and Gavshon, op. cit., p. 115.

89. See *Malvinas: La Trama Secreta*; see also Wallace *HC II-iii*, para. 393. For a contrary view see Rice and Gavshon, op. cit., especially p. 92.

90. Rice and Gavshon, op. cit., chapter 5.

91. See *HC II*, Appendix 2, which specifies the differences between the proposals of 1 and 2 May and those rejected by Argentina on 6 May, pp. 132–4.

92. Henderson, 'America and the Falklands. Case Study in the Behaviour of an Ally'; Parsons, 'The Falklands Crisis in the United Nations'; and the evidence which each gave to the Foreign Affairs Committee, *HC 268–iv* and *HC 268–v*, especially para. 344. See also Wallace, *HC II-iii*, para. 393; *Malvinas: La Trama Secreta*; and *HC II*, 'Majority Report' paras 5.31–5.35.

93. *Caveat*, p. 293.

94. *HC II*, Appendix 12, p. 177.

95. Rice and Gavshon, supplementary memorandum to the Foreign Affairs Committee *HC II*, p. 41.

96. 'There clearly was an inherent conflict between the protection of our own Task Force and the opportunities which might develop for further peaceful negotiations. That was always present, but in the last resort I saw my overriding duty, and indeed, the whole War Cabinet did unanimously, as being the protection of our Task Force.' *HC II-v*, para. 586.

97. Hastings and Jenkins, op. cit., pp. 194–7.

98. *Digest of Debates*, p. 219.

99. Ibid., pp. 219–20. The details of the British response can be found in *HC II*, Appendix 2, Annex A, p. 134.

100. Ibid., p. 222.

101. Ibid., p. 219.

102. See Rice and Gavshon, op. cit., pp. 123–6, for a fuller account of this telephone conversation.

103. Hastings and Jenkins, op. cit., p. 197.

104. The Argentine Commission of Inquiry was known as the Rattenbach Commission and for its conclusions see Rice and Gavshon op. cit., pp. 175–7. See also *Malvinas: La Trama Secreta*. Despite their general line of argument this view can also be read between the lines of Rice and Gavshon's account, *The Sinking of the BELGRANO*.
105. *Digest of Debates*, pp. 230, 241 and 274–305.
106. Ibid.
107. Parsons, *HC 268–v*, para. 354.
108. The terms were reviewed in detail by the Prime Minister in the Commons Debate on 20 May, *Digest of Debates*, pp. 275–9.
109. *HC 268–v*, para. 354. Thompson reports that he received the order on 12 May, *No Picnic*, p. 26.
110. For an analysis of the concept of 'dependency' and the South Atlantic Dependencies see Dr D. J. Murray, 'Dependencies in the South Atlantic Territories', memorandum submitted to the Foreign Affairs Committee, *HC 31–xv*, Appendix 30, pp. 494–6.
111. Rice and Gavshon, op. cit., pp. 125–6.
112. *Digest of Debates*, pp. 275–81.
113. Sir Geoffrey Vickers, *The Art of Judgement* (London: Methuen, 1965), for example; or Desmond Keeling, *Management in Government* (London: Allen and Unwin, 1972).
114. *Digest of Debates*, p. 325.
115. See Henderson, 'America and the Falklands. Case Study in the Behaviour of an Ally', p. 58.
116. WEU, *The Falklands Crisis*, p. 7.
117. Parson, 'The Falklands Crisis in the United Nations'; and *HC 268–v*, para. 350.
118. WEU, *The Falklands Crisis*, p. 7.
119. Ibid.

6   War Cabinet Military Policy

1. *Franks Report*, pp. 67–70. Hastings and Jenkins, *The Battle for the Falklands*, chapter 4, pp. 85–7.
2. See chapter 2, and *Franks Report*, pp. 12–13.
3. *Franks Report*, pp. 31–2. See, in addition, Lewin's response to the House of Commons Foreign Affairs Committee, *HC II–iv*, para. 444.
4. Hastings and Jenkins, op. cit., pp. 89–90.
5. *Franks Report*, para. 258.
6. *HC II–iv*, paras 442 and 457.
7. For some classic studies of civil military relations see S. Huntington, *Changing Patterns of Military Politics* (New York: Free Press, 1962); J. Van Doorn, (ed.), *Armed Forces and Society* (The Hague: Mouton, 1968); J. Van Doorn and G. Harries-Jenkins (eds) *The Military and the Problem of Legitimacy* (New York: Sage, 1976); and A. Perlmutter, *The Military and Politics in Modern Times* (New Haven: Yale University Press, 1977).
8. See especially Hastings and Jenkins, op. cit., pp. 85–90, 100–1 and 128–9.
9. Ibid.

10. Ibid., p. 86.
11. All accounts of the War emphasise the degree to which the British reaction was improvised as the Task Force sailed to the Falklands with reliance placed upon such publications as *Janes Fighting Ships*, as well as confidential sources, to supplement the scant knowledge of Argentine forces. In addition to Hastings and Jenkins, see also Woodward's account in which he admits, 'initially we knew little of the threat—our Intelligence effort is not normally focussed in that direction'. Woodward and Moore, 'The Falklands Experience', p. 25. See also Insight's *The Falklands War*; Robert Fox's *Eyewitness Falklands*; C. Dobson *et al.*, *The Falklands Conflict* (London: Coronet Books, 1982); Hugh Tinker, *A Message From The Falklands: The Life and Gallant Death of David Tinker, Lieut. R.N. From His Letters and Poems* (London: Junction Books, 1982).
12. See, for example, R. Eveleigh, *Peacekeeping in a Democratic Society: Lessons of Northern Ireland* (London: C. Hurst, 1978); and D. Hamill, *Pig In the Middle: the Army in Northern Ireland, 1969–84* (London: Methuen, 1985).
13. Hastings and Jenkins as well as Gavshon and Rice remark upon the close relationship which was formed between Thatcher and Lewin in particular; see, *The Battle for the Falklands*, pp. 128–9; and *The Sinking of the BELGRANO*, p. 100. Woodward also paid tribute to the level of domestic support in Woodward and Moore, op. cit., as did Thompson in *No Picnic* p. xviii.
14. *No Picnic*, p. 50.
15. These developments can be traced through F. A. Johnson, *Defence by Committee* (London: Oxford University Press, 1960); F. A. Johnson, *Defence by Ministry* (London: Duckworth, 1980); M. D. Hobkirk, *The Politics of Defence Budgeting* (London: Macmillan, 1983); M. Edmonds 'Central Organizations of Defence in Great Britain' in M. Edmonds (ed.) *Central Organizations of Defence* (London: Frances Pinter, 1985).
16. Lewin to the Foreign Affairs Committee, *HC II–iv*, para. 439.
17. Ibid.
18. See also the description of the command structure in Thompson, *No Picnic*, p. 17.
19. Hastings and Jenkins, op. cit., p. 129.
20. Lewin, *HC II–iv*, para. 441.
21. Michael Heseltine to the Foreign Affairs Committee, *HC II–i*, para. 136.
22. The texts of the British warnings may be found in *HC II*, Appendix 5.
23. See *Digest of Parliamentary Debates*.
24. Hastings and Jenkins, op. cit., p. 141.
25. See in particular Lewin's evidence *HC II–iv*; and Michael Heseltine, *HC II–i*.
26. Only an Enlightenment rationalist would maintain that it could or should be. See Raymond Aron, *Clausewitz, Philosopher of War* (London: Routledge and Kegan Paul, 1983); and Anatol Rapaport's introduction to the 1968 Penguin edition of Clausewitz's, *On War*.
27. M. Walzer, *Just and Unjust Wars* (New York: Basic Books, 1977), p. 36. See also the discussion in Ian Clark, *Limited Nuclear War* (Oxford: Martin Robertson, 1982).

28. Quoted in Hastings and Jenkins, op. cit., p. 145. See also *No Picnic*.
29. See Belaunde's conversation with Galtieri quoted in Rice and Gavshon, *The Sinking of the BELGRANO*, chapter 5. In addition see the Argentine accounts of the war, in particular Robert L. Scheina, 'The Malvinas Campaign', *United States Naval Institute Proceedings* (1983). Reprinted in *HC II*, Appendix 6.
30. Hastings and Jenkins, op. cit., p. 149. See also Lewin's evidence in *HC II–iv*.
31. Julian Thompson describes air superiority as 'one of the prerequisites for carrying out an amphibious operation', *No Picnic*, p. 23. See also Lewin *HC II–i*; and Woodward and Moore, 'The Falklands Experience'.
32. See especially the detailed account given in *No Picnic*, chapters 1–4.
33. Ibid.
34. Ibid.; see also, Woodward and Moore, op. cit.
35. This was evident from Lewin's insistence on the limited air strength of the Carrier Group and his account of the purpose of the Exclusion Zones, *HC II–iv*.
36. Detailed accounts of this period can be found in most of the initial descriptions of the campaign but the point is documented best in Woodward and Moore, op. cit.; Thompson, op. cit.; and Hastings and Jenkins, op. cit.
37. Woodward and Moore, op. cit., pp. 27–32.
38. Ibid., p. 25.
39. Ibid., p. 27.
40. Lewin, *HC II–iv*, 'Timing and the Falklands Crisis. Supplementary Memorandum by Admiral of the Fleet Lord Lewin', p. 96; hereafter referred to as 'Lewin Memorandum'.
41. *HC II–i*, 'Changes in the South Atlantic Rules of Engagement During Operation Corporate April–June 1982 (Fl 48) Memorandum by the Ministry of Defence', p. 1.
42. *HC II–i*, 'Changes in the South Atlantic Rules of Engagement During the Falklands Conflict (F1 90) Memorandum by the Ministry of Defence', p. 27. See also Lewin's evidence in *HC II–iv*, para. 465.
43. *HC II–i*, p. 27, para. 4.
44. *HC II–iv*, paras 462 and 465.
45. Woodward and Moore, op. cit., p. 28.
46. *HC II–i*, para 5.
47. *Digest of Debates*, p. 210.
48. *Digest of Debates*, p. 66.
49. Lewin, *HC II–iv*, para. 446.
50. Heseltine, *HC II–i*, para. 67.
51. Lewin, *HC II–iv*, para. 456.
52. Ibid., para. 446.
53. Heseltine, *HC II–i*, para. 67.
54. See Lewin, *HC II–iv*, paras 447-9. This discussion of the origins of the Zones also relies on R. P. Barston and P. W. Birnie, 'The Falkland Islands/Islas Malvinas conflict. A question of Zones', *Marine Policy* (January 1983).
55. Hastings and Jenkins, op. cit.

56. The account in this paragraph is drawn from Lewin, *HC II–iv*, para. 450.
57. Ibid., para. 446.
58. See, for example, Scheina, op. cit.
59. This chronology of events has been compiled from Hastings and Jenkins, op. cit.; Woodward and Moore, op. cit.; and Thompson, op. cit.
60. Thompson, op. cit., p. 26.
61. Ibid.
62. Woodward and Moore, op. cit., p. 29.
63. Ibid.
64. See especially Lewin, *HC II–iv*, paras 446 and 512 in particular; and Woodward and Moore, op. cit. The following account is based upon these two sources as well as Thompson, op. cit.
65. Woodward and Moore, op. cit., p. 28.
66. Hastings and Jenkins, op. cit., p. 141.
67. This is especially evident from Lewin, *HC II–iv*.
68. A list compiled from Lewin, *HC II–iv*; and from Woodward and Moore, op. cit.
69. Lewin, *HC II–iv*, para. 455.70. Ibid., para. 462.
70. The phrase was also used by John Nott, who confirmed that the carrier was the main preoccupation, *HC II–v*, para. 611.
71. See Scheina, op. cit.; and Juan Carlos Murguizur, 'The South Atlantic Conflict: An Argentinian Point of View', *International Defence Review, 2* (1983).
72. Hastings and Jenkins, op. cit., p. 71.
73. Woodward and Moore, op. cit., p. 28.
74. See Hastings and Jenkins, op. cit., p. 155 for a discussion of the press conference given by Woodward after the recapture of South Georgia; and Woodward in Woodward and Moore, op. cit., p. 28.
75. Woodward and Moore, op. cit., p. 25.
76. Ibid.
77. Thompson, op. cit., p. 27.
78. *HC II–i*, MOD Memorandum (F1 48)', p. 1.
79. See Thompson, op. cit., chapter 3.
80. Scheina, op. cit., in *HC II*, Appendix 6, p. 164. (All references to this article will be based on its reprint in the House of Commons Report).
81. Haig, *Caveat*, pp. 290–3. See also *HC II*, 'Majority Report', paras 7.14–7.17.
82. Rice and Gavshon, op. cit., especially chapter 5.
83. See especially his supplementary memorandum to *HC II–iv*.
84. Woodward and Moore, op. cit., pp. 27–28.
85. Hastings and Jenkins, op. cit., p. 150.
86. Woodward and Moore, op. cit., p. 28.
87. *HC II*, Minority Report, para. 3.23.
88. Quoted in *HC II*, Minority Report, para. 3.23.
89. The bulk of which can be found in *HC II*.

7 The Climax of the Conflict

1. The evidence is contained principally in *HC II–iv*, although Lewin's

personal account, which is given there, only serves to document in more careful and balanced detail the general impression given in such accounts as that by Hastings and Jenkins, op. cit.

2. There remains some dispute about whether HMS *Conqueror* also attacked the *Belgrano*'s escorts. The Minority Report of *HC II* maintain that the *Hipolito Bouchard* was hit by a torpedo which failed to explode. See para. 7.12.

3. For a discussion of the nuclear issues raised by the conflict see George H. Quester, *The Falklands and the Malvinas: Strategy and Arms Control* (Los Angeles: University of California Center for International and Strategic Affairs, ACIS Working Paper No. 46, May 1984).

4. Lewin, *HC II–iv*, para. 455.
5. For the texts see *HC II*, Appendix 6, pp. 142–3.
6. Lewin, *HC II–iv*, para. 455.
7. *HC II*, Minority Report, para. 3.28.
8. *HC II*, Appendix 6, para. 142.
9. See below.
10. Ponting, *The Right to Know*, p. 94.
11. *HC II–iv*
12. For the text of this warning see *HC*, Appendix 6, p. 144.
13. *Digest of Debates*, pp. 122–5.
14. Ibid., p. 129.
15. Ibid., p. 133.
16. Ibid., p. 137.
17. Ibid., pp. 143–81.
18. Ibid., p. 147.
19. In an interview with Gavshon and Rice reported in *HC II*, Minority Report, para. 3.42.
20. *HC II–iv*, para. 482.
21. Including John Nott apparently; see his evidence, *HC II–v*, para. 582.
22. *HC II–iv*, para. 484.
23. Ibid., para. 512.
24. Ibid., para. 479.
25. Including Woodward in Woodward and Moore, op. cit., p. 28, and John Nott in *HC II–v*, para. 620. Nott maintained, in response to questioning, that 'The change on the Sunday morning of May 2nd was a major change, yes'.
26. *HC II–iv*, para. 476.
27. *HC II–iv*, para. 462.
28. Ibid., para. 455.
29. Ibid.
30. Ibid., para. 462.
31. Rice and Gavshon, op. cit., pp. 66–7.
32. *HC II–iv*, para. 479.
33. Ibid., para. 487.
34. *HC II*, Appendix 17, 'House of Commons Foreign Affairs Committee. Events of the weekend of 1 & 2 May 1982. Memorandum by the Ministry of Defence', p. 184.
35. *Cmnd. 8758*, para. 109.

36. *HC II–iv*, para. 464.
37. *HC II–v*, para. 611.
38. *HC II–iv*, para. 477.
39. Ibid., para. 538.
40. *HC II*, Majority Report, para. 4.6.
41. *HC II–iv*, para. 515.
42. In an interview with a national newspaper, the *Daily Mirror*, later reported in Rice and Gavshon, op. cit., p. 100; and Ponting, op. cit., p. 86.
43. Woodward and Moore, op. cit., p. 28.
44. See also John Nott's evidence, *HC II–v*, para. 607.
45. *HC II–iv*, para. 511.
46. Ibid., para. 532.
47. Scheina, op. cit., p. 151.
48. Ibid.
49. Peter Greig (a pseudonym), 'Revelations', in *Granta*, No. 15 (Spring 1985), (Cambridge: Granta Publications Ltd., distributed by Penguin Books) p. 255.
50. This account of the day's engagement was compiled from Lewin, *HC II–iv*, especially para. 512; Scheina, op. cit.; and Murguizur, op. cit.
51. Greig, op. cit., p. 259; Ponting, op. cit., p. 83; and *HC II*, Minority Report, para. 6.2. All times have been standardised to British Summer Time (BST) as in the previous chapter.
52. Scheina, op. cit., p. 151.
53. Ibid., p. 152.
54. Greig, op. cit., p. 259; however, this source claims that intelligence assessments based on these intercepts wrongly concluded that the *Belgrano* formed an offensive part of Argentine strategy.
55. Scheina, op. cit., pp. 151–2.
56. O. R. Cardoso, R. Kirschbaum and E. Van de Kooy, *Malvinas: La Trama Secreta*, quoted in *HC II* Majority Report, para. 4.15. and Report, para. 6.2.
57. Scheina, op. cit., p. 152.
58. *La Trama Secreta*, quoted in *HC II* Majority Report, para. 4.15.
59. *HC II*, Minority Report, para. 6.2. See also Greig, op. cit., pp. 259–60.
60. Greig, op. cit., pp. 259–60; however, again this pseudonymous account claims that there was confusion over the receipt and interpretation of these interceptions.
61. Rice and Gavshon, op. cit., pp. 81 and 161. See also *HC II*, Majority Report, para. 4.15.
62. *La Trama Secreta*; and Scheina, op. cit.
63. Rice and Gavshon, op. cit., p. 71, quoting the diary of Lt. Sethia, an officer aboard HMS *Conqueror*.
64. Although official accounts first reported that *Conqueror* detected the *Belgrano* on 2 May, the Prime Minister revised the official line, in response to Opposition questions, in a letter to the Labour Party's Defence spokesman Denzil Davies. See *HC II*, Minority Report, paras 1.16–1.17.

65. Ponting, op. cit., p. 83; confirmed by *HC II*, MOD Memorandum, p. 184.
66. Ibid. The sighting and the signal from the SSN's confirmed by *HC II*.
67. Ponting, op. cit., p. 83.
68. See MOD Memorandum, *HC II*, p. 184.
69. Woodward and Moore, op. cit., p. 28.
70. Including, for example, the shallower waters of the Burdwood Bank referred to by Woodward which would have made *Conqueror* more vulnerable to detection by the *Belgrano*'s escorts. See Woodward and Moore, op. cit.,p. 28.
71. The *25 de Mayo* was not detected by the British and Woodward must have remained extremely concerned about its whereabouts.
72. MOD Memorandum, *HC II*, p. 184.
73. Lewin, *HC II–iv*, para. 543; Nott, *HC II–v*, paras 640–41; and Majority Report, para. 4.29.
74. Lewin, *HC II–iv*, para. 515.
75. Ibid.
76. *HC II*, p. 184.
77. Lewin's evidence is conclusive on this point, see *HC II–iv*, especially paras 501, 502, 511, 512, 513, 515, 534, 538 and 543.
78. Greig, op. cit., p. 260; Ponting, op. cit., p. 86; Lewin, *HC II–iv*, para. 511.
79. Always assuming that these signals had been intercepted. Lewin, *HC II–iv*, para. 511.
80. *HC II*, Majority Report, para. 4.24.
81. Ibid.
82. Ibid., para. 4.27.
83. *HC II*, Majority Report, para. 4.16.
84. *Guardian* (5 January 1985); *Observer* (6 January 1985); Greig, op. cit., p. 260.
85. See especially Scheina, op. cit.
86. *HC II*, Majority Report, para. 4.23.
87. See note 173 and *HC II*. Majority Report, para. 4.22.
88. Ponting, op. cit., p. 86.
89. MOD Memorandum, *HC II*, p. 184.
90. *HC II–iv*, para. 513.
91. Ibid.
92. Ibid., para. 543 and para. 511.
93. MOD Memorandum, *HC II*, p. 184.
94. Ponting, op. cit., pp. 87–8.
95. *HC II*, Minority Report, para. 5.28.
96. Woodward and Moore, op. cit., p. 28.
97. Ponting, op. cit., p. 87.
98. *HC II*, Minority Report, para. 5.28.
99. *HC II*, Appendix 5, para. 145.
100. *HC II*, Majority Report, para. 2.9; Ponting, op. cit., p. 87.
101. MOD Memorandum, *HC II*, p. 184.
102. Ponting, op. cit., p. 88.
103. Lewin, *HC II–iv*, para. 537.

104. Ponting, op. cit., p. 88; the MOD Memorandum *HC II*, p. 184, records that *Conqueror* signalled Northwood at 18.30 confirming receipt of the order and recording its 'intention to attack'.
105. *HC II*, Majority Report, para. 2.9. The MOD Memorandum records that *Conquerer* signalled its hit at 20.30 BST.
106. *HC II*, Majority Report, paras 2.9, 4.4 and 4.5; Minority Report, para. 7.9.
107. *HC II*, Minority Report, para. 5.6.
108. *HC II–v*, para. 631. See also para. 627.
109. *HC II–iv*, para. 544.
110. Ibid., para. 568.
111. House of Commons, *Official Report*, 3 April 1982, Vol. 21, Col. 650.
112. *HC II–iv*, para. 505.
113. Ibid., para. 568.
114. MOD Memorandum, *HC II*, p. 184.
115. Greig, op. cit., p. 260.
116. *HC II*, Majority Report, para. 4.18.
117. See Rice and Gavshon, op. cit. The submarine had damaged its radio aerial in a storm.
118. On the loss of submarine logs see Heseltine, *HC II–i*, para. 58.
119. *HC II–iv*, para. 505.
120. *HC II*, Minority Report, para. 6.4.
121. Ibid., para. 6.1.
122. Ibid., para. 6.4.
123. Ibid.
124. *HC II–iv*, para. 542.
125. Lewin, *HC II–iv*, paras 446-52; and Heseltine, *HC II–i*, paras 67–71.
126. Heseltine, *HC II–i*, para. 446.
127. Lewin, *HC II–iv*, para. 446.
128. Woodward and Moore, op. cit., p. 28.
129. Lewin, *HC II–iv*, para. 449. See also paras 456–7.
130. *HC II*, Majority Report, para. 6.20.
131. Lewin, *HC II–iv*, para. 447.
132. Quoted in *HC II*, Majority Report, para. 6.11.
133. Woodward and Moore, op. cit., p. 28.
134. *HC II*, Majority Report, para. 6.16.
135. See *HC II*, Majority Report, para. 6.17.
136. Greig, op. cit., p. 258.
137. Ibid.
138. Ibid.
139. Nott, *HC II–v*, paras 598–9.

8 Conclusion

1. Maurice Pearton, *The Knowledgeable State: Diplomacy, War and Technology since 1830* (London: Burnett Books, 1982).
2. On policy-making in the United Kingdom see, for example, Richard Rose (ed.) *The Dynamics of Public Policy: A Comparative Analysis* (London:

Sage, 1976); Martin Burch and Bruce Wood, *Public Policy in Britain* (Oxford: Martin Robertson, 1983); Martin Burch and Michael Clarke, *British Cabinet Politics* (Ormskirk, Lancs.: G. W. and A. Hesketh, 1980); and H. H. Heclo and A. Wildavsky, *The Private Government of Public Money* (London: Macmillan, 1974).

3. The idea alluded to here has informed much of the foregoing analysis. It can be stated very simply but it has yet to be developed into a fully formed alternative model of policy-making. Nonetheless, it is this. We live in and through the act of discourse. Policy-making too is discourse and decision-making is conducted by language communities. Power is exercised through language in action, but the basic idiom of all institutionalised policy-making is the written word—the text. However, as Ricoeur argued, not only is a 'text' 'a tissue of quotations drawn from innumerable centres of culture', its career also 'escapes the finite horizons lived by its author'. Quoted in Michael Shapiro, *Language and Political Understanding* (London: Yale University Press, 1981) p. 106. Finally, for those attracted by the parallel between Victor Turner's idea of a social drama and the Falklands War (see below, note 8), language in action is drama.

4. John Morley in his account of Lord Walpole, quoted in Michael Rush, *The Cabinet and Policy Formation* (London: Longman, 1984), p. 89. A classic account of leadership is contained in P. Selznick, *Leadership in Administration* (New York: Harper and Row, 1967).

5. Richard E. Neustadt, *Presidential Power: The Politics of Leadership* (New York: John Wiley and Sons Inc., 1960) p. 46. The following discussion draws heavily on Neustadt's shrewd analysis of the political nature of the discourse of policy-making. See especially chapter 3, 'The Power to Persuade' and chapter 4, 'Professional Reputation'. For another quite excellent, but more theoretical, account of political judgement and political reputation see Ronald Beiner, *Political Judgement* (London: Methuen, 1983).

6. George Steiner, *Language and Silence* (London: Faber and Faber, 1967) p. 259.

7. Particularly with respect to the conduct of Cabinet politics and Prime Ministerial leadership in the Westland affair of 1985–86, when the same questions about leadership, individual style and Ministerial politics were raised once again. See, for example, Magnus Linklater and David Leigh, *Not With Honour: The Inside Story of the Westland Scandal* (London: Sphere Books Limited, 1986); and also *House of Commons Third Report from the Defence Committee Session 1985–86. The Defence Implications of the Future of Westland plc* (London: HMSO, 23 July 1986), HC 518 and HC 519, together with *HC 169*; the minutes of evidence and appendices.

8. Victor Turner, *Dramas, Fields and Metaphors* (London: Cornell UP, 1974). See also *The Ritual Process. Structures and Anti-Structure* (London: Cornell UP, 1973); and *From Ritual to Theatre: The Human Seriousness of Play* (New York: The Performing Arts Journal, 1983).

9. All the first-wave Falklands War books contain some account of the narrowness of Britain's advantage. The hurried assembly and despatch of the Task Force is dealt with in chapter 6. See, however, the following: Max

Hastings and Simon Jenkins, *The Battle for the Falklands*, which is perhaps the best account of the conflict. Others include *The Falklands War*, by the Sunday Times Insight Team; Dobson *et al.*, *The Falklands Conflict*; John Laffin, *Fight for the Falklands* (London: Sphere, 1982). See in addition, *Falklands/Malvinas: Whose Crisis?*; Mary Cawkwell, *The Falkland Story 1592–1982*, a slim volume by a Falkland Islander updating an earlier work by her and other authors, *The Falkland Islands* (London: Macmillan, 1961). For another domestic history of the Islands see Ian Strange, *Falkland Islands*. For some additional reviews of the Falklands literature see Simon Collier, 'Argentine Falklands Literature', in *International Affairs*, Vol. 59, No. 3 (Summer 1983); Geoffrey Wheatcroft, 'The Fighting and the Writing', *Times Literary Supplement* (13 May 1983); and Neil Ascherson, 'By San Carlos Water', *London Review of Books* (1 December 1982).

10. Notably with respect to the relevance and value of overseas interventionary capabilities. See Appendix, *The Price of Victory*.

Appendix: The Price of Victory

1. See also the following two articles on Fortress Falklands: P. E. de la C. de la Billière, 'The Falkland Islands: The Strategic and Military Aspects', *Royal United Services Institute Journal*, Volume 131, No. 1 (March 1986); and Sir Rex Hunt, 'The Falkland Islands: The Political and Economic Aspects', Ibid.
2. *Report by the Comptroller and Auditor General. Property Services Agency: Defence Works in the Falkland Islands* (London: HMSO, 13 November 1984), para. 23, p. 6.
3. *Official Report*, 30 January 1985, Col. 181.
4. *Statement on the Defence Estimates 1983 Cmnd 8951-I*, para. 114.

Select Bibliography

Government Papers

Britain and the Falklands Islands. A Documentary Record (London: Central Office of Information, 1982).

The Falkland Islands. The Facts (London: HMSO, 1982). *The Disputed Islands. The Falklands Crisis. A History* (London: HMSO, 1982).

Falkland Islands. Economic Study 1982, Cmnd. 8653 (Second Shackleton Report), (London: HMSO, September 1982).

The Falklands Campaign. The Lessons, Cmnd. 8758 (London: HMSO, December 1982).

Falkland Islands Review. Report of a Committee of Privy Counsellors, Cmnd. 8787 (Chairman: The Rt Hon The Lord Franks), (London: HMSO, January 1983).

Ministry of Defence. The Handling of Press and Public Information During the Falklands Conflict. Observations presented by the Secretary of State for Defence on the First Report from the Defence Committee, HC 17–I–II 1982–83. Cmnd. 8820 (London: HMSO, March 1983).

Ministry of Defence. The Future Defence of the Falklands Islands. Observations presented by the Secretary of State for Defence on the Third Report from the Defence Committee, HC 154, 1982–83. Cmnd. 9070 (London: HMSO, October 1983).

Ministry of Defence. The Protection of Military Information. Report of the Study Group on Censorship. Cmnd. 9112 (Chairman: General Sir Hugh Beech), (London: HMSO, December 1983).

Ministry of Defence. The Protection of Military Information. Government response to the Report of the Study Group on Censorship. Cmnd. 9499 (London: HMSO, April 1984).

House of Commons Papers

The Falklands Campaign. A Digest of Debates in the House of Commons, 2 April–15 June 1982 (London: HMSO, 1982).

First Report from the Defence Committee. Session 1982–83. The Handling of Press and Public Information During The Falklands Conflict, Volume I, Report and Minutes of Proceedings. Volume II, Minutes of Evidence. HC 17–I–II (London: HMSO, 8 December 1982).

Minutes of the Proceedings of the Foreign Affairs Committee. Session 1982–83 (including 'Chairman's Draft Report On A Policy For The Falkland Islands') HC 380 (London: HMSO, 11 May 1983).

Second Report from the Foreign Affairs Committee. Session 1982–83. Falkland Islands Inquiry (together with the Proceedings of the Committee Relating to the Special Report). HC 378 (London: HMSO, 11 May 1983).

Foreign Affairs Committee. Session 1982–83. Falkland Islands. Minutes of Evidence Wednesday 10 November 1982. HC 31–i (London: HMSO, November 1982).

Ibid. *Monday 15 November 1982.* HC 31–ii (London: HMSO, November 1982).
Ibid. *Monday 22 November 1982.* HC 31–iii (London: HMSO, November 1982).
Ibid. *Monday 6 December 1982.* HC 31–iv (London: HMSO, December 1982).
Ibid. *Monday 13 December 1982.* HC 31–v (London: HMSO, December 1982).
Ibid. *Monday 17 January 1983.* HC 31–vi (London: HMSO, January 1983).
Ibid. *Monday 24 January 1983.* HC 31–vii (London: HMSO, January 1983).
Ibid. *Evidence Taken In The Falkland Islands.* HC 31–viii–xii (London: HMSO, February 1983).
Ibid. *Monday 14 February 1983.* HC 31–xii (London: HMSO, February 1983).
Ibid. *Monday 21 February 1983.* HC 31–xiv (London: HMSO, February 1983).
Ibid. *Appendices to the Minutes of Evidence.* HC 31–xv (London: HMSO, 11 May 1983).
Third Report from the Defence Committee. Session 1982–83. The Future Defence of the Falklands Islands. HC 154 (London: HMSO, 12 May 1983).
First Report from the Defence Committee. Session 1983–84. Statement on the Defence Estimates 1984. HC 436 (London: HMSO, 22 May 1984).
Fifth Report from the Foreign Affairs Committee. Session 1983–84. Falkland Islands, Volume I, Report and Minutes of Proceedings. Volume II Minutes of Evidence and Appendices (including HC 268–i to HC 268–viii). HC 268–I–II (London: HMSO, 25 October 1984).
Report by the Comptroller and Auditor General. Property Services Agency: Defence Works in the Falkland Islands. National Audit Office (London: HMSO, 13 November 1984).
Third Report from the Defence Committee. Session 1984–85. Defence Commitments and Resources and the Defence Estimates 1985–86. HC 37–I–II–III (London: HMSO, May 1985).
Third Report from the Foreign Affairs Committee. Session 1984–85. Events Surrounding the Weekend of 1–2 May 1982. Report together with the Proceedings of the Committee; Minutes of Evidence; and Appendices (including HC II–i to HC II–v). HC II (London: HMSO, 22 July 1985).

Other Papers

Lord Shackleton, *Economic Survey of the Falkland Islands* (First Shackleton Report), (London: Economist Intelligence Unit, 1976). Assembly of Western European Union. Thirty Eighth Ordinary Session (Second Part), *The Falklands Crisis* (Paris: Report submitted on behalf of the Committee on Defence Questions and Armaments, 8 November 1982, Document 935).

Books

Anthony Barnett, *Iron Brittania* (London: Allison and Busby, 1982).
Lucinda Broadbent *et al.,* *War and Peace News* (Milton Keynes: Open University Press for the Glasgow Media Group, 1985).

Peter Calvert, *The Falklands Crisis: The Rights and the Wrongs* (London: Frances Pinter, 1982).

O. R. Cardoso, R. Kirschbaum and E. Van der Kooy, *Malvinas: La Trama Secreta* (Buenos Aires: Sudamericana/Planeta, 11th ed., January 1984).

Mary Cawkell *et al.*, *The Falkland Islands* (London: Macmillan, 1961).

Mary Cawkell, *The Falkland Story* (London: Anthony Nelson, 1983).

Tam Dalyell, *One Man's Falklands* (London: Cecil Woolf, 1982).

Tam Dalyell, *Thatcher's Torpedo. The Sinking of the BELGRANO* (London: Cecil Woolf, 1983).

Christopher Dobson *et al.*, *The Falklands Conflict* (London: Coronet Books, 1982).

Falklands/Malvinas. Whose Crisis? (London: Latin American Bureau, 1982).

H. S. Ferns, *Britain and Argentina in the Nineteenth Century* (New York: Arno, 1970).

H. S. Ferns, *Argentina* (London: Ernest Brown, 1969).

Robert Fox, *Eyewitness Falklands* (London: Methuen, 1982).

Julius Goebel, *The Struggle for the Falkland Islands* (New Haven: Yale University Press, 1982 ed.).

Jozef Goldblat and Victor Millan, *The Falklands/Malvinas Conflict—A Spur to Arms Build-ups* (Stockholm: SIPRI, 1983).

Alexander Haig, *Caveat* (London: Macmillan, 1984).

Robert Harris, *Gotcha! The Media and the Falklands Crisis* (London: Faber and Faber, 1983).

Max Hastings and Simon Jenkins, *The Battle for the Falklands* (London: Pan, 1983).

Adrian F. J. Hope, *Sovereignty and Decolonization of the Malvinas (Falkland) Islands* (Boston: Boston College International and Comparative Law Review, Volume 6, No. 2, 1983).

John Laffin, *Fight for the Falklands* (London: Sphere, 1982).

Clive Ponting, *The Right to Know* (London: Sphere, 1985).

George H. Quester, *The Falklands and the Malvinas: Strategy and Arms Control* (Los Angeles: University of California Center for International and Strategic Affairs, ACIS Working Paper No. 46, May 1984).

Desmond Rice and Arthur Gavshon, *The Sinking of the BELGRANO* (London: Secker and Warburg, 1984).

Brad Roberts, *The Military Implications of the Falklands/Malvinas Islands Conflict* (Washington: Congressional Research Service Report, No. 82–140F, February 1983).

Michael Stephen, *The Falklands. A Possible Way Forward* (London: Bow Group Publications Ltd., March 1984. A Bow Group Memorandum).

Ian Strange, *Falkland Islands* (London: David and Charles, rev. ed. 1983).

Sunday Times Insight Team, *The Falklands War* (London: Sphere, 1982).

Testing the Power of a Media Consensus: A Comparison of Scots and English Treatment of the Falklands Campaign (Glasgow: Strathclyde University Paper on Government and Politics, no. 17, 1983).

Julian Thompson, *No Picnic* (London: Secker & Warburg, 1985).

Articles and Reviews

'America's Falklands War. A Relationship Sweet and Sour', *The Economist* (3 March, 1984).

Neil Ascherson, 'By San Carlos Water', *London Review of Books* (1 December 1982).

Major General P. E. de la C. de la Billière, 'The Falkland Islands: The Strategic and Military Aspects', *Royal United Services Institute Journal*, Volume 131, No. 1 (March 1986).

R. P. Barston and P. W. Birnie, 'The Falkland Islands/Islas Malvinas. A Question of Zones', *Marine Policy* (January 1983).

Peter J. Beck, 'Co-operative Confrontation in the Falkland Islands Dispute. The Anglo-Argentine Search for a Way Forward', *Journal of Interamerican Studies and World Affairs*, Volume 24, No. 1 (February 1982).

Peter J. Beck, 'Research Problems in Studying Britain's Latin American Past: The Case of the Falklands Dispute 1920–1950', *Bulletin of Latin American Research*, Volume 2, Part 2 (1983).

Peter J. Beck, 'The Anglo-Argentine Dispute Over Title to the Falkland Islands: Changing British Perceptions on Sovereignty Since 1910', *Millenium Journal of International Studies*, Volume 12, No. 1 (Spring 1983).

Peter J. Beck, 'The Future of the Falkland Islands: A Solution Made in Hong Kong', *International Affairs,* Volume 6, no. 4 (Autumn 1985).

Alfredo Bruno Bologna, 'Argentinian Claims to the Malvinas under International Law', *Millenium*, Volume 12, No. 1 (Spring 1983).

Peter Calvert, 'Latin America and the United States During and After the Falklands Crisis', *Millenium*, Volume 12, No. 1 (Spring 1983).

Peter Calvert, 'Sovereignty and the Falklands Crisis', *International Affairs*, Volume 59, No. 3 (Summer 1983).

Duncan Campbell, 'Falklands War. The Chilean Connection', *New Statesman* (25 January 1985).

Simon Collier, 'Argentine Falklands Literature', *International Affairs*, Volume 59, No. 3 (Summer 1983).

Denzil Dunnett, 'Self-Determination', *International Affairs*, Volume 59, No. 3 (Summer 1983).

Malcolm Deas, 'Falklands Title Deeds', *London Review of Books* (19 August–2 September 1982).

Margaret Doxey, 'International Sanctions: Trials of Strength or Tests of Weakness', *Millenium*, Volume 12, no. 1 (Spring 1983).

Geoffrey Edwards, 'Europe and the Falklands Crisis', *Journal of Common Market Studies*, Volume 22, No. 4 (1984).

James Fawcett, 'Legal Aspects' in *The Falkland Islands Dispute. International Dimensions*, London: Chatham House Special Paper, RIIA (April 1982).

James Fawcett, 'The Falkland Islands and the Law', *World Today* (June 1982).

L. Freedman, 'The Falklands War 1982', *Foreign Affairs* (Fall 1982).

L. Freedman, 'British Falklands Literature', *International Affairs*, Volume 59, No. 3 (Summer 1983).

Norman Friedman, 'The Falklands War: Lesson Learned and Mislearned', *Orbis*, Volume 26, No. 4 (Winter 1983).

Bruce George and Walter Little, 'Options in the Falklands-Malvinas Dispute', *South Atlantic Council Occasional Papers*, No. 1 (London: April 1985).

Peter Greig (pseudonym), 'Revelations', *Granta*, 15 (Spring 1985).

Sir Nicholas Henderson, 'America and the Falklands. Case Study in the Behaviour of an Ally', *The Economist* (12 November 1982).

Sir Rex Hunt, 'The Falkland Islands: The Political and Economic Aspects', *Royal United Services Institute Journal*, Volume 131, No. 1 (March 1986).

International Commission of Jurists, 'The Argentinian Claim to the Falkland Islands', *The Review*, No. 28 (June 1982).

Julian S. Lake, 'The South Atlantic War: A Review of the Lessons Learned', *Defence Electronics*, Volume 15, No. 11 (November 1983).

Ned Lebow, 'Miscalculation in the South Atlantic: The Origins of the Falklands War', *Journal of Strategic Studies*, Volume 6, No. 1 (March 1983).

Walter Little, 'The Falklands Affair. A Review of the Literature', *Political Studies*, Volume xxxii (1984).

Guillermo Makin, 'The Military in Argentine Politics', *Millenium: Journal of International Studies*, Volume 12, No. 1 (Spring 1983).

Guillermo Makin, 'Argentine Approaches to the Falklands/Malvinas: Was the resort to force foreseeable?' *International Affairs*, Volume 59, No. 3 (1983).

J. C. J. Metford, 'Falklands or Malvinas: The Background to the Dispute', *International Affairs*, Volume 44, No. 8 (1968).

Major General Sir Jeremy Moore and Admiral Sir John Woodward, 'The Falklands Experience', *Royal United Services Institute Journal* (March 1983).

Juan Carlos Murguizur, 'The South Atlantic Conflict. An Argentinian Point of View', *International Defence Review*, 2 (1983).

J. D. Myhre, 'Title to the Falklands-Malvinas under International Law', *Millenium Journal of International Studies*, Volume 12, No. 1 (Spring 1983).

Sir Anthony Parsons, 'The Falklands Crisis in the United Nations 31 March–14 June 1982', *International Affairs*, Volume 59, No. 2 (Spring 1983).

Joan Pearch, 'The Falkland Islands Negotiations 1965–82', *The Falkland Islands Dispute: International Dimensions*, London: Chatham House Special Paper, RIIA (April 1982).

Robert S. Scheina, 'The Malvinas Campaign', *United States Naval Institute Proceedings* (1983).

Robert S. Scheina, 'Where Were Those Argentine Subs?', *United States Naval Institute Proceedings* (1984).

Ronald Slaughter, 'The Politics and Nature of Conventional Arms Transfers During a Military Engagement: The Falklands-Malvinas Case', *Arms Control* (May 1983).

Christopher Wain, 'The Belgrano Incident Will Not Go Away', *The Listener* (25 October 1984).

William Wallace, 'The Franks Report', *International Affairs*, Volume 59, No. 3 (1983).

Geoffrey Wheatcroft, 'The Fighting and the Writing', *Times Literary Supplement* (13 May 1983).

Philip Williams, 'Miscalculation, Crisis Management and the Falklands', *World Today* (April 1983).

Philip Windsor, 'Diplomatic Dimensions of the Falklands Crisis', *Millenium: Journal of International Studies*, Volume 12, No. 1 (Spring 1983).

Robert Worcester and Simon Jenkins, 'Britain Rallies Round the Prime Minister', *Public Opinion* (Washington: June/July 1982).

Derek Wood and Mark Hewish, 'The Falklands Conflict Part 1: the Air War', *International Defence Review*, 8 (1983). 'The Falklands Conflict Part 2: missile operations', *International Defence Review*, 9 (1983). 'The Falklands Conflict Part 3: naval operations', *International Defence Review*, 10 (1983).

Index

284 *Index*